DATE DUE			

The Main Stream of Mathematics

The
Main Stream
of
Mathematics

EDNA E. KRAMER

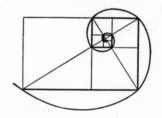

New York • Oxford University Press • 1951

Copyright 1951 by Oxford University Press, Inc.

Printed in the United States of America

то Benedict Taxier Lassar

Preface

EVENTS in August 1945 and thereafter have revealed that mathematics holds one of the most important keys to the future of the human race. The common man is curious to know how and why the science of numbers plays this basic role. *The Main Stream of Mathematics* attempts to appease this curiosity.

Modern mathematics with its ramifications into every conceivable area of thought is like a tree. We shall mount, climb out on a few sturdy limbs, return to the trunk, ascend a little higher, then branch out once more. Most of our time will be spent exploring the branches, which will support us between the periodic intervals of rising on the trunk. Since we are not climbing on a dare or running a race, but are engaged in our activities for pleasure, we shall, in human fashion, look outside and beyond. We shall not attempt to reach the summit or to venture out to every twig and leaf, for that would require a profound and monumental treatise.

Answers to questions like the following are simple and will be found in this volume:

How did primitive man anticipate modern electronic brains?

How does the H-bomb indicate that $2+2$ does not always equal 4?

What is the formula for beauty invented by a Harvard professor?

What sort of mathematics flourished by the waters of Babylon?

What distinguished algebraist owes his fame to the composition of a single poem?

How can playing poker help to win hot or cold wars?

What does a scale on the piano have in common with a chain reaction?

Wherein lies the charm of the 'Helen of Geometry'?

Who is the only outstanding mathematician in history who was also a wife and mother?

What was the nature of the 'Russian revolution' in mathematics?

A special feature of the book is the historical or legendary material, which has been included both to show the evolution of science, and because the facts are so full of surprises. There are few who do not know Einstein as a mathematician, but how many have heard of Hilbert? Again, most laymen have never read a word about the Hindu mathematicians whose influence on our daily lives is probably greater than that of Henry VIII or Napoleon. In a few instances we have combined fiction with fact in narrating biographical incidents. The men of mathematics come alive in association with their surroundings. It is surprising that they have almost never figured in historical fiction.

We shall, of course, discuss ordinary arithmetic and algebra. Our objective, however, will be to examine their relationship to other systems of numeration and symbolism, systems that have some factors in common with the everyday species but diverge in ways rendering them more suitable for certain scientific applications. Geometry will be considered at first in relation to art and the inspiration of art—nature itself—leaving the notion of pure geometry for a later chapter. Trigonometry as a tool can stand some deemphasis in favor of its characteristic of mirroring the eternal periodicity of nature. Statistics is no longer glorified bookkeeping but a means of testing hypotheses, controlling industrial processes, and describing the nature of matter. Calculus concepts, freed of manipulative detail, are within the reach of all.

Relativity is a natural climax to mathematical discussions. Today a comprehensible outline of this subject can be offered to the layman —yet less than fifty years ago it had been mastered by only a handful of savants. The man in the street can even gain some understanding of the objectives of Einstein's new unified field theory. Finally, we must touch on a major issue of mathematical philosophy—the infinite, with its intriguing paradoxes and its inevitable association with the most profound problems of modern mathematics.

At this point, I should like to express my gratitude to the late John A. Swenson for being the first to stimulate in me a love of mathematics and a desire to undertake a mathematical career. Throughout his lifetime he acted as a source of inspiration.

Many thanks are due to Bernard Jaffe for reading the manuscript and urging that it be offered for publication, to Professor H. S. M. Coxeter of the University of Toronto for constructive criticisms, to the members of the staff of the Oxford University Press for their valuable editorial assistance, to Bernard Handelman for the preparation of diagrams, to Byron Steel for the index, to the students, too numerous to list, who helped with a variety of clerical tasks, and finally to Benedict T. Lassar, without whose inspiration, encouragement, patience, and assistance, this book could not have been written.

EDNA E. KRAMER

New York, New York
March 1951

Table of Contents

The Main Stream of Mathematics

1

Mathematical Genesis

We lack but open eye and ear
To find the Orient's marvels here.

WHITTIER

WHEN as a boy Bhaskara was not absorbed in the study of mathematics, he would brood on the nature of the society about him. The adamant wall of custom had always been a source of pain to him. He chafed under the system that forbade him to share his scientific knowledge with youths of lower caste, or to seek companionship outside of Brahmin ranks. Bhaskara had feared to confide his unorthodox views to others, lest he be outlawed. But it had comforted him to learn from the writings of an earlier day that men had once lived a freer life and a happier one.

Often in his later years his nervously active mind would turn suddenly, by some train of association, from serious scientific considerations to sentimental memories. Now this old pattern of thought recurred with good reason, for today his only daughter was to be married. He thought for a moment of the two ancient astrologers who, when Lilavati was born, had been paid to cast her horoscope; bent with age, and shorn of their dignity in his presence— Bhaskara even then had been renowned for his wisdom—they had seemed uneasy and timid, and had spoken of many things other than their business. Finally they had predicted that Lilavati was to be his only daughter, and that she should never marry; and when they had delivered this prediction, they left hurriedly, fearful of the rage which they expected their prophecy would call forth. But Bhaskara had sent gifts after them and a message of blessing.

Today Bhaskara recalled how Lilavati, even at the age of eleven, had preferred to remain at home and read to him her childish compositions or listen to his recitals of myths and puzzles, while her playmates celebrated, as they had every year since the age of seven, the festival of Molakata, in order to ensure the speedy winning of a husband. Bhaskara had been pleased. More and more she had become the comfort and delight of those leisure moments which he stole from his endless work on mathematics.

But suddenly she changed. The books, the puzzles, the lessons, all seemed to bore her. Now she played all day with her friends at games that she had always scorned as childish. And when in her twelfth year the festival days of Molakata came, she celebrated with the other girls of her age. Soon Bhaskara perceived that he could not change the course of nature.

Lilavati did not then know that the astrologers had been unable to discover any time when the gods would permit a marriage for her; and when Bhaskara saw that her heart was set upon marriage and that to be denied this would cause her great misery, he laid aside his books, and for one whole day and night studied the child's horoscope and the heavens.

At last he found an hour on a certain day when the gods would receive the marriage favorably. He called Lilavati to his side, and telling her first that he had found a propitious date, related the findings of the old astrologers so many years before. Then he went to a friend in a near-by village and arranged a match with the delighted friend's son. All this had happened three months ago. And today Bhaskara realized with a start that within a few hours the ceremony must begin.

Soon the noisy wedding procession arrived and the great rooms were filled with chatter and laughter. Lilavati was seated in the embrace of her uncle, as was the custom, with a screen still barring her first glimpse of her husband to be. Then the astrologers set up the hour glass beside her, to determine the exact moment that the heavens had decreed for the performance of the ceremony. From time to time Lilavati leaned over and gazed at the floating cup, to see how near the hour was.

To Bhaskara the preliminaries seemed endless. Several times he approached the priest, to ask whether the propitious moment had not already come. Then suddenly Vatsaraja, the old astrologer, bent over the hour-cup and cried out! A silence fell on the group as he lifted the vessel from the water. No liquid flowed through the cavity, just as no liquid had entered it. As Lilavati in her anxiety had bent over the cup, a pearl had dropped from her costume and stopped the opening through which the fluid should have passed. And so, unnoticed, the hour had gone, and now that the accident was discovered, it was forever too late.

It was the will of heaven, Bhaskara said. And he took into his arms the child who could not restrain her weeping, and caressed her; he mustered all the words of comfort he could find; among other things, he whispered to Lilavati that the great book upon which he had been laboring for years would bear her name through the centuries. Thus, by the promise of immortal fame did he hope to console her for the accident that had prevented her marriage.

* * *

Whether Lilavati realized the significance of Bhaskara's great tribute, we do not know. It is certain, however, that the spirit if not the name of Lilavati is ever with us. Each day we make use of one of the most important inventions of all time—the one Bhaskara named *Lilavati* (the beautiful). Each day we doubtless overlook the great significance of this remarkable tool, much as the fates overlooked Lilavati. Our ingenious number system is that great instrument of scientific progress which Bhaskara and his Hindu predecessors developed. A presentation of the facts will show that no anticlimax is involved in mentioning Hindu arithmetic in the same breath as wedding bells, stargazing, and social customs.

To understand the development of mathematics, we must have a picture of the men who made the science. We must see Bhaskara (1114–85) as he really was—the practical mathematician *par excellence* and at the same time the naive romantic, working with one of the greatest mathematical ideas of all time on the one hand, and participating on the other in primitive beliefs and customs characteristic of his environment. Bhaskara's performance was the outcome of more than fifteen hundred years of Hindu mathematical culture and almost a thousand years of Hindu social degeneration.

Mathematics was functioning in India even before the time (600 B.C.) when Buddha preached his spiritual message, and by his own arithmetic work initiated a mathematical tradition. At an early period the Hindus were skilful calculators even where large numbers were involved. Thus, one of the Buddhist sacred books, the *Lalitavistera,* relates that when Buddha was of the age to marry, the father of Gopa, his intended bride, demanded that an examination be given the five hundred suitors, the subjects to include writing, arithmetic, music, and archery. Having vanquished his rivals in all else, Buddha was matched against Arjuna, a great mathematician of the day, and asked to demonstrate his scientific knowledge.

To do so, he proceeded to describe the number of 'primary atoms' which, placed end to end, would form a line with length equal to the ancient Hindu equivalent of a mile. He stated: 'Seven primary atoms make a *very* minute grain of dust, seven of these make a minute grain of dust, seven of *these* a grain of dust whirled up by the wind.' Thus he continued until he reached the length of a mile. The multiplication of all the 7's listed by Buddha would give an answer of more than 50 digits, and hence, although Buddha's estimate of 'atomic' size was in error by being, from the modern point of view, very much too large, we may infer, even after discounting for the glorification of Buddha's talents, that large numbers were no novelty in Hindu science in 600 B.C.

There are many charming legends of this type, but actual knowledge of the history of Hindu mathematics is slight. A few scientific manuscripts bear witness to the fact that the Hindus attained a lofty height but the path of ascent is no longer traceable. The mathematical historian, Otto Neugebauer, has proposed the theory that through some channel, probably trade, the great mathematical achievements of the Babylonians of the first two millennia before the Christian era were transmitted to India, and that the Hindu mathematicians were not entirely original in their work. There is reason to believe that they were merely building on a firm Sumerian foundation. That commercial relations existed between the East and the Near East has some verification in archaeological findings in India and Mesopotamia. Among these are seals of the type used in Babylonia in the third millennium B.C. for the witnessing of business transactions.

We can only conjecture what the names were of the men who invented the ideal symbolism that led to modern arithmetic. It would seem that a 'latter-day' Babylonian astronomer, Naburianu (*c*.400 B.C.), mastered the zero, which is the crux of modern arithmetic symbolism, as we shall shortly see. The names of the early workers, in the days from 2000 B.C. to 400 B.C., are completely unknown to us. An interval of a thousand years separated Naburianu from his first great Hindu successor, Aryabhata (A.D. 475–550).

Historians lack exact details of the gradual evolution of Hindu arithmetic during this millennium. It is likely, however, that the maximum progress occurred before the original Aryan myth had frozen Hindu society into the caste system. By the day of Aryabhata only the privileged Brahmins and Kshatriyas had the right to mathematical knowledge. The stifling effect of the caste system resulted from the secretiveness it engendered. The same principle that encouraged mathematicians to keep their knowledge secret from the masses made them hide it even from their fellow scholars, causing tremendous waste through repetition of discovery. For six centuries after Aryabhata, Hindu mathematicians duplicated not only his work but also that of other predecessors and contemporaries. This seems all the stranger since so many of these scientists worked in the same city, Ujjain, a center of scientific culture.

In spite of the smoke screen of secrecy, there is evidence that Bhaskara was the greatest Hindu of them all. Except for the legend concerning Lilavati, the only details that have come down to us about his personal life are summarized in an ancient temple inscription: 'Triumphant is the illustrious Bhaskaracarya whose feet are revered by the wise, eminently learned . . . a poet . . . endowed with good fame and religious merit . . .' The same inscription relates that Bhaskara's grandson, Changadwa, was chief astrologer to King Simghana, and that in his time a college was founded to expound the doctrines of Bhaskara.

The *Lilavati* was primarily a text on arithmetic—the fundamental processes, fractions, interest, commercial rules—but it also included some algebra. In the style, if not in the subject matter, there is evidence of Bhaskara the poet. Religious, fanciful, poetic wording was the classic style of mathematical writing. Aryabhata had dedicated a mathematics text thus:

Having paid homage to Brahma, to Earth, to the Moon, to Mercury, to Venus, to the Sun, to Mars, to Jupiter, to Saturn and to the constellations, Aryabhata, in the City of Flowers, sets forth the science venerable.

Bhaskara wrote not only the *Lilavati* but also three other great treatises—the *Bija Ganita* ('seed arithmetic'), the *Siddhanta Siromani* (Head Jewel of Accuracy), and the *Goladhia* (Theory of the Sphere).

To understand why, from the point of view of scientific progress, the Hindu number system was as great a factor in the history of civilization as atomic fission promises to be, we must, in our own way, do what the Ujjain thinkers did—start from the beginning. Modern scientific knowledge requires us to go back further in the story than Hindu or even Babylonian thought could, and to consider an era long before the golden age of Sumer and Akkad and a setting more universal than the Tigris-Euphrates valley. Even prehistoric times are too late a date for the origin of the number notion; even the location of the missing link will not give geographic orientation to mathematical beginnings. We must go back to a time before genus homo existed and seek our material in bushes and treetops.

Naturalists claim that a number sense exists in birds and insects. If, for example, a bird's nest contains four eggs, one may be safely taken; but if two are removed, the bird becomes aware of the fact and generally deserts. As another illustration we may cite an incident recounted by the English naturalist Lubbock. A man was anxious to shoot a crow. To deceive the bird, he sent two men to the watch house, one of whom left, while the other remained; but the crow seemed able to count, and so kept her distance—the next day he sent three and had two leave; but still she refused to return to the house. Finally it was found necessary to send five or six men to the watch house to upset her counting. From this it might possibly be concluded that the crow could count up to four. Lubbock cites another example, in the case of the wasp, of what might be judged a number sense. A certain species of wasp supplies the cells in which the young are to hatch with five caterpillars apiece; another species furnishes ten, another fifteen, and still another twenty-four. The number is constant in each species. Of course this might be mere instinct, but Lubbock doubts it. In one genus the males are smaller than the females. Hence the mother supplies the cell of the male egg with five victims, the female egg with ten. Does she count?

What is the next stage in number history?

We have ample evidence that primitive man hardly excels birds and insects in his number notions, for some primitive tongues show a complete lack of number words. Such is the case with some of the South American languages. Most primitive tongues, however, do contain words for 'one' and 'two' but describe every larger quantity by 'heap.' This paucity of number knowledge is found today among the forest tribes of Brazil, the Bushmen of South Africa, the native races of Australia and Polynesia.

Even such an elementary number concept represents centuries of progress. Philosophers believe that it may require untold ages for a primitive tribe to conceive the notion that a set of twins, a pair of eyes, and a couple of days are all instances of the general concept two. What usually happens is that a tribe evolves a word for 'two' to refer to a pair of human beings, a different word 'two' for a couple of animals, still another 'two' for inanimate objects, and so on. The Thimshian language of a tribe in British Columbia illustrates this very point but nevertheless indicates progress toward complete abstraction. There are seven sets of words for each number they know—that is, seven different words for 'two,' seven others for 'three,' etc., as far as they count. One set is for animals and flat objects, one for time and round objects, one for human beings, one for trees and long objects, one for canoes, one for measures, and one for miscellaneous objects not in the other six categories. The last of these, of course, may eventually become the general number word if the tribe progresses to a better number comprehension. Although civilization advances and arithmetic progress is a concomitant, the language of a people may retain primitive number inconveniences. If this occurs in a small way, we merely have the use of special synonyms such as brace, pair, couple, for two, and score for twenty, for example. On the other hand, the original failure to master the number concept completely may remain as permanent evidence in the language. Modern Japanese contains fourteen or more different classes of number words to be used for various types of object.

To modern man it seems a commonplace, requiring no philosophic elaboration, that the word 'four' or the symbol 4 does not mean four chairs, four nations, four telephones, four electrons, four dreams, but is simply a verbal or written way of characterizing all possible sets of things of a certain type. Yet something that appears as simple as formulating the concept of 'twoness' or 'threeness' or 'fourness' illustrates the basic nature of what modern scientists call 'pure' mathematics. To progress in the mathematics of science and practical affairs we must not be confused by images of adding 10 ancestors to 37 dollars or of multiplying 6 senators by 1,000,000 electrons. We must have no conflict between arithmetic procedure and physical reality when asked: If 10 men can build a cottage in a month, how long will it take 3,000 men? We perform arithmetic with ease just because it is disentangled from sensations, emotions, and concrete pictures; that is, pure mathematical thought consists of the abstraction or removal of a concept from the very many different things it may simultaneously describe, however useful or beautiful these concrete instances may be. Having abstracted ideas, pure mathematics tries to provide the simplest words, the most suitable symbols, the most logical and economical operations for the handling of abstract concepts. The pure mathematician works with these abstract tools, confident that his friend, the *applied* mathematician, will be able to apply them to many and varied important concrete situations—sounds and smells, stars and microbes, taxes and airplanes. Thus the abstractness of pure mathematics makes it general and is the key to its power as 'queen of the sciences.' Primitive man and his more civilized successors practiced applied arithmetic first, gradually made it pure, then reapplied it. Repetition of this pattern occurred in other branches of mathematics, although it was not the only sequence, or even the best one for scientific discovery.

Early man struggled by gradual steps from physical situations to pure numbers. First he abstracted 'two' and used 'heap' for anything beyond. But when he progressed beyond the hunting and food-gathering stage and reached the point of keeping herds and flocks, there was a need to count, which he did in 'applied' or concrete fashion. Instead of counting herds, primitive man tallied them with notches cut in a tree, knots tied in a rope, pebbles spread on the ground or grain kernels piled into a heap. This procedure involves setting up what mathematicians call a 'one-to-one correspondence,' a technical name for matching. We mention it here only so that we can refer, in chapter 13, to the fact that even now modern higher mathematics makes tallying of this sort the basis of advanced number concepts. Two sets in one-to-one correspondence are said to contain the same *cardinal number* of objects.

Eventually, instead of relying on a random model for matching—a pile of pebbles, a bunch of sticks, or a string of shells—man came to use ever-ready standard models—his eyes for *two*, the legs of an animal for *four*, the fingers of one hand for *five*. Then the one-to-one correspondence usually became a matching with fingers and/or toes. Every child reverts instinctively to the primitive when he first learns to count and turns to his fingers, until parents and teachers wean him of the procedure.

In his next step toward abstraction, man progressed to the *number word*. The choice of words is evidence that they were made in connection with finger-counting. The savage usually counts on his fingers until he has reached the end of one hand, or both. If he wishes to proceed further, some mark is made, or a knot is tied, or a stick laid aside. Then he starts counting again and repeats the same number words. He is very likely to repeat the name of the first halting place in making this second count. If he calls the number five 'hand,' six becomes 'hand and one,' seven is 'hand and two,' ten is 'two hands,' eleven is 'one on the foot,' twenty is 'hands and feet' or 'man.' We use a similar method for our thirteen, fourteen, fifteen, which are merely contractions for three and ten, four and ten, five and ten.

In the case of our modern Indo-European tongues, the number words have a long past and, in most cases, all trace of their origin has been lost. Of course, the similarity of the words for numbers in the various languages must please the linguists who hold to the theory of a mother Indo-European tongue as the root of all modern Indo-European languages. The chart below illustrates this fact.

Modern English	French	German	Old English	Latin	Greek
one	un	ein	an	unus	oinos
two	deux	zwei	two	duo	duo
three	trois	drei	threo	tres	treis
seven	sept	sieben	seofon	septem	hepta
eight	huit	acht	ahta	octo	okto
nine	neuf	neun	nigon	novem	ennea

Whether the series of numbers used by a particular tribe will be developed into an arrangement that may be called a 'number system' depends once more on the progress of the tribe in other respects. If social advances occur, a time may come when greater accuracy is a necessity. Perhaps the number eleven is to be indicated exactly. At this stage, our primitive man may use 'all the fingers and one more' or 'one of another man's fingers' or some equivalent expression, meaning ten and one. When this step is taken, we say that the *base* of the tribal number system has been established. This base may be any number; that is, a fresh start in counting can be made at any point. Since fingers and toes are used for counting, five, ten, and twenty are the most likely bases, and ethnological studies bear out the fact that the savage will, in general, follow nature and actually select *five, ten,* or *twenty.*

There are, however, interesting exceptions of tribes who have used *two, three,* or *four* as base. The Yuki Indians in California count by fours because they use the spaces between the fingers instead of the fingers themselves. The 'binary' or 'dyadic' scale (base *two*) is rather pronounced among Australian tribes, but is found in South America and Africa as well. One observer of Australian tribes reports that if a native were shown seven pins in a row, and then two were removed without his knowledge, he would not know the difference. But if a single pin were removed, he would realize that something was amiss because of the Australian habit of counting by pairs—pointing two fingers again and again. This develops the ability to discover whether any number within reasonable limit is odd or even. If we stop to consider what a language nuisance a binary scale must be, we can realize how low an intellect will select such a system. Take, for example, one of the dialects found among the Western tribes of the Torres Straits. The method of counting in this dialect is

1. urapun
2. okosa
3. okosa urapun = 2 + 1
4. okosa okosa = 2 + 2
5. okosa okosa urapun = 2 + 2 + 1
6. okosa okosa okosa = 2 + 2 + 2

Anything above six they call *ras,* a lot. We can understand why they have no number words higher than six, if we consider that ten would be *okosa okosa okosa okosa okosa,* or that the African Basutos, who are not lingually lazy, refer to ninety-nine as Machoume-**arobilen**gmonoolemon**g**ametso**arobilen**gmonoolemon**g**.

Although the choice of a base like two can hardly be called an indication of great progress, the selection of some larger base is an actual milestone in the mathematical history of a race. The enumeration of large quantities is inevitably easier if we can merely indicate the distance we have progressed beyond our base, and not the distance from the original starting-point. It also makes vocabulary easier. Suppose that in youth we had to commit to memory one thousand completely different number words (all in order) for the purpose of counting one thousand things! And then, how would we count beyond one thousand, if we made no choice of a base? Thus the establishment of a base is absolutely essential in any society where there is need for any sort of enumeration except the most elementary.

The next step in abstraction was logically the creation of the *number symbol.* As civilization progresses, there is always the necessity for carrying on business transactions, keeping government records, and engaging in many activities requiring the use of written numbers as well as techniques of operating with these numbers.

Figure 1 shows the number symbols that characterized the Egyptian hieroglyphic or picture writing. Figure 2 shows the number 32,536 written with these symbols. The hieroglyphic symbols stood for concrete objects, just as the words had. Ten was an arch, 100 a

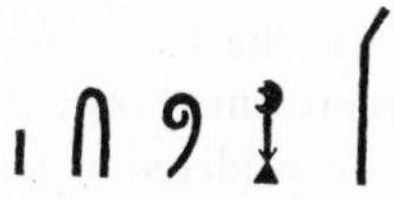

Fig. 1. Numbers in Egyptian hieroglyphics.

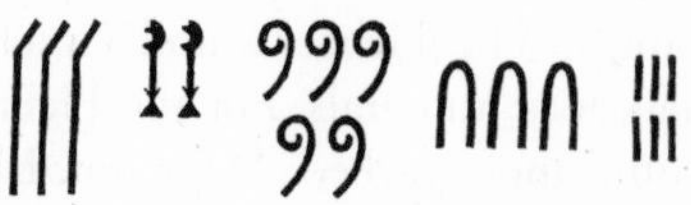

Fig. 2. The number 32,536 as written by the early Egyptians.

coiled rope, 1,000 a lotus flower, 10,000 a finger pointing upward, 100,000 a pollywog, 1,000,000 a man with arms outstretched with wonder at so large a number. Evidently the Egyptians had more coiled ropes than arches, many lotus flowers, but still more pollywogs on the Nile's marshy banks.

Most ancient peoples—the Babylonians, Egyptians, Greeks, and the natives of India—used a numeral like our 1 to represent 'one.' Since sticks were used constantly as aids in calculating, perhaps this symbol was suggested by a vertical stick. Another conjecture is that it stood for the lifted finger. The 'one' was sometimes a horizontal stick, thus —. Two was **ll** or **=**, two vertical or horizontal sticks. When written rapidly **ll** became **N**, and later **ʱ**, the symbol used by the Arabs and later Persians. The **=** became **ᴢ**, when written rapidly, which is not unlike our 2, into which it may have developed. The three was **lll** or **☰**. In China and Japan today **≋** still represents three. Again the blurring of a pen would convert **☰** into **3**, which may explain our 3. The pen gradually turned **lll** into **ⱳ** which finally became the Arabic **ʰ** of nowadays. Figure 3 shows the early 'matchstick' notation used by the Chinese, later adopted by the Japanese and used by them as recently as the eighteenth century.

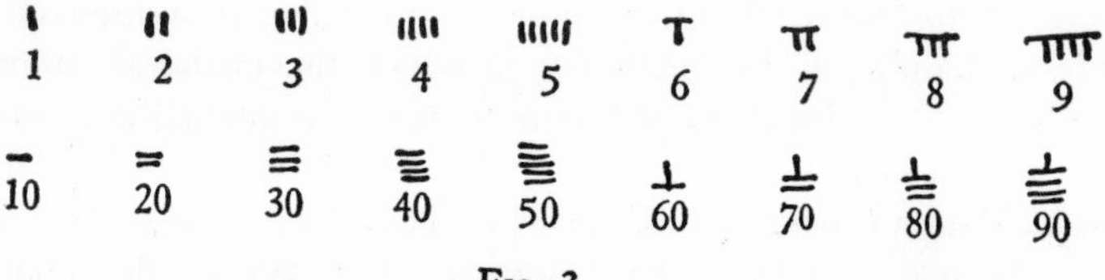

Fig. 3.

We have seen the general similarities in the symbols that some ancient peoples used. The Hebrews, the later Greeks, and the Romans form another group who used the letters of their alphabet to represent numbers. We are all familiar with the Roman numerals that persist on clockfaces, college seals, and the cornerstones of buildings. The Hebrews and Greeks also used the letters of their alphabets as numerals. For the Hebrews א represented one, ב two, etc. until they reached י for ten. Eleven was considered as ten and one and hence written יא, twelve was ten and two, etc. The Hebrews made two exceptions to this procedure. In the order of things, fifteen would be written as ten and five or יה, which initiates the word for Yahve or Jehovah meaning God, the utterance of whose name is forbidden in the Hebrew religion. Hence fifteen is considered as nine and six. In the same way sixteen was construed as nine and seven, because the symbols for ten and six are typographically similar to the initial letters of Yahve.

Such use of the letters of the Hebrew, Roman, and Greek alphabets may be one reason why these peoples came to associate numbers and words in a numerological pseudo-science called *Gematria*. (This word probably derives from the same root as *grammar*.) The sum of the numbers represented by the letters of the word was considered to be the *value* of the word. If we work with the Roman alphabet, Roosevelt, Churchill, Stalin have the numerical values 131, 94, 75 respectively. Therefore, according to Gematria, Roosevelt was the greatest political figure of the three.

The Greek letters for 'Amen' would be αμην. These letters stood for 1, 40, 8, 50 in Greek numeration. Their total is 99. Hence in certain manuscripts one finds 99 written at the end of prayers. On many ancient tombstones a man's Gematria number as well as his name is found.

Gematria led to a favorite pastime of the Middle Ages and Reformation. This little piece of fun was the trick of 'beasting' your archenemy. In the book of Revelations in the Bible, 666 is mentioned as the 'number of the beast.' It has been surmised that this number referred to 'Nero Caesar,' which has this value if written in the Hebrew alphabet. The extremes to which the medievals went in beasting—the substitution of letters from various alphabets, arbitrary numbers taken away or thrown in for good measure—show them to have been experts at proving what they set out to do.

Anyone can give a Gematria proof on the spur of the moment.

Once the author was challenged on this statement by fellow members of the Statistical Research Group at Columbia University. It was easy to prove that the success of the war work of the Group was inherent in the names of the workers. *Wal*lis directed, *Wol*fowitz and *Wal*d were assisting mathematicians. Now everyone knows that *l* and *r* are interchangeable in baby talk, Chinese, etc., and *a* and *o* are often confused. Hence the names of each of the chiefs started with *War*. When one added to this the fact that the director-in-chief was *War*ren *Weaver,* whose name made him naturally able to *knit* together WAR activities, the success of our project, according to Gematria, was inevitable.

We come now to our own number symbols, which will bring us back to Bhaskara. We have already explained our 1, 2, 3. Although our numerals are frequently referred to as Arabic, this is a misnomer. They come to us, with many changes, from the Hindus. The Arabs were merely the intermediaries through whom Hindu mathematics reached Europe. At the time when the caste system was stifling Hindu science completely, the Arabs transplanted Hindu mathematics and astronomy to Baghdad. The Arabs kept ablaze the torch of Greek and Indian science during the dark ages in Europe, and later transmitted this knowledge to the countries of the Occident.

The number system the Hindus gave us employs the base *ten,* which means that there are ten, and only ten number words, and hence ten, and only ten symbols:

$$0, \ 1, \ 2, \ 3, \ 4, \ 5, \ 6, \ 7, \ 8, \ 9$$

With these all possible numbers can be written. The same few ciphers have different significance according to *position.* In Hindu counting the objects are grouped into tens, and tens of tens (hundreds) and tens of tens of tens (thousands), etc. This method of grouping involves an iteration of the choice of a base. In Hindu writing, the grouping is indicated by the position of the symbol. Thus 3,275 means 3 thousands, 2 hundreds, 7 tens, and 5 units.

If man had had six fingers, the Hindus might have used *six* as the base of their number system. The written symbols would have conveyed different meanings but the abstract mathematical concepts and procedures would have been the same. They (and hence we) would have used six symbols and only six—0, 1, 2, 3, 4, 5—to write all numbers. We should write six as 10 (1 six and 0 units); twelve would be written as 20 (2 sixes and 0 units); thirty-five would be 55 (5 sixes and 5 units). Since this is the largest two digit number we can write with the six symbols available, thirty-six, the next higher number, would have to be written as 100. We leave as an exercise for the reader the task of figuring out what numbers in our system would be written as 1,000 and 10,000 in the system with base six.

On the other hand, if man had had six fingers on each hand, we might have had *twelve,* not six as base. Although the Aphos of Benue, an African tribe, do not have twelve fingers, they use twelve as their number base and thereby seem to indicate some remarkable arithmetic intuition in the choice of a superior base. For the use of the base twelve, we would need twelve symbols:

$$0, 1, 2, 3, 4, 5, 6, 7, 8, 9, *, \#$$

and we should write twelve as 10 (1 twelve and 0 units); thirteen would be 11, twenty-four would be 20 (two twelves and 0 units); one hundred forty-three would be # # (eleven twelves and eleven units). As this is the largest two-digit number that can be represented with the twelve symbols available, the next number, one hundred forty-four, would be written 100.

The reader may amuse himself by checking the following sample exercises.

System with base six

35	Five + two = seven, written as 11 in this system.
+ 52	Put down 1 and carry 1.
131	Three + five + one = nine, written as 13 in this system.

43	Three × three = nine, written as 13 in this system.
× 3	Put down 3 and carry 1.
213	Four × three = twelve. Twelve + one = thirteen, written as 21.

System with base twelve

8*	Ten and one are eleven. Eight and four are twelve.
+ 41	
10#	

35	Eleven five's = fifty-five, written as 47 in this system.
× #	Put down 7 and carry 4. Eleven three's = thirty-three.
317	Adding four, the result is thirty-seven, written as 31 in this system.

Mathematicians have differed about what the best base would be. Some have agreed that twelve, since it has the divisors 2, 3, 4, 6, would have made fractional work easier than it is with base ten (divisors 2 and 5). It would have involved learning only two additional symbols, and this would be worth while, in consideration of the tremendous saving in other arithmetic effort. Some pure mathematicians have indicated that a prime base (one with no divisors but one and itself) would have led to greater uniformity in arithmetic procedures. It is said that Charles XII of Sweden was actually contemplating, at the time of his death, the abolition of the decimal system in all his dominions, in favor of the duodecimal. A universal change to the base twelve, or to any base, however, is just as impracticable as the general use of Esperanto, or the adoption of the exclusive use of the metric system in the United States and the British Empire. A duodecimal or a prime system is the scale of civilization, while quinary, decimal, and vigesimal systems are the scales of nature and have become traditional.

We must mention in passing that Leibniz, great mathematician and philosopher of the seventeenth century, co-inventor of calculus, advocated the binary system, the type of numeration with two as base, which is used by the most primitive of primitive races. He attached mystic significance to this system. He believed that it was 'the image of Creation'; he imagined that Unity (One) represented God, and Zero the void from which the Supreme Being drew all things, just as unity and zero are the only symbols needed to express all numbers in binary form.

For this realization of the simplicity of the binary system, but more for certain powerful concepts of Leibniz's logic and philosophy, Professor Norbert Wiener of the Massachusetts Institute of Technology has called the German mathematician the 'patron saint' of *cybernetics* (so-named from the Greek word *kybernetes,* meaning steersman). This is the modern science of control and communication in the animal as well as in the machine. It deals with electronic calculators, 'mechanical brains,' and the like. Professor Wiener anticipates that, in the course of its development, we may gain light on the functioning of the human mind and emotions, both normal and abnormal. At present, machines like BINAC, with the aid of 1400 vacuum tubes and a mercury 'memory,' calculate 12,000 times as fast as man, while the electronic brain now being designed by Professor John von Neumann of the Institute for Advanced Study will be able to add or subtract in 1/100,000th of a second.

What advantages did Leibniz see in binary notation and how are these carried out in current thinking machines? In the first place, there are only the symbols 1 and 0, the 'on' and 'off' of the banks of telegraph-type relays and radio-type tubes in the machine. Children studying binary arithmetic would find no tax in learning the number symbols. The addition rules reduce to

$$0 + 0 = 0 \qquad 0 + 1 = 1 \qquad 1 + 1 = 10$$

All multiplication tables are embodied in the three statements:

$$0 \times 0 = 0 \qquad 0 \times 1 = 0 \qquad 1 \times 1 = 1$$

But then there is the *length* of a number! Our thousand would have to be written as

$$1, \; 111, \; 101, \; 000$$

In calculating machines based on the binary system it is necessary initially to convert decimal numbers to binary form and finally to reverse the process. This phase of the machine's work is a concomitant of the game 'Nim,' a favorite of mathematicians. Three (or more) numbers in the decimal system are written down, and two players move alternately. Each player may reduce one and only one of the integers by any amount he wishes, except zero. The winning player is the one who obtains all zeros, that is, the set (0, 0, 0) when the game is played with three numbers.

A system of winning this game has been proved to depend on first expressing the set of numbers in the binary scale, then adding them in the everyday way (decimally). A winning combination is one in which the sums of the columns are each *even*. To illustrate, suppose we start with (13, 7, 5). Remembering that the successive columns from right to left in the decimal system signify units, tens, ten × tens, ten × ten × tens, etc. those in the binary system will represent units, twos, two × twos, two × two × twos, etc. Then, in the latter system, the numbers from one to ten would be written as 1, 10, 11, 100, 101, 110, 111, 1000, 1001, 1010.

$$
\begin{array}{rl}
\text{thirteen} = & 1101 \\
\text{seven} = & 111 \\
\text{five} = & 101 \\
\hline
\text{decimal sum} = & 1313
\end{array}
$$

This is an unsafe combination, since all the columns give odd totals. The first player, A, changes the 13 in the original set to a 2 and thus arrives at a safe set, for

$$
\begin{aligned}
\text{two} &= 10 \\
\text{seven} &= 111 \\
\text{five} &= 101 \\
\hline
\text{decimal sum} &= 222
\end{aligned}
$$

and all the columns have even sums. Let us imagine the remaining moves as B $(2, 0, 5)$; A $(2, 0, 2)$; B $(1, 0, 2)$; A $(1, 0, 1)$; B $(1, 0, 0)$; A $(0, 0, 0)$.

We leave it to the reader to verify that A plays safe each time. It has been proved that if the initial set of numbers is unsafe, then A, the one who plays first, can maintain safe combinations throughout and eventually win. On the other hand, if the initial set is safe, it can be shown that any move whatsoever must make the position unsafe and it is B who can win by careful playing. Since the original combination determines the outcome, providing the player favored moves correctly, these first numbers should be dealt from a shuffled pack or selected in some other random fashion. Then in order to give a chance to the player not favored, the game can be played with large numbers (making conversion to binary form more difficult) or with a large set of numbers; the time for moves can be limited and it can be required that all figuring be mental. Thus players anxious to win may find it advantageous to memorize safe combinations.

The essential advantage of a position system and the choice of a base of reasonable size is that a small number of symbols will accomplish the compact representation of any arithmetic number, however large or small. Recent studies of cuneiform tablets, such as those made by Otto Neugebauer, indicate that the Babylonians, as early as 2000 B.C., were great mathematicians and among other accomplishments actually did select a number base and evolve a position system. Their weakness was in failure to master completely the idea of *zero*. To put the Babylonian weakness into modern dress, let us imagine our system without a zero. We write

$$1 \qquad 2 \qquad 3$$

Is this one hundred twenty-three, or one thousand two hundred thirty, or ten thousand two hundred three? The Babylonians had a sexagesimal system (sixty as base) as the result of the use of their arithmetic in astronomy and their estimate of the year as 360 days. When they wrote ▼ , it represented not only one but sixty, thirty-six hundred (sixty × sixty) or sixty multiplied any number of times. How could one tell which number was meant? Only from the context. Eventually, as some cuneiform tablets show, they evolved a symbol for a void. Although Naburianu apparently understood the meaning of zero, Babylonian computers did not use the symbol in computation; that is, they did not accord it the rank of a number. It was more a mark of punctuation, like our dash.

The idea of position is the essence of a good system of numeration, and this conception was mastered early in the West as well as in the East. The Maya Indians of Yucatan had a positional notation using a vigesimal system (base twenty). To the Hindu mathematicians must go all credit for carrying the idea to completion—not only symbolizing numbers, but computing with them successfully. One of the most significant instances of this is the fact that they alone, of all peoples, first included the concept *zero* and the symbol *0* among other cardinal numbers and did not think of it merely as a dash or *sunya* (void). Zero is the most civilized of the cardinals, for it represents the greatest degree of abstraction. One can see two hands, two trees, two stones, etc. There are concrete images from which to abstract 'twoness.' But who goes to market to buy zero chickens? This may be the end result, but certainly not the initial aim of a business transaction. The concept of zero was not abstracted from concrete images, but from the consideration of other abstractions—the symbols for the cardinals themselves: 1, 2, 3, 4, etc. In writing and reckoning, these symbols had the common attribute of positional significance and a common difference of one in magnitude of successive cardinals. When arranged in order of size, they are thought of as *ordinal* numbers. To care for an absence of a cardinal symbol in reckoning, some symbol was needed. When created, it had to be placed ordinally, and so was put as lowest in rank, and the number system became 0, 1, 2, 3, 4, etc.

Even the greatest mathematical minds could not conceive of zero as being a number. Diophantus (*c.* A.D. 275), the leading algebraist of antiquity, worked out puzzles of this sort in connection with algebraic theory: what number, multiplied by itself, gives itself as answer? 'Obviously one,' said Diophantus. 'Also zero,' we would add, but this solution did not exist for Diophantus, because to him zero was not a number, just a dash.

Various explanations have been offered why the idea of zero as a number came more readily to the Hindus than to other peoples. One interpretation connects the zero concept with the Hindu picture of Nirvana, the ideal state of 'nothingness.' Some materialists suggest that the widespread poverty of Indian natives furnished the concrete situations abstracted in the zero. At any rate, even Bhaskara, at the summit of Hindu arithmetic achievement, was still not at ease in computations involving zero. One reason for this is that zero is actually exceptional in some of its behavior.

In all the years of elementary schooling of all the many generations of children who have been exposed to arithmetic, it is doubtful whether any child stumbling over a division example thought of using as a substitute for the usual '*I* can't do this' the novel '*No one* can do this—it is really impossible.' If we ask for the answer to $8 \div 2$, we can check it by the multiplication $4 \times 2 = 8$. If we ask for $8 \div 0$, however, there is no answer that will check, since there is no number that when multiplied by 0 will give 8. If we try $5 \div 0$, $\frac{1}{2} \div 0$, etc. we are just as badly off. Division by zero is impossible! For the particular quotient $0 \div 0$, any answer will do, since any answer will check. The result of $0 \div 0$ is *indeterminate*.

No wonder Bhaskara was puzzled! In 1152 he wrote: '$1 \div 0$ is like the infinite invariable God who suffers no change.' Translated into less mystic language, $1 \div 0$ is *infinite*. Bhaskara's reasoning was as follows: If we perform the series of divisions, $1 \div 0.1$, $1 \div 0.01$, $1 \div 0.001$, $1 \div 0.000001$, etc., the answers 10, 100, 1,000, 1,000,000, etc. become increasingly large. Hence, he thought, if we divide by *nothing at all,* the answer should be inconceivably large or infinite. A more accurate statement would be:

$$1 \div 0 \text{ is meaningless}$$

and 1 divided by a variable quantity approaches no definite limit as this variable gets smaller and smaller, but exceeds all bounds.

Nothing of the Hindu mathematics would be ours if it were not for the Arabs, who carried the Hindu thought back to the region from which it had originally come and then transmitted it to Europe. It is this historic fact that often causes the erroneous naming of our numerals as Arabic. After the death of their Prophet (A.D. 632), the Mohammedans obtained successively possession of Egypt, North

Africa, part of Spain, and Sicily. Later they extended their conquests to the East as far as India, a fact that explains their opportunity for contact with Hindu culture. Toward the end of the eighth century, a Hindu astronomer was summoned to Baghdad to translate certain trigonometric tables into Arabic. It is thought that these tables brought about the use of the Hindu numerals by the Arab mathematicians.

Those were the days of Harun-al-Rashid, the Caliph of the Arabian nights. Harun must have given some thought to scientific progress, for he had the mathematical classics translated into Arabic and encouraged mathematical activity in general. Al-Mamun, the son of Harun-al-Rashid, succeeded him. He was not only a patron of mathematics but an astronomer in his own right. The greatest of his associates was Al-Khowarazmi, who wrote a mathematics book in which the Hindu numerals were used. This work had great influence throughout Europe and was one means of introducing the Hindu numerals to the Continent. The title of another of Al-Khowarazmi's treatises, *ilm al-jabr wa'l muqabalah,* meaning transposition and removal of terms in an equation, was often quoted in abbreviated form, and the *al-jabr* became our *algebra.* Later, the Moorish universities in Spain continued the work of spreading the Hindu numerals and arithmetic to Europe.

2

Nature, Art, and Geometry

Mighty are numbers, joined with art, resistless.

EURIPIDES

IN THE early hours of the day the group has gathered more than its quota of the ripe fruit, but now efforts lag in proportion to the sun's elevation. The laborers search the August sky for some kindly cloud, some momentary shadow to shield them from the relentless glare.

The tenant-farmer grows impatient. He circulates among the bare-torsoed, muslin-skirted men and shouts, 'Hurry, hurry!'

In obedience, the workers leap over irrigation ditches and fall into ranks.

Dusty breezes bearing the vague perfume of vegetation drift toward the adobe shelters at the edge of the field. From the doorway of one of these dwellings a poet regards the toilers. His eye follows the parallel paths of cultivation to their terminus in the arid sadness of the plain bordering the horizon. He seeks to extract from the scene some association for the next stanza of a poem.

In the town, an advocate in the security of his study appears well-satisfied with his prose efforts. He rereads the preamble he has prepared. He asks himself if he has covered all points.

He reads aloud: 'This legislation is designed to make justice prevail, to prevent the strong from oppressing the weak, to enlighten the land, and to further the welfare of the people.'

An astronomer arises from his daytime slumbers. Some dream, some compulsion, drives him to examine at once his records of heliacal risings and settings of Venus.

The office of the statistician is a place of conferences. A matter of investment is at issue.

The computer consults the stacks of tablets, fretting, 'That boy never arranges them in proper order.'

Although the exponential tables are located, the clerk receives the customary rebuke.

At school, having devoted the cooler morning hours to 'three R' routine, the children are listening once more to the familiar legends on which they are to be catechized: how through erring in the matter of forbidden fruit, Man came to forfeit everlasting life; how later the Deity brought about a flood to destroy mankind except for one righteous man and his family.

*　　*　　*

No, not southern California in mid-twentieth century, but the Tigris-Euphrates plain in the second millennium before the Christian era! Here, at an earlier date, was the cradle of all civilization; here mathematics had taken firm root and was to flourish well nigh to full bloom. For many centuries prior to 2500 B.C. the non-Semitic people who lived just north of the Persian Gulf had developed a culture in which mathematics played a prominent role. Semites who lived near these early Sumerians eventually conquered them, absorbed their mathematics and general mores, and developed their civilization to greater heights.

From our initial tale of the triumphs of Hindu arithmetic we now go back to the probable setting of *all* mathematical origins. In exegetical spirit, we explain some facts of our introductory sketch. As for the school children and the legends that their priest-teachers were inculcating—scholars have always admitted that Mesopotamian myths resembled Biblical stories.

We have alluded to the story of Noah. The Biblical and Babylonian versions are in almost complete agreement. What locale could be more natural for a devastating deluge than a land between two mighty rivers? There was even a Sumerian parallel to the birth of Moses. Sargon I related, 'My humble mother conceived me; in secret she brought me forth. She placed me in a basket-boat of rushes.' Sargon was then rescued by a worker and the rest of the tale is a success story, climaxed by his rule over the first great empire in history.

The legal extract of our sketch is drawn from the classic Code of Hammurabi, model for latter-day law, which in turn stems in good part from an earlier Sumerian code. The greatest king of Ur (Abraham's city), King Ur-engur, had boasted (*c.*2400 B.C.), 'By God-inspired laws of righteousness, forever I established justice.'

The astronomer in our picture is one in the chain of patient observers and inspired theoreticians who laid the foundation for the work of the Babylonian Copernicus and Kepler, whose names were Naburianu and Kidinnu and whose dates are estimated at present as some time about the fourth or fifth century B.C. Exact dates and names of other Mesopotamian astronomers must await further archaeological findings, but it now appears that the Alexandrian Greeks, Hipparchus and Ptolemy, who for 1900 years have been called the founding fathers of theoretical astronomy, leaned heavily on the work of Babylonian forefathers.

Closely allied to the work of these observers of the heavens was that of the conscientious compilers of all sorts of mathematical tables. The 'statistician' of our sketch might be pictured appropriately as using a chart to estimate maturity dates on loans. Babylonian rates would seem usurious to us for they ranged from 20 to 33 per cent. Another type of table (see chapter 5) helped students to solve cubic equations. Still another evolved from theorizing on 'Pythagorean' numbers (chapter 4) a thousand years before Pythagoras lived and in a subtler fashion than the Greek himself was to achieve. As for the tables associated with the forte of the Babylonians, they indicate to what a great extent the early science of the stars stimulated mathematical development. At the pinnacle of Babylonian progress, these tables included the sexagesimal equivalent of a twenty-nine-place decimal. Such was the computational ability of the era of Kidinnu and the precision associated with his cosmic theories. By the time Babylonian astronomy merged with Greek, the method of 'harmonic analysis' (see chapter 7) was being applied to the theory of the moon and other complicated periodic phenomena, thus anticipating by some 1800 years ideas of the French mathematician Fourier.

In our first chapter we touched on man's debt to the Babylonians for a position system of numeration and the arithmetic that grew out of it. Later in our story we shall reveal the subtleties of the algebra that flourished in Mesopotamia and was doubtless the greatest mathematics of antiquity. Let us now, however, examine one of the lesser Babylonian contributions, the applied geometry that enabled this early people to stem the inundations of their great rivers, channelizing the outbursts to enrich the land, or to construct architectural marvels like the famed Palace of Bel and the oft-described Hanging Gardens.

At school, students are usually told that geometry originated in Egypt and was perfected in Greece, but it is now believed that the Nile merely borrowed from the Tigris and Euphrates, and that the mathematical glory of Greece probably drew a strong draught of inspiration from Babylonian springs. Even in the first century after Christ the Jewish historian Josephus wrote that Abraham had brought arithmetic from Chaldea to Egypt.

If engineering geometry had reached an advanced point in Babylonia and Egypt more than three thousand years ago, how far back are we to go for the roots? It is our belief that 20,000 B.C. would be a good approximation. The Aurignacian men of the

FIG. 4. Fragment of reindeer's antler found in the Hautes Pyrenees showing spirals carved by late Aurignacian men (from Cook, T. A. *Curves of Life,* New York, Henry Holt & Co., 1914).

Third Paleolithic Period evidently had a knowledge of the geometry of form, as remains of their art indicate (see fig. 4). They observed, imitated, and standardized shapes they saw in nature and so climbed the first rung of the ladder we call the scientific method. Remains found in the Old World, Mexico, and Peru furnish ample evidence that such geometry was practiced universally at a very early date, antedating the more abstract numerical activities discussed in the previous chapter. In textiles, architecture, personal ornaments, and pottery, primitive man demonstrated a cognizance of geometric form.

The figures that were basic in ancient art and industry are still fundamental. These are the *regular polygons* or plane straight-line figures having all sides and angles equal, the angles being convex (less than 180°). The simplest regular polygons are obviously the equilateral triangle and the square. The petals of flowers, the bodies of starfish are arranged so as to form regular pentagons (5 sides), regular hexagons (6 sides), or other regular polygons.

The regular hexagon seems to be a special favorite of nature, for we find it in snow crystals, in the cells of the beetle's eye, in the comb of the honey-bee, and elsewhere. It can be proved by mathematical methods that the honey-bee's choice of the regular hexagonal cell is a most remarkable one, for only in this way can a maximum amount of honey be stored with a minimum use of wax.

Since nature is admitted to be the original for all classic art work, we should expect to have the regular polygon occur in design. And thus it is the basis of ancient and modern tile patterns; it appears in the six-pointed star of David and the five-pointed star of the American flag.

The regular decagon (ten sides) is of special interest to the artist. In figure 5 the side of the decagon was measured, and *OB* was laid off equal to this length. In mathematics the radius is said

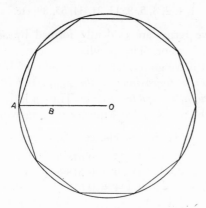

FIG. 5. The regular decagon. The side divides the radius in golden section.

to be divided in *golden section,* or according to *divine proportion.* A crude approximation of the ratio which *OB* bears to *BA* is 5:3.[1] The ratio of the two parts of *OA* is of miraculously frequent occurrence in nature, and hence the term 'divine proportion.' It would follow, then, that the same ratio should prevail in classic art.

Before explaining Nature's divine proportions, let us make acquaintance with the *Fibonacci sequence* of numbers, named after an outstanding Italian mathematician of the thirteenth century, Leonardo of Pisa. He was the son (*figlio*) of Bonaccio, hence the

---

[1] The exact incommensurable value of the ratio is given in chapter 4, page 85, where golden section is discussed more fully.

name *Fibonacci*. In his noted *Liber Abaci*, appears the following problem:

How many pairs of rabbits can be produced from a single pair in a year if it is supposed that every month each pair begets a new pair which from the second month on becomes productive?

The number of pairs living at the end of each month are: First—1; second—1; third—2 (because the pair recorded for the first month begets a new pair); fourth—3 (because the pair recorded for the first and second month begets another pair); fifth—5 (because the 2 pairs recorded for the third month beget 2 new pairs); etc. This leads to the number sequence

$$1, 1, 2, 3, 5, 8, 13, 21, 34, 55, 89, \text{etc.}$$

where successive terms are evidently formed by adding the last term to its predecessor. The peculiar property of the Fibonacci sequence is that if we go out far enough the *ratio of any successive pair of numbers is approximately the same, and is approximately equal to the ratio of the golden section*. Thus, a little arithmetic will show that for the terms of the sequence starting with 34, namely

$$34, 55, 89, 144, \text{etc. we have}$$

$$34/55 = 0.618+$$
$$55/89 = 0.618+$$
$$89/144 = 0.618+$$

These ratios agree with one another, as well as with the golden section, in the third decimal place.[2] Ratios of numbers further out give still closer agreement. Now it is surprising to find that the numbers of the Fibonacci sequence occur constantly in plant growth. The curves on a daisy disc, for example, run in two sections, 13 one way and 21 the other. The rows of florets on a sunflower disc may show 34 in one direction, and 55 in another, or even as high as 89 and 144 (see fig. 6). Note that 13 and 21, 34 and 55, 89 and 144 are successive pairs in the Fibonacci sequence and offer approximations to divine proportion. In our illustrations, we have shown the sunflower head with a 34, 55 system of growth, as well as a pine cone with a 5, 8 system (fig. 7).

The English botanist Church offered a theory (1901) to explain these phenomena. He found that such growth as occurs in the daisy

[2] Again, see page 85.

and sunflower discs, cones, and similar formations can be plotted as in fig. 8 by criss-crossing two sets of spirals (*logarithmic spirals,* to use a more exact mathematical description), one set winding one way, the other the opposite way. The number of spirals in each set

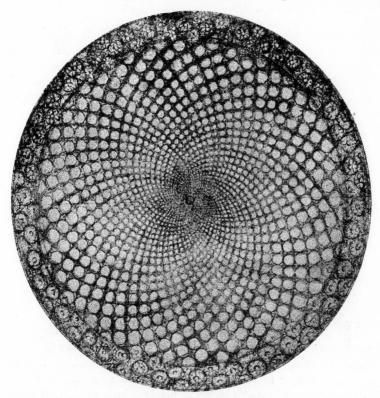

Fig. 6. Head of giant sunflower showing spiral curves on which the seeds are planned (from Colman, S. and Coan, C. A. *Proportional Form,* New York, Putnam, 1920).

is fixed by the Fibonacci sequence and the law of golden section. Thus there may be 5 in one set and 8 in the other, 8 in one set and 13 in the other, 13 in one set and 21 in the other, and so on. The spirals form a network of curvilinear 'rectangles,' and if we fill these with circles as in figure 8 we can get a good picture of how nature seems to plan the growth of plants.

Church has a hypothesis why plant growth and animal as well

should occur in just this way. He forms an analogy between electrical energy and living energy and suggests that the distribution of living energy follows lines identical with those of electrical energy, and that such things as a leaf arrangement and the plan of a nautilus are comparable with *electrical lines of equipotential.*

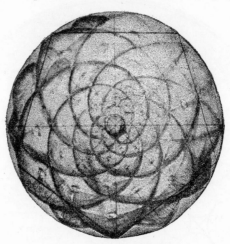

Fɪɢ. 7. Pine cone with 5, 8 system (from Colman, S. and Coan, C. A. *Proportional Form,* New York, Putnam, 1920).

The divine proportion of nature is everywhere in evidence in Greek art and was also used by many of the great masters of a later day. The sculpture of Phidias is typical. If the work of this renowned sculptor of the Golden Age is used as a model, then a well-proportioned man 68 inches in height is built as follows: From the ground to his navel is 42 inches; from his navel to the crown of his head is 26 inches; from the crown of his head to the line of his breasts is 16 inches; and from his breasts to his navel is 10 inches. The ratios of these measurements are

$$10/16 = 5/8 \qquad 16/26 = 8/13 \qquad 26/42 = 13/21 \qquad 42/68 = 21/34$$

These are those approximations to golden section given by the successive terms 5, 8, 13, 21, 34 of the Fibonacci sequence.

Some schools of art teach that divine proportion is something to be used deliberately by artists in their compositions. They feel that the Greeks and later artists made conscious use of golden section.

It is more likely, however, that such use was unconscious, and that the artist, who must always be a most sensitive observer of nature's forms, absorbs a feeling for those proportions which nature uses. Rather than interpret classic art as a mere copy of natural forms,

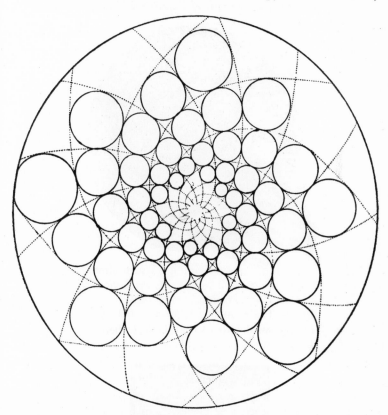

Fig. 8. Theoretical diagram of logarithmic spiral construction for 8, 13 system (from Church, A. H. *Relation of Phyllotaxis to Mechanical Laws*, London, Williams & Norgate, 1901).

we can view it as the creative work of masters who had absorbed so thorough a knowledge of nature's proportions that they imitated them unconsciously. The use of golden section is, to use the words of Goethe, like all the work of an artist, 'a revelation working from within; a synthesis of world and mind.' 'Art does not exactly imitate that which can be seen by the eyes, but goes back to that

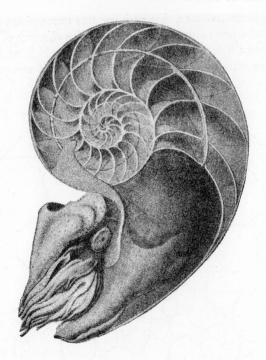

FIG. 9. The nautilus exhibits a perfect logarithmic spiral (from Cook, T. A. *Curves of
Life,* New York, Henry Holt & Co., 1914).

FIG. 10. Spirals in the horns of the eland (from Cook, T. A.
Curves of Life, New York, Henry Holt & Co., 1914).

Fɪɢ. 11. Spiral Nebula M51 Canum Venaticorum. *By permission of Lick Observatory.*

element of reason of which Nature consists and according to which Nature acts.'

In connection with a discussion of geometric form, we must mention a curvilinear figure that occurs with great frequency in nature. It is the spiral. We have already seen its association with plant growth. Other instances are to be found in shells, horns of animals, human anatomy, nebulae, etc. (figs. 9, 10, 11). Hence it is not surprising to find the spiral occurring in carvings made 20,000 years ago (fig. 4) by the Aurignacian men living in the French Pyrenees, as well as in all ornamentation from the Golden Age of Greece to the present time, in the work of Leonardo, Dürer, and other artists, and in columns and staircases.

Other geometric forms observed in nature and imitated in art at a very early date are the regular polygons previously mentioned. The *regular solids,* or regular three-dimensional forms, illustrated

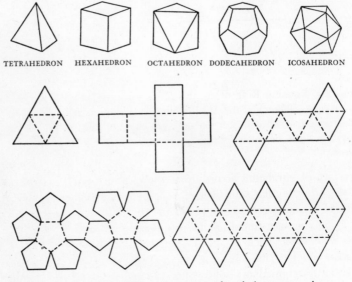

TETRAHEDRON   HEXAHEDRON   OCTAHEDRON   DODECAHEDRON   ICOSAHEDRON

FIG. 12. Regular solids and patterns for their construction.

in figure 12 (which contains patterns for their construction), by contrast, are man-made discoveries. The Greeks (probably the Society of Pythagoras) proved, by logical methods, that a maximum of five such solids is possible. Regular solids contrast with regular polygons in two ways. First, there are regular polygons of 3, 4, 5, 6 . . . *any* number of sides; that is, the variety is infinite. Secondly, man observed such polygons in nature and later abstracted the general concept. The number of regular solids is *finite,* and although these forms do occur in nature—that is in crystal structure—mathematics discovered them first by abstract methods and then constructed and applied them. Very much later in the history of science, natural regular solids were found. In this instance and in many others pure mathematics predicted natural phenomena.

A regular solid has regular polygons of the same kind as faces and has all its 'solid angles' (polyhedral angles) convex and equal. The regular *tetrahedron* and *cube* were known to the Babylonians and Egyptians, but no jeweler to date seems to have fashioned a

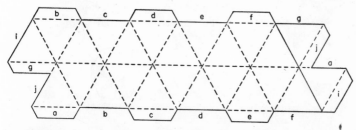

Fig. 13. Rotating Ring of tetrahedra (discovered by J. M. Andreas and R. M. Stalker). If the edges of this pattern are joined, a solid will be formed which constitutes a necklace of tetrahedra. It will not be rigid and can be rotated round and round.

necklace of tetrahedra according to the plan of figure 13. The use of the other regular solids became frequent in design even though natural models were originally lacking. In addition to their artistic function they are important in modern higher algebra, strange as this may seem. Each of the star solids shown in figure 14 has a regular solid as its core. Star solids (figs. 14, 15, 17) and semi-regular (Archimedian) solids (fig. 16) might be termed 'regular' by us, but they did not conform to Greek (artificial) rules for polygons and polyhedrons which permitted only *convex* angles, and forbade *reflex* angles, whether plane or solid.

Nowadays a pure mathematician feels confident that his abstract discoveries will be useful some day, and a physicist or a chemist is willing to prophesy and wait. When gaps were found in the periodic table, chemists were reasonably confident that the missing elements would turn up sooner or later, and, if not, felt they would be willing to modify chemical theories. The ancients, however, were less experienced scientists and could not wait. They were too accustomed to the pattern

$$\text{nature} \longleftrightarrow \text{mathematics}$$

Fig. 14. Star Solids (from Ball, W. W. R. *Mathematical Recreations and Essays,* London, Macmillan, 1940).

and wanted their applications at hand. When they were unable to find them, they resorted to imagination. So it was that the Society of Pythagoras (540 B.C.) held that earth had been produced from the regular hexahedron or cube; fire from the regular tetrahedron; air from the regular octahedron; water from the regular icosahedron; and the heavenly sphere from the regular dodecahedron.

Fig. 15. Stellated Dodecahedron as drawn by Leonardo da Vinci (from Ghyka, M. C. *Le Nombre d'Or,* Paris, Librairie Gallimard, 1931).

Pythagoras had spent considerable time in the Orient, and it is possible that he acquired a taste for mystic interpretations there. The great philosopher Plato (430–349 B.C.) found the fictional notion of the natural occurrence of regular solids pleasing and helped to perpetuate it—and unfortunately, along with it, a tradition of mystic application of pure mathematical discoveries.

If mysticism revealed the emotional streak of Babylonians and Egyptians, their geometry indicated that they were fundamentally down-to-earth. They worked out essentially the particular geometric facts called for by their practical needs, and it was left to the Greeks, at a later date, to make of geometry a true science. 'Whatever we Greeks receive, we improve and perfect,' said Plato. About

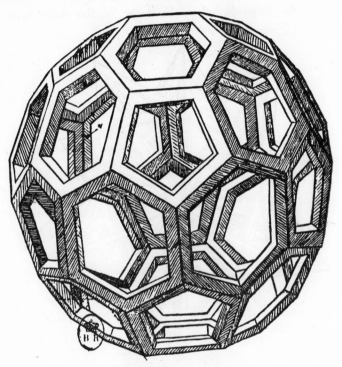

Fig. 16. A semi-regular or Archimedean solid as drawn by Leonardo da Vinci (from Ghyka, M. C. *Le Nombre d'Or,* Paris, Librairie Gallimard, 1931).

300 B.C. Euclid showed that this was no idle boast. He compiled all the mathematical work (both geometric and geometro-algebraic) of the Greeks, including his own, into the *Elements,* a text which, totaling all copies sold, is second only to the Bible in circulation in the Western world. We shall postpone a discussion of the Euclidean technique until much later in our story and limit ourselves at present to the practical mathematics of the Near East.

As an imitation of Babylonian experimental geometry, we might

FIG. 17. Artistic composition based on the Icosahedron (from
Ghyka, M. C. *Le Nombre d'Or,* Paris, Librairie Gallimard,
1931).

use a protractor to indicate that the sum of the angles of a triangle is 180°, or that in an isosceles triangle (one with two and only two sides equal), the angles opposite the equal sides are equal. Incidentally, Babylonian astronomers were the first to assume that the Sun moves uniformly in a circular path around the Earth in 360 days. Thus it became customary to divide a circle into the 360 equal parts we now call *degrees,* and embody this fact in the protractor and other tools.

As the ancients applied their geometry to surveying, it was a relatively simple matter. Crude instruments seemed to meet the

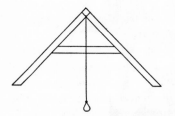   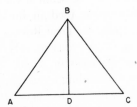

Fɪɢ. 18. Egyptian level.   Fɪɢ. 19. Isosceles triangle.

needs of the era remarkably well. One early requirement was a device for running a horizontal line. For this the Egyptians used a wooden framework shaped like the letter A (fig. 18), with a plumb line suspended.

To understand the Egyptian trick, notice that in isosceles triangle *ABC, BD* is drawn from the vertex to the midpoint of the base (fig. 19). With a protractor or the corner of a piece of paper, you can check the fact that the angles at *D* are *right angles,* or as we sometimes say, line *BD* is *perpendicular* to *AC.* Thus the Egyptians held the level of figure 18 so that the plumb line would hang opposite the midpoint of the crossbar. They knew that the line and the bar must meet at right angles, and, since the plumb line always hangs in a vertical position, the bar in the *A* always furnishes the horizontal.

The Greeks proved in rigorous fashion the fact that the base angles of an isosceles triangle are equal. The Euclidean proof of the equality of the base angles represented the limit of the work in geometry at the medieval universities and was often referred to as the *Pons Asinorum* or Bridge of Asses, with the inference that the students could not cross it. They countered with the rhyme:

> If this be rightly called the Bridge of Asses,
> He's not the fool that sticks but he that passes.

Although the Egyptians did not prove, but merely surmised from experiment the equality of the base angles of an isosceles triangle, the primitive level was used satisfactorily in first-class irrigation projects in Egypt and Babylonia, as well as in some remarkable engineering feats such as the construction of a set of water gauges in the Nile Valley. The same instrument, which can be seen in the Museum at Cairo or pictured on the tombs of Roman surveyors, was used in building canals in Mesopotamia and in constructing the great Roman aqueducts.

Some of the ancient surveying problems were concerned with finding distances or lengths. But the fundamental land problem was that of finding areas. The Egyptian pyramids and our skyscrapers are evidence that geometry must also concern itself with volumes. We should classify these problems as one-dimensional, two-dimensional, and three-dimensional geometric questions. In the world of practical or 'physical' geometry, even early history shows that the study of form and size in nature went hand in hand with the measurement of time. Babylonian geometry especially was concerned with time. The study of astronomy and the creation of some types of clock and calendar even among early peoples show that the measuring of time and of space have always been associated intuitively and practically. To say that time is *the* fourth dimension would be incorrect pure mathematics. To say that the space-time continuum used by Einstein is four-dimensional is correct. It is like saying that four means a certain set of apples; four may be *illustrated* by a particular set of apples but by many other concrete situations as well. In the world of pure mathematics there is four-dimensional, five-dimensional, one hundred-dimensional, even infinite-dimensional measurement. The mathematician feels no need to limit his imagination and likes his geometry to serve in situations with any number of dimensions. These are abstract and not actually geometric in the ordinary sense. But geometric vocabulary is a convenience and it is a surprising fact that modern science is able to make 'practical' application of the geometries of these many-dimensional worlds.

All measurement, whether it is concerned with distance or time or weight or electric current or intelligence or beauty, is merely comparison with a standard. In measuring length the Egyptians used a wooden rod or else knotted a rope so that all the sections were of equal length (their standard). Solomon's temple was three-score cubits in length. Nowadays our length standards are foot or meter. The unit area has a *square* form—in recent times, the square foot or square meter. The unit volume is a *cube*. It is surmised that the square rather than some other area was chosen for a standard because it was suggested by the square-tiled floors that existed at an early date. It was doubtless a common thing to estimate the number of tiles needed to cover a floor, and in this way to measure its area. The cube, as the regular solid with square faces, was the natural generalization for the standard volume.

Does anything as elementary as the measurement of length merit discussion? What could be simpler than applying a yardstick to a piece of cloth, or a foot-rule to the edge of a building? Well, then, how would you measure the length of the spiral segments we have mentioned or the distance a zig-zagging baseball travels? When lines are curved, does the surveyor lay off the standard foot or yard? Does he attempt to bend his unit in a suitable manner, or is there some other way out of this difficulty?

Would it ever be impossible to measure the length of a simple straight segment with any ruler, even if we were free to select any type of fractional subdivision (not necessarily halves, quarters, etc., or tenths, hundreds, etc.) and subdivide to any degree of submicroscopic fineness? In other words, are there absolutely *incommensurable* lengths from the point of view of ordinary arithmetic? The answer is 'Yes.' The question never occurred to the practical-minded Babylonians and Egyptians but nearly drove the Greeks mad. Eventually, it did lead to significant advances in mathematics. Incommensurability turns out to be the *rule* rather than the exception.

If the diameter (or any fractional part of it) is the unit of measure, pure mathematics proves that the circumference of a circle is incommensurable, that is, if the diameter is 1 unit, no fraction in the realm of elementary arithmetic will give the length of the circumference. Yet your childhood method of measuring the circumference is not too bad for practical purposes. Perhaps you constructed a cardboard circle with 7-inch diameter, rolled it, without sliding, until it had made one complete revolution, and then measured the length of its path, which turned out to be 22 inches (approximately). Thus you measured the *straight line path,* instead of the *curved* circumference. You found that the ratio of circumference to diameter is $22/7$ or $3\frac{1}{7}$ and assumed that if you

FIG. 20. Level on a funeral mosaic of Pompeii (from Ghyka, M. C. *Le Nombre d'Or,* Paris, Librairie Gallimard, 1931).

were to repeat the experiment carefully with many circles of different sizes, you would find the ratio of circumference to diameter to have approximately this same value each time. You obtained by *induction* the rule: *Circumference is approximately $3\frac{1}{7}$ times the diameter.* For more precise practical work a refinement of the fraction $1/7$ in the $3\frac{1}{7}$ ratio would be called for. Egyptians did fairly well in estimating the ratio of circumference to diameter as 3.16.

Babylonians and Hebrews used 3 as the value, just as we might in crude computations.

Greek or other pure mathematical methods will prove *deductively* that in all circles the ratio of the circumference to the diameter has the same value. This constant ratio of which $3\frac{1}{7}$ is an approximation is customarily symbolized by the Greek letter π. The Greeks originally used π (the Greek letter *p*) merely to represent the perimeter or periphery (*peri*—around) of a *standard circle,* one with *unit diameter.* Its circumference would be π multiplied by 1 and hence just π. It is evident that if a circle had a diameter 4, its perimeter would be 4 times as large as the standard circle or 4π and the ratio of 4π (circumference) to 4 (diameter) would be π. Hence π is the perimeter of a standard circle as well as the ratio of circumference to diameter in any circle.

Although π can be shown experimentally or logically to be a constant ratio connected with a circle, this is not the last word on this interesting number. No measuring tools, however refined, can give a precise value for π, for it turns out that it is not an ordinary fraction, which is another way of saying that the standard circle has an incommensurable length. After centuries of study by mathematicians, the final judgment on π was given in 1882 by Lindemann, who proved conclusively that it is 'transcendental.' This term has no mystic significance. It is just the appellation for a number that transcends not only ordinary fractional representation but even the domain of algebra. By the use of modern mathematical expressions for π we can approximate it to any degree of precision, to hundreds, to thousands of decimal places. One form of expression is the infinite series:

$$\pi = 4(1 - 1/3 + 1/5 - 1/7 + 1/9 - 1/11 + 1/13 - 1/15 + \cdots)$$

Carry out the series in the parenthesis as far as you like, noting that the addition and subtraction signs alternate and the denominators differ by two. Then total the parenthesis and multiply this total by 4. The more arithmetic you like, the better the approximation you will obtain. Twentieth-century engineers and other practical workers seldom require an excessively precise estimate of π. For the fun of it, some have invented mnemonics to assist the recall of an approximation, such as:

> See I have a rhyme assisting
> My feeble brain its tasks oft-times resisting.

Substitute the number of letters in each word for the word itself and you will get

$$\pi = 3.141592653589 \text{ (approximately)}$$

The letter π has become classic because it occurs in so many situations which, at first glance, appear to have no connection whatsoever with circles. A story on this point is told by the mathematical philosopher De Morgan ($c.1850$). He was explaining to an actuary what the chance was that a certain part of a group would be alive at a given time, and quoted a formula involving π. The actuary exclaimed in astonishment, 'My dear friend, that must be a delusion. What can a circle have to do with the number of people alive at a given time?' (A modern actuary would be more sophisticated in his mathematics.) De Morgan does not tell us what explanation he gave, but we shall give our own. If the original association of π with a circle is not connected with its other appearances, their fre-

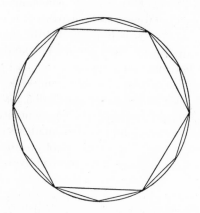

Fig. 21. Regular polygons inscribed in a circle of unit diameter. As the number of sides is increased indefinitely, the perimeter of the polygon approaches closer and closer to the circumference of the circle, whose length is symbolized by π. It can be proved that the following approximations hold true.

No. of sides	Perimeter of in-scribed polygon
6	3.000
12	3.106
24	3.134
384	3.142

quency will make a substantial group of scientific laws seem 'delusions' to many.

The fact is that π can be described as a *summing* or totaling number. There are other numbers like this in mathematics, but π gets the most publicity because of its venerability. The infinite series above, which expresses π, shows it as a sum of an infinite number of terms. The actuarial formula would involve a total of a large number of probabilities. Even the proof for the circumference of a circle, Greek style, involved summing an infinite series. In figure 21 we see a circle of unit diameter in which a regular hexagon and then a regular polygon of 12 sides are inscribed. In each case, the perimeter of the polygon approximates the circumference of the circle, the latter polygon yielding the better approximation. Measure the perimeters of the polygons with a ruler if you desire a crude value for π. Now, in our minds, if not in our drawings, we can increase the number of sides of the inscribed regular polygons to 24, 48, 96, 192, etc. (We need not double their number—just have them get smaller and increase their number.) The approximation would then, in theory, improve each time. The circle is the *limit* approached by the variable inscribed polygon as the number of sides is increased more and more, or in a sense, a circle is a regular polygon with an infinite number of sides. To find π, the circumference of the standard circle, we should thus have to sum an infinite number of infinitesimal values.

The concepts of limit and 'infinite' summation are mathematically sophisticated and we shall give them more attention later in our story. In those branches of mathematics where it is possible to perform 'infinite' summation, namely integral calculus and its extensions and applications, π is likely to appear. Hence the actuary in the story should have anticipated rather than been startled by its occurrence in the formula in question.

The next rung in the ladder of mensurational geometry is the consideration of an *area* rather than a length. The triangle, being the polygon with the smallest number of sides, is fundamental, and a formula for its area is derived in figure 22a. With the use of this formula the surface of a plot of land of any shape can be measured, provided its boundaries are straight lines (see fig. 22b). If an area has a curvilinear boundary, it can be approximated by using rectangles or triangles. By making these numerous and small, good estimates can be obtained. As such a procedure is difficult to carry out with accuracy, Archimedes (250 B.C.) tried to obtain a mathematical technique that would total all the small rectangular or triangular areas without measuring them. The fruition of this idea did not occur until the eighteenth century, when Newton and Leibniz perfected Archimedes' procedure, arriving at the technique called *integral calculus* (see chapter 10).

The area to be measured need not lie in a single plane or be flat. If the surface is that of a pyramid or a box form there is no prob-

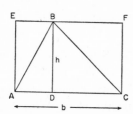 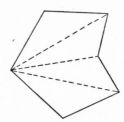

Fig. 22a. The area of *any* triangle is one half the product of base and height, for triangle *ABD* is one half of rectangle *AEBD* and triangle *DBC* is one half of rectangle *DBFC,* making the entire triangle *ABC* one half the entire rectangle.

Fig. 22b. Any polygonal area can be subdivided into triangles.

lem, because it is merely a case of measuring triangular or rectangular areas. Again, an approximation, or else the integral calculus, will take care of curvilinear surfaces. In all cases the idea is to measure areas *indirectly*. In the simple cases of the rectangle and triangle, area depends on measuring two lengths, those of base and altitude. Thus two-dimensional measurement is reduced to one-dimensional.

The next step in measurement is to obtain volumes by measurements of three lengths, thus reducing three-dimensional measurement to one-dimensional. Continuing the process there will be four-dimensional, five-dimensional, etc., 'hypervolumes.' The domain of measurement is unlimited and will take us far beyond oriental empiricism. Even the logical methods of Euclid will furnish exact answers in only a few simple cases.

Modern mathematics goes even further. Generalization is not all in the direction of higher dimensions. Mathematicians have generalized the idea of measure itself. Instead of considering lengths, areas, volumes, hypervolumes, they have investigated other entities closely related to these, which have become as vital in recent mathematics and science as earth-measure was to the ancients.

3

The Binding Energy of Thought

> These three notions, of the *variable,* of *form,* and of
> *generality,* comprise a sort of mathematical trinity
> which preside over the whole subject.
>
> WHITEHEAD

Mr. 'Chad' and Mr. 'Clem' are two of the pseudonyms for a doodle
that British and American soldiers of the Second World War
scribbled indiscriminately all over Europe, usually with some mild
'gripe' in Cockney lingo or G.I. slang appended: 'Wot, no bloomin'
fish?'; 'Wot, no dial tone?' Credit for Chad's creation has been
argued hotly in the public press by Army and Air forces, Tommies
and Yanks. His origin has been sought with the same zeal with
which a historian might look into the beginnings of geometry, and
by a strange quirk the whole story of the winking gremlin has
some actual connection with scientific thought.

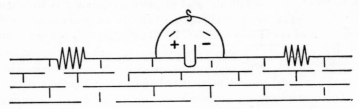

Wot, no PEACE?

As to Chad's origin: One story is that a REME (Royal Electrical
and Mechanical Engineers, popularly pronounced rem-may) in-
structor was explaining diagrammatically the charging of a condenser and indicated the condenser plates and the resistors in the
circuit by the customary electric symbols $\|$ and $\sim\!\!\wedge\!\!\sim$ respectively;
he also used the signs $+$ and $-$ to indicate the opposite charges
on the condenser plates, so that initially he drew on the black-
board:

Next he indicated the short-circuiting of the condenser by putting in Chad's dome, and, alternatively, the discharging of the condenser through the 'schnozzle'; then, with a question mark to please the 'doubting Thomases,' the whole became

Elaborations were added by addicts of the figure, and its quick adoption by the younger generations proved its appeal. Chad was probably named after the REME training school, which the boys referred to as 'Chad's Temple.'

Now Chad is mathematical in several respects. In the first place his quips about the *lack* of something ('Wot, no PEACE?') indicate that the man in the street recognizes zero as a number; the quip substitutes a Cockney symbol for a Hindu one. Going back to Chad as used by the REME teacher, he is merely an assemblage of certain electrical symbols that have been made standard for the sake of economy in verbal expression. In addition, it is far simpler

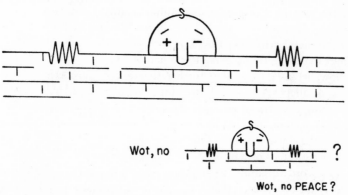

Fig. 23. Chad of a Chad.

in theoretical electricity to reason from a 'Chad' than from the apparatus itself. Thus one use puts Chad into the class of an arithmetic symbol, and another partakes of the character of geometric abstraction.

If idealization is one habit of the pure mathematician, *generalization* is another. The most mathematical doodler among the REME was the one who inscribed the message 'Wot,-no *Chad*?' below the customary cartoon when a superior officer forbade the drawing of the gremlin as a defacement of property. The disobedient youth was 'iterating' the idea of 'lack of something' to the lack of a lack of something. His act was like the generalization to tens of tens in arithmetic history, after the base ten had been selected. The Tommy should have created a new sort of gremlin, or placed the usual one in a different position, or added an additional question mark, or put a Chad within a Chad, or done something in order to symbolize the increased generality (see fig. 23).

Algebra is often referred to as generalized arithmetic. Let us see why. The use of literal symbols in algebra is proverbial. When we say, 'In this process, formula, or problem, the letter n symbolizes a *variable* number, in this case any cardinal number,' then we mean the n stands simultaneously for

$$0, 1, 2, 3, 4, 5, 6 \ldots 1000 \ldots 1,000,000 \ldots$$

Conceiving of all cardinal numbers in this way and representing them by a single act of thought and a single symbol may once again be described as an iteration of a previous process, namely that of formulating the concept, cardinal number, and creating a symbolism for the different cardinals. We recall, for example, that the abstraction 'fiveness,' symbolized by 5, is the essence of all possible sets of things matching the fingers of one hand.

Now, let us go one step further. Instead of considering the essence of all possible sets of five things or of one or two or three, etc., things, we try to consider the essence of all the 'essences' one, two, three, four, five, etc., and we symbolize this new concept by some letter, in this case n. This sort of generalization is not strictly analogous to tens of tens or 'No Chad.' It is more like the invention of the word 'gremlin' to indicate what are already abstractions, namely all the 'spirits' that make things go wrong; 'Chad' is only one species—the spirit of things lacking. The mathematician has to deal with the concept of variables so frequently that he needs a standard symbolism and uses an n or an x, or any letter he may choose to represent a *set* or *class of numbers*.

In an algebraic statement, formula, problem, or proof, we may consider sets of numbers other than the infinite class of cardinals. We may assign to x the task of representing all fractions, or all incommensurables, or all integers larger than 0 and less than 10, or all numbers in the range of atomic mass, or all numbers in the range of stellar distance, or every number that, when multiplied by itself, gives itself as an answer. The advantage of literal algebraic notation lies in the fact that the letters possess the power of working simultaneously with *all* numbers in some special set. When the 'all' is as inclusive as the set of cardinals, or the set of fractions, the variety of different situations that a *single* algebraic procedure will cover is, infinite.

Elementary algebra could be carried on even if the mathematician were to write *Number* or *Numero* or *Zahl* or *Res* (the Latin for thing—a customary usage even as late as the sixteenth century) instead of using *n* or *x*. The Greeks did not refer to a variable number as such or represent it by a letter. To them it was always a *length*. Instead of giving as an algebraic problem: Find a number that when multiplied by itself gives an answer of 9, they would have asked for the length of the side of a square with *area* nine square units. Multiplying the unknown length by itself again leads to the volume of a cube. To repeat the multiplication once more is a procedure they would never have considered because there was nothing geometric connected with the end picture. The Babylonians, however, had more imagination and did consider some algebraic questions that had no geometric analogues.

But what we wish to stress is that Babylonians and Greeks were algebraists without benefit of shorthand or literal symbolism. This was not their chief handicap. Instead, they suffered from inadequate abstractness in the concept of *variable number*. If they had progressed in making the variable notion pure, they might have developed their algebra to greater heights.

The use of literal symbols in algebra came much later in the history of mathematics and was originated by the French mathematician François Viète (1540–1603), better known under his Latin pen name Vieta. Vieta was a lawyer by profession and took up mathematics merely as a hobby, distributing his writings on the subject among his personal friends. He was first a member of the Bretagne parliament and later a member of the king's privy council. Cryptograms were a special mathematical pastime in which he indulged, and during a war between France and Spain he found the key to a Spanish code—by magic, the Spanish said.

Although Vieta's use of letters to represent variable numbers has become a simple matter to modern man, it really was a remarkable contribution to mathematics and marks the beginning of modern algebra. The value of the literal notation, like modern arithmetic, is difficult to appreciate. It is on the scene, and we cannot imagine a world without it any more than we can visualize existence without railroads, automobiles, and electrical appliances.

Since algebraic facts are merely whole *sets* of arithmetic facts 'in a nutshell,' laws inherent in arithmetic can be stated in *general* literal form and characterize ordinary algebra. Thus

$$3 + 4 = 4 + 3 = 7$$
$$\tfrac{2}{3} + 1\tfrac{1}{2} = 1\tfrac{1}{2} + \tfrac{2}{3} = 2\tfrac{1}{6}$$

illustrate the fundamental law

$$a + b = b + a$$

where *a* and *b* represent any and all integers and fractions. In fact they can also stand for the 'incommensurable' numbers to which we have made brief allusion.

This is called the *commutative law of addition*. Verbally, the *order* of terms in addition is immaterial. As algebraists invented new types of number and created rules for their 'addition,' they aimed to have this new addition obey the commutative law, as we shall see shortly.

In arithmetic the addition

$$3 + 4 + 2$$

signifies either

$$7 + 2 = 9$$

or

$$3 + 6 = 9$$

that is,

$$(3 + 4) + 2 = 3 + (4 + 2)$$

the parentheses indicating that the enclosed additions should be performed first. Hence, in the algebra of integers, fractions, incommensurables, and later of certain new types of number, it is assumed that

$$(a + b) + c = a + (b + c)$$

This is called the *associative law of addition*. To state this verbally would be a linguistic nuisance. The symbolic notation might be called a 'shorthand,' but more accurately, its function is rather a matter of clarification and exact expression.

Multiplication is also commutative and associative in everyday arithmetic and ordinary algebra. With some of the newest types of number, one or the other of these laws may not hold, since maintaining it would spoil the application to physical situations. There are *non*-commutative or *non*-associative algebras.

Obviously commutative and associative laws do not hold for the operations of subtraction and division.

$$4 - 3 \text{ does not equal } 3 - 4$$

The latter subtraction is impossible if we are dealing with the numbers of ordinary arithmetic. With the use of negative numbers an answer can be given for $3-4$, but it will still not be the same as $4-3=1$. The fact that division is not commutative is illustrated by

$$4 \div 2 = 2 \qquad 2 \div 4 = \tfrac{1}{2}$$

You may consider the discussion of commutative and associative laws as 'much ado about nothing.' Many years of contact with ordinary arithmetic make these things seem obvious. If we select illustrations from a field like quantum theory, the situation is quite different. Basic in quantum theory and all modern physical science is the fact that multiplication of the 'numbers' involved is *not* commutative.

$$q \times p \text{ does not equal } p \times q$$

and there is a famous formula:

$$qp - pq = \frac{ih}{2\pi}$$

that is, the two products always differ by the same quantity. The symbols q and p are not everyday numbers. Each stands for a *matrix* or a systematic arrangement of a whole set of numbers, and matrix 'multiplication' has a special meaning. In the formula we recognize the constant π which, as we have seen, is bound to appear in many mathematical situations. The quantities h and i are also fundamental in science and we shall have more to say about them presently.

Let us return to everyday affairs and take as 'numbers' chemical compounds or mixtures of these. In baking a cake with a recipe that calls for butter, sugar, eggs, flour, and baking-powder, you will have a flat cake if you put in the baking-powder first instead of last, and the order of adding the other ingredients will also affect the texture of the cake. The order of terms in baking or in any chemical experiment is certainly not immaterial. The sum of the terms (where $+$ means 'followed by' in the mixing process)

$$water + concentrated\ sulphuric\ acid$$

gives dilute sulphuric acid with slight heat of dilution, while

$$concentrated\ sulphuric\ acid + water$$

will bring about a tremendous production of heat and a very dangerous spattering of acid. Thus we would expect a sum of chemical symbols to differ for different arrangements of the terms.

For multiplication and division, *distributive laws* hold, which means that in the multiplication or division of a sum (or difference) the operation is applied to each of the terms to be added (or subtracted):

$$a(b + c) = ab + ac \qquad \text{or} \qquad a(b - c) = ab - ac$$

$$\frac{b + c}{a} = \frac{b}{a} + \frac{c}{a} \qquad\qquad \frac{b - c}{a} = \frac{b}{a} - \frac{c}{a}$$

if a, b, c are the numbers of ordinary arithmetic. These laws are generalizations of such arithmetic as the fact that doubling the subway fare for a city consists of doubling it for each person. Addition and subtraction are not distributive in the sense above. A \$100 gift to, or tax on, a group does not enrich or impoverish each member to that extent.

Failure to apply distributive laws on the one hand, or to use them where they do not apply, on the other, produces common 'boners.' There is the student with a cancellation complex, who says that

$$\frac{2 + x}{2x} = \frac{\overset{1}{\cancel{2}} + \overset{1}{\cancel{x}}}{\cancel{2}\cancel{x}} = 2$$

asserting as 'proof' such arithmetic as

$$\frac{1\cancel{6}}{\cancel{6}4} = \frac{1\cancel{66}}{\cancel{66}4} = \frac{1\cancel{666}}{\cancel{666}4} = \text{etc} \cdots = \frac{1}{4}$$

The latter example is not law but lucky accident. As for the former, its incorrectness as a general statement is indicated by taking different values for x. If $x = 1$

$$\frac{2 + x}{2x} = \frac{3}{2}$$

which is obviously not 2, as claimed. If the distributive law of division is used correctly

$$\frac{2 + x}{2x} = \frac{1}{x} + \frac{1}{2}$$

and this quotient will vary with x. Only for $x = \frac{2}{3}$ will it have the value 2.

Again, once a distributive law is mastered, there is a tendency to distribute everything.

$\sqrt{9 + 16}$ does *not* equal $\sqrt{9} + \sqrt{16}$, that is, 7

$\sqrt{9 + 16} = \sqrt{25} = 5$

The operation of taking square root (or cube root or any root) is not distributive with respect to addition or subtraction. On the other hand, taking of roots is distributive with respect to multiplication or division.

$$\sqrt{4 \times 9} = \sqrt{4} \times \sqrt{9} = 2 \times 3 = 6$$

$$\sqrt{\tfrac{16}{25}} = \sqrt{16 \div 25} = \sqrt{16} \div \sqrt{25} = \frac{4}{5}$$

A large portion of time in elementary algebra courses is spent gaining practice in manipulating literal symbols so as to follow the fundamental laws. Our point of view leads away from such mechanical procedures, since it is our purpose to stress the meaning of algebraic symbolism and its power in practical scientific applications rather than to drill on technical aspects.

Just as the surprises and contrasts of foreign travel are cultural experiences that bring into relief the virtues and faults of the traveler's native land, a brief examination of laws in some other type of algebra will give us perspective about ordinary arithmetic and algebra. The latter are concerned with numbers. Modern mathematics, however, has penetrated into fields that are not purely numerical but contain material that can be handled profitably through abstract symbolism. Such a domain is the *algebra of classes* or Boolean algebra, named after George Boole, an English mathematician whose book *The Laws of Thought* (1854) was a significant contribution to the progress of mathematical foundations. This algebra is useful in problems dealing with complex arrangements of electrical circuits, legal testimony, validity of detailed actuarial data, mathematical logic, probability theory, etc.

In Boolean algebra there is a *universe of discourse;* this universe may consist of all the members of the American Mathematical Society or all the types of atomic particle known at the present time, etc., depending on the subject of the problem. If u symbolizes the universe, then the letters a, b, c, etc. are used to stand for classes or groups of things in it.

Then ab, the *intersection* or *logical product* of a and b, consists of the common part of classes a and b. It is termed 'logical' because the algebra of classes is applied in the field of logic. If

u = all inhabitants of the United States
a = all Democrats
b = all residents of New York City
ab = all Democratic residents of New York City

The *union* or *logical sum* $a + b$ consists of all elements belonging to either a or b or both. With the concrete meanings just used, membership qualifications for $a + b$ are: being a Democrat *or* being a New Yorker. There is no objection to being doubly qualified, that is being a Democrat and a New Yorker. Then

$a + b$ = all residents of New York City as well as Democrats living elsewhere in the United States

Using $N(a)$ to mean the number of elements in a,

$$N(a + b) \text{ does not usually equal } N(a) + N(b)$$

for the total number of Democrats includes New York City Democrats, and if this is added to the number of residents of New York City, there will be duplication. Measurement is not distributive with respect to addition unless $ab = 0$, that is, unless a and b have no element in common. If a and b are North American and South American inhabitants

$$N(a + b) = N(a) + N(b) \text{ because } ab = 0$$

In general

$$N(a + b) = N(a) + N(b) - N(ab)$$

as illustrated by the fact that the number in the group, New Yorkers and Democrats elsewhere, can be found by adding the numbers for all Democrats and all New Yorkers and then subtracting the number of Democratic New Yorkers to avoid duplication.

The commutative, distributive, and associative laws of ordinary algebra transfer to additions and multiplications in the algebra of classes. New York Democrats are the same as Democratic New Yorkers, etc. but manipulative techniques differ to some extent from ordinary algebraic procedures. For example, $ab = 0$ when a and b represent inhabitants of North and South America respectively, although neither a nor b is zero. This could not occur in ordinary arithmetic, which requires that one factor be zero if a product vanishes. Also

$$a + a = a$$
$$a + a + a + a + \cdots = a$$

for if we add the class of United States citizens to itself again and again, we have the same class with no new elements in it. Also

$$aaaaa \ldots = a$$

since any class has all its elements in common with itself. Because

$$a + a + a + \cdots = a$$
$$aaa \ldots = a$$

there is no need for coefficients and exponents in this algebra, that is, symbols like $5a$ and a^2 will not appear.

There are laws of *absorption,* like

$$a(a + b) = a$$

(The part common to a class and a larger class including it is the first class.) If

$$a = \text{all United States Democrats}$$
$$b = \text{all United States Republicans}$$
then $\quad a + b = \text{all United States Democrats and Republicans}$
$$a(a + b) = \text{elements common to the two classes } a \text{ and } a + b$$
$$= \text{all United States Democrats}$$
$$= a$$

A special symbol is used for *complementation.* If a is a class, a' indicates its complement, that is all elements in the universe of discourse except those in a. If

$$u = \text{all United States citizens}$$
$$a = \text{United States citizens with incomes less than \$3000}$$
$$a' = \text{United States citizens with incomes of \$3000 or more}$$

To give an especially simple, and hence somewhat artificial, instance of how the algebra of classes is used to analyze statements,

consider the problem of two librarians who are told to sort a pile
of books just returned by borrowers. The first librarian is told to
collect all political works by American authors and all books over
500 pages by foreign authors. The second is told to take political
works exceeding 500 pages and novels by Americans, provided they
are not political in nature. Will there be any books claimed by both
librarians? If

$$u = \text{all books in the pile}$$
$$a = \text{books by Americans}$$
$$b = \text{books over 500 pages}$$
$$p = \text{books of political nature}$$
$$n = \text{novels}$$
then
$$a' = \text{foreign books}$$
$$b' = \text{books of 500 pages or less}$$
$$p' = \text{non-political works}$$
$$n' = \text{books other than novels}$$

The first librarian will call for

$$ap + a'b$$

The second will claim

$$bp + anp'$$

Both will claim the intersection of these two sets, namely

$$(ap + a'b)(bp + anp') = abpp + aanpp' + a'bbp + aa'bnp'$$

Since, according to the law of absorption

$$pp = p \qquad bb = b$$

and because complementary classes have nothing in common

$$pp' = 0 \qquad aa' = 0$$

the number of books claimed reduces to

$$abp + a'bp$$

which equals

$$bp(a + a') = bpu = bp$$

since the elements common to the universe and any class in it is
the class itself. Hence both librarians will claim political books of
over 500 pages.

After this short journey into another algebra, let us return to the
everyday variety. In it a symbol like x stands for a class or set of

numbers. A symbol like $x+y$ also represents a set of numbers, namely that formed by taking the arithmetic sum of any number in one set and the corresponding number in another. For example if

x represents the set of prices of all articles in a store, and
y represents the set of sales taxes on each, then
$x + y$ represents the set of actual costs to the purchaser.

What does $x+x$ mean? It signifies that there are two identical sets of numbers and addition is performed by pairing equal numbers. Then, since $1+1=2$, $2+2=4$, $6\frac{1}{2}+6\frac{1}{2}=13$,

$$x + x = 2x$$

leading to the *coefficient* symbolism of ordinary algebra. Iterating the procedure

$$2x + x = 3x, \text{ etc.}$$

and other coefficients appear. Since $x+x+x+x+x=5x$, we may think of any integral number y of such terms as yx, symbolizing *multiplication*. Even when y is not an integer we accept the juxtaposition of the two letters to symbolize multiplication. If x and y are numerically equal, the product is xx or x^2. Thus *exponents* make their appearance. By reversing addition, multiplication, and raising to a power (use of an exponent), we are led to subtraction, division, and root extraction. Hence, since algebraic addition leads to all other fundamental processes and symbolism, all of algebra, philosophically speaking, has its roots in the simple formula

$$z = x + y$$

From this and the fundamental laws it is possible to deduce additional rules that lead to the familiar manipulative processes of algebra and at certain points demand the creation of additional definitions and auxiliary symbolism. This is the body of pure mathematical material that goes by the name of elementary algebra. The manifold practical uses of this abstract subject are too well known to demand elaboration. Nevertheless the relationship of *applied* mathematics to the pure phases of the mother subject is something with which mathematicians of today are concerned.

In pure algebra, the only concern is *logical consistency*. In applied algebra, the focus of attention is the field to which application is made. The question in the latter case is: Do the numerical entities behave like the x's and y's? If the answer is 'Yes,' ordinary algebra is applicable. A 'No' may be more stimulating, for then it will demand a search for more appropriate mathematics and, if this does not exist, for something altogether new.

To give a simple indication of algebraic application, we now cite a set of examples from varied fields. We might have selected concrete instances of the basic addition formula but we have decided to pause one step higher in the development of algebra and study some of the many situations described by the multiplication formula

$$z = xy$$

We have two points to make—that, by analogy, all mathematical formulas and processes can be expected to describe a large body of scientific fact; and secondly, that the mathematical symbols, formulas, and techniques, whether elementary or advanced, are secondary in applications. When mathematics is applied it is the subject matter of the field involved upon which attention is focused.

Application I: Wave Phenomena

It is well known that sound is a wave phenomenon. Light and other forms of electromagnetic radiation can no longer be described adequately as waves. Nevertheless they partake of certain wave properties and hence the mathematical vocabulary of waves is still retained in discussing them.

To understand such usage, think of wave propagation as being somewhat like the blowing of soap bubbles one after another at uniformly timed intervals, each bubble to expand at the same speed forever in our mind's eye unless some obstacle is encountered (see fig. 24). If our 'waves' are electromagnetic, then the bubbles can be pictured as having a speed of radial expansion equal to 186,000 miles or 300,000,000 meters per second. We can in imagination blow 1 bubble each second. Then in fig. 24, as the bubbles expand, their radii will always differ by 186,000 miles. If, in our mind's eye, we blow 2 per second, the radial difference will be 93,000 miles. If we blow 3 per second, the difference will be 62,000 miles. The number blown each second is called the *frequency* of the radiation, and the radial difference is called the *wave length*. Obviously

$$\text{speed} = \text{frequency} \times \text{wave length}$$
$$\text{or} \quad z = xy$$

with this special interpretation of the variables.

In nature's electromagnetic radiation there are no such tiny frequencies as 1 or 2 or 3. The longest useful electromagnetic waves are about a hundred miles in length with frequencies around 2000

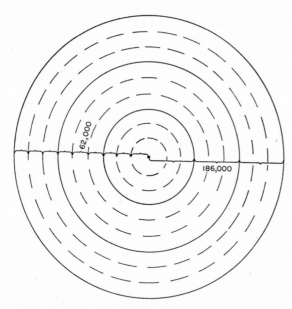

FIG. 24. Wave propagation. Heavy lines represent a hypothetical frequency of 1 wave per second. Dotted lines represent a frequency of 3 per second.

(product = 186,000 miles). The shortest radiations are cosmic rays with wave lengths of about 0.000,000,000,000,3 centimeters and frequencies of 100,000,000,000,000,000,000,000 (product = 30,000,000,000 centimeters).[3]

The speed of sound in air at 20° C is 1130 feet per second. Middle 'C' in music has a frequency of 256 and a wave length of about 4.41 feet. Hence

$$256 \times 4.41 = 1130 \text{ (approximately)}$$

Application II: Radar

The word RADAR is shorthand, RA standing for RADIO, D for DETECTION (or direction finding), A for AND, R for RANGING: Radio De-

[3] See page 90 for condensed representation of these figures.

tection (or Direction Finding) and Ranging. It is a palindrome, reading the same backward and forward, to symbolize that the radio beam or pulse behaves the same way going and returning. It was one of the superweapons of World War II and holds great promise of peacetime safety in navigation and aviation, in addition to all sorts of exploration by remote control.

Radar operates by projecting into space a pulse of ultra-high frequency radio energy. Traveling with the velocity of all electromagnetic radiation, 186,000 miles per second, the beam continues on its path unless it strikes an interfering object—a ship or iceberg or plane or mountain peak—in which case it bounces back; that is, it is reflected by the obstacle, and echoes in a receiver, all within a split second. If the tiny interval between broadcast and return is 0.001 second, which is a relatively long time in radar operation, then the pulse took 0.0005 second to reach the reflecting surface and the same time to return. If a man's walking speed is 3 miles per hour, and he walks for 2 hours, he will cover 6 miles. Speed multiplied by time will give distance. Hence, in the radar ranging illustrated the pulse traveled

$$186,000 \times 0.0005 = 93 \text{ miles}$$

and in every case the *range* will be given by multiplying the speed of light by half the interval between broadcast and return of pulse. A little 'pip' or hump (see fig. 25) will appear in the indicator of

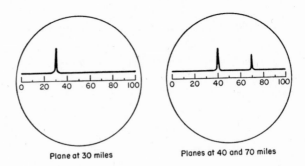

Plane at 30 miles   Planes at 40 and 70 miles

Fig. 25. Radar indicator.

the radar set opposite the appropriate range (the multiplication is done automatically by ruling this indicator to a proper scale).

It is again a case of

$$z = xy$$

where x is *constant* and $= 186,000$ miles per second

> y *varies* over the set of possible half-intervals between broadcast of pulse and returning echo.

> z varies from 50 ft. upward.   The upper limit for z will be the distance to the Moon, or the record to date for radar ranging. The lower limit for z will eventually be less than 50 ft., for it is anticipated that pocket radar sets may, in the future, serve as 'seeing eyes' for the blind.

The mathematician is fond of certain letters. He likes to use the letter c to symbolize constants, and in particular, that most important constant, the velocity of light. He likes t for time and s for distance. Therefore he would be more likely to symbolize the radar range formula by

$$s = \tfrac{1}{2}ct$$

Application III: Einstein Mass-Energy Formula

We are being told regularly these days that atomic energy is obtained by annihilating matter, or rather converting matter into energy. Accounts of A-bomb and H-bomb describe the conversion of subatomic particles into vast amounts of energy. The future possibilities of atomic energy are envisioned, and there are contrasting expectations. Perhaps the *Queen Elizabeth* will be sent on a round-trip across the Atlantic on the energy of annihilation of an ounce of coal. Perhaps there will be destruction of all life on earth through H-bomb energy combined with subsequent radioactive effects. The figures for either contingency would be a consequence of the *equivalence of mass and energy* as expressed by the Einstein *mass-energy* formula, which is nothing more than our multiplication function. Once again

$$z = xy$$

with proper limitations on the variables. Before furnishing these numerical restrictions, however, let us examine the general implications of the mass-energy law. Prior to relativity, three 'conservation' laws ruled physics and chemistry—the laws of conservation of *matter,* of *mass,* and of *energy.* Einstein has reduced these to one, the law of conservation of *energy.* Matter and mass are considered merely forms of energy. To elaborate the older concepts, we recall that science pupils were taught that matter could neither be created nor destroyed; at most, its chemical form could be changed, as in burning coal and obtaining carbon dioxide and ashes, but, as it was classically put, *two plus two must always equal four*. Or the sum total of matter in the universe is constant.

Now, for the conservation of *mass:* Mass is not merely a measure of matter. It is a numerical evaluation of the *inertia* or laziness of matter, of its resistance to being moved when at rest, or to slowing down or altering its path when in motion. Formerly physicists asserted: Every substance has a constant, unalterable mass. J. J. Thomson showed theoretically, and other scientists demonstrated experimentally, that the mass of an electron *increases* with its speed; that is, the faster the electron moves, the harder it is to push it out of its course. Another way of putting this is to say that increased mass accompanies greater *kinetic energy* (energy due to motion). Then Einstein showed that *every* form of energy has an equivalent mass, that an increase in the energy of a body always represents an increase in mass. If a 200 ton locomotive moves at a speed of 60 miles an hour, its mass is slightly greater than when at rest. In motions of subatomic particles, in the speeds of particles ejected in radioactivity, and in cosmic-ray energies, substantial mass increases appear. Total mass is no longer one of nature's constants. The total energy of the universe, however, is still considered an invariant. Einstein's mass-energy formula is

$$z = xy$$

where x is constant and equal to 900,000,000,000,000,000,000,[4] which is the speed of light in centimeters per second, multiplied by itself.

y is variable and equal to the number of *grams* of *mass*

z is variable and equal to the corresponding number of *ergs* of *energy* (An erg is the energy of a 2-gram mass moving 1 centimeter per second.)

Thus $z = 900,000,000,000,000,000,000y$

or, to use the letters of which physicists are fond

$$E = mcc$$

where E represents energy
                        m represents mass
                        c represents the speed of light

[4] See page 87 for algebraic condensation of this number.

Since the multiplier of y is so huge, the size of mass will be magnified enormously when it is converted into energy. The masses and energies dealt with in atomic physics are so small that grams and ergs are not suitable units of measure. The unit of energy employed is the *electron volt,* which is the amount of energy acquired by an electron moving through a potential difference of one volt. It is less than 1/500,000,000,000 of an erg.

Long ago chemists planned to take as the unit of mass the lightest atom, that of the element hydrogen. Later experiments showed that this would produce uncomfortable arithmetic in dealing with other atomic masses. Hence they took the mass of the oxygen atom as 16 units and postulated an artificial mass unit equal to one-sixteenth the mass of an oxygen atom. The mass of the hydrogen atom in this system is 1.0081, which is slightly larger than the abstract unit of atomic mass.

Now when an American buys so many yards of goods at so much per yard and a Frenchman buys so many meters at so many francs per meter, the transactions differ numerically, but the same operation is involved in totaling the cost, namely multiplication. Hence, in the same way, the form

$$z = xy$$

of the Einstein mass-energy function does not change if atomic units of mass and energy are employed, but the *conversion factor,* or constant multiplier, will have to be modified. For atomic transformations

 x is *constant* and equal to 933,000,000

 y ranges over subatomic masses (upward from 0.00005 for a positron)

and z furnishes corresponding energies in electron volts

That is,

$$z = 933,000,000y$$

To see how this formula will reveal H-bomb energy, consider first the present picture of the hydrogen atom. There is a central *nucleus,* containing one *proton,* which holds practically all the mass of the atom (1.0081 units) and carries *one positive* unit of electric charge. In addition, there is an extranuclear revolving *electron,* relatively large in volume compared to the proton, but having almost no mass in comparison, since its mass is only about 1/1840 that of the proton.

It bears, however, an electric charge equal to that on the proton, but opposite in effect; that is, *one negative* unit. The hydrogen atom enlarged might be pictured as a small tenuous cloud (the electron), whirling around at tremendous speed (more than 600 miles per second) in a portion of space as large as Notre Dame Cathedral, the only other matter present in the region being a microscopic but heavy speck of dust (the nucleus).

The helium atom is next in order of simplicity. The nucleus of ordinary helium contains two protons and two *neutrons*. An isolated neutron has a mass of 1.0089 and no electric charge whatsoever. In the helium atom there are two extranuclear electrons whirling about. Now what is the total mass of the helium atom? Ordinary arithmetic dictates:

$$\text{mass of 2 protons} = 2 \times 1.0081 = 2.0162$$
$$\underline{\text{mass of 2 neutrons} = 2 \times 1.0089 = 2.0178}$$
$$\text{total} = 4.0340$$

The mass of the two electrons has been omitted from the total, since it is relatively so small.

But measurement shows that the mass of the helium atom is not 4.034, but 4.004. Thus 'two and two do not make four' in atomic addition. Somehow 0.03 units of mass have disappeared in the transaction. This is reconciled by the Einstein theory, which says that an equivalent amount of energy should be released in the fusion of the four nuclear particles, and by the formula

$$z = 933,000,000 \times 0.03$$
$$= 27,990,000$$

or approximately 30,000,000 electron volts.

It is not surprising then to learn that present theories about the source of solar or stellar energy state that it comes from the union of hydrogen nuclei to form those of helium. Here then in our life-giving Sun was the inspiration for the death-dealing H-bomb. 'Let's try to create a miniature Sun,' the physicists said, as a grim sort of joke. They did not actually believe they could duplicate the Sun's fusion of hydrogen nuclei, since this takes place at about 20,000,000° C, and before 1945 there were no such temperatures on earth. The creation of uranium and plutonium A-bombs now makes such 'hell on earth' a possibility.

The Sun's process of conversion of hydrogen into helium is a patient one, requiring 6,000,000 years and the presence of carbon as a cementing agent. Therefore nature's example is not adequate for designers of speedy lethal weapons. Present H-bomb schemes call for the use of either of two types of *heavy* hydrogen, called *deuterium* and *tritium*. The deuterium nucleus, or *deuteron,* contains one proton and one neutron. If two deuterons are fused, they will form a helium nucleus. The detonation of an A-bomb will furnish the heat requisite to force deuterons or tritons (tritium nuclei) to fuse. The plan is to use sufficient heavy hydrogen to bring about huge numbers of nuclear fusions in a short time, with relatively great destruction of matter and creation of energy within this brief interval.

We have said that 30,000,000 electron volts of energy are released in forming a helium nucleus from two protons and two neutrons. In reverse, it would take the same amount of energy to smash the nucleus and resolve it into component protons and neutrons. Hence, physicists say that the *binding energy* of the helium nucleus is 30,000,000 electron-volts. At present no one has succeeded in disintegrating a helium nucleus this way.

The nuclei of atoms of other elements have different binding energies. Binding energy is a variable, being less for the lighter and heavier atoms than for the 'average' ones. This is very significant because it explains two alternative plans for creating atomic energy, both based on the ancient alchemist's idea of *transmutation* of elements. The plan was to transmute either the lighter or the heavier elements into the 'middling' ones, since the nuclei of the latter have greater binding energies; hence greater quantities of energy would be released when they are formed. So the nuclear physicist tries either to build up the lighter elements into the average ones or uses *fission* (splitting) on the heavier ones to break them up into the middling elements, as in the fission of uranium or plutonium in the atom bomb. The energy emitted per single fission is of the order of 2,000,000,000 electron volts. If many uranium or plutonium atoms undergo fission, as in the bomb, there is a large-scale release of atomic energy.

From the applications above of the simple formula $z = xy,$ it is evident why mathematics in pure form is bound to be simpler than its practical uses. The genius of a Planck or an Einstein lies in fitting nature with so elementary a mathematical garb, and in selecting the precise size of nature's figures, whether very large or very small.

Once a scientist has found a suitable formula, he will consult pure mathematics once more for further uses. The Einstein mass-energy formula is used to show just how much energy will be obtained by the destruction of a certain amount of matter. In the form

$$z = 933,000,000y$$

where y represents atomic mass

and z represents energy in electron volts

it is natural to ask if the formula will work *in reverse*. Matter can be created from energy as previously remarked. Will the same formula give the mass equivalent to the energy used in creation? The answer is 'Yes.' *Cosmic rays* are at present considered to be high energy radiation (some rays exceed billions of electron volts) coming from sources outside the earth's atmosphere. When they come in contact with our atmosphere or other matter in their path, changes take place that involve the creation of matter. Cosmic-ray energy will sometimes create *positrons,* which have the same mass as electrons, but carry a positive electric charge; sometimes it creates *mesons,* which have about 200 times the mass of an electron and may be positively *or* negatively charged. Again the high energy *gamma* radiation, which is emitted by radioactive substances, can give birth to two particles of matter, an electron and a positron. To compute mass from energy, we merely perform division instead of multiplication, or *change the subject* of the formula above. We think of it as

$$y = \frac{z}{933,000,000}$$

and see from this form that it will require huge energies (large values of z) to create any noticeable mass (y).

This is still the multiplication formula $z = xy$, but we see that it can be transformed into two division formulas, namely

$$y = \frac{z}{x} \quad \text{or} \quad x = \frac{z}{y}$$

all depending on the subject that applied science demands. We comment that there is only one restriction on such a transformation.

While $z = xy$ has meaning even if $x = 0$ or $y = 0$ or both are 0, we have seen in chapter 1 that the transformation to the division form would be meaningless in these cases. In the Einstein formula this exception would not arise, since x is constant and equal to 933,000,000, while we would hardly be interested in $y = 0$, for 0 mass will of course convert into 0 energy and vice versa.

Before leaving the question of the uses of that elementary formula $z = xy$ in its transformed division forms, $x = \dfrac{z}{y}$ or $y = \dfrac{z}{x}$ we must mention one recent, very novel application. The late Professor Birkhoff (1884–1944) of Harvard, who was considered by some to be the dean of American mathematicians, gave

$$x = \frac{z}{y}$$

as the formula for *aesthetic measure*. Since he preferred to use the first letters of words, he wrote it as

$$M = \frac{O}{C}$$

where O represents the 'order' of the aesthetic object, C its 'complexity' and M its aesthetic 'measure.' This use of the division formula is not in a class with the other uses in this chapter. Those are scientifically accepted. In this case the formula represents Professor Birkhoff's aesthetic theory, which has not, at the present time, gained widespread acceptance in the world of art, music, or literature. The formula was applied by Birkhoff to a great variety of aesthetic objects, such as ornaments, tilings, vases, melodies, and poems.

An examination of $M = \dfrac{O}{C}$ shows that the greater the numerator and the smaller the denominator of $\dfrac{O}{C}$, the greater the aesthetic value; or, put concretely, order enhances and complexity detracts from aesthetic appeal.

Birkhoff stated that in the typical aesthetic experience a preliminary effort of attention is necessary in perceiving the object; that this effort increases with the complexity of the material to be perceived, and so detracts from enjoyment, even though the act of perception seems automatic. Although the reaction to a tile in the form of a regular polygon may seem instantaneous, there is a slight feeling of tension accompanying each adjustment of the eye as it follows the sides of the polygon. The greater the number of sides of a polygon, the less its aesthetic appeal. Thus, considering only the element of complexity, the triangle would have greater appeal than other polygons.

There is, however, the question of order as well. Birkhoff pointed to our intuitive pleasure in symmetric figures, consonant musical intervals, and moderately alliterative poetry. An isosceles triangle appeals more than a scalene (three sides unequal) and an equilateral triangle appeals more than an isosceles.

Birkhoff subjected O and C to exact numerical measurement, and we refer the reader to his work [5] on this subject for details about how O and C are computed for each class of aesthetic objects. In applying his formula to poetry a number of selections were analyzed. Of those tested, the following lines of Coleridge rate highest:

> In Xanadu did Kubla Khan
> A stately pleasure-dome decree:
> Where Alph, the sacred river, ran
> Through caverns measureless to man
> Down to a sunless sea.

'Little Boy Blue' and an excerpt from Amy Lowell's 'Night Clouds' receive the median rating. The selection with the lowest aesthetic appeal is one from Edgar A. Guest's 'Contribution.'

Turning to another set of aesthetic objects, the formula gives the square first rating among polygonal forms. Rectangles of certain shape, including the 'golden rectangle,' which we shall discuss shortly, come next, followed by the equilateral triangle. The regular hexagon, star of David, five-pointed star, Greek cross, rate high. The swastika gets a middling rating, for Professor Birkhoff analyzed figures in purely formal fashion without regard to connotative factors. At any rate, Hitler's choice of a symbol was merely of moderate aesthetic appeal, while the emblems he tried to degrade were superior. The two upper forms in figure 26 are about on a par with the swastika, and the other two have lowest rank among the forms analyzed.

In spite of the many varied uses of the multiplication and division formulas in their elementary or generalized forms, neither nature

---

[5] Birkhoff, George D. *Aesthetic Measure,* Cambridge University Press, 1933.

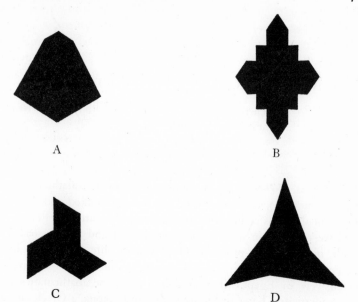

Fig. 26. Birkhoff's aesthetic theory rates A and B median in appeal and C and D lowest (reprinted by permission of the publishers from George D. Birkhoff. *Aesthetic Measure,* Cambridge, Mass., Harvard University Press, 1933).

nor the pure mathematician can be satisfied under most circumstances by such elementary formulation, and thus we must go on with our story to see what scientific problems arise and what mathematics is needed to furnish the answers.

4

The Mathematics of the Forbidden

There is no excellent beauty that hath not some strangeness in the proportion.

FRANCIS BACON

PYTHAGORAS, (569–500 B.C.), if not one of the greatest mathematicians of ancient times, is certainly one of the most talked about. Since many of the facts connected with his biography are largely legendary, we relate them mainly for their interest and their association with mathematical progress. Of his early life we know little except that he was born on the Greek island of Samos and traveled extensively in Egypt, where he absorbed some mathematics but more mysticism. Later in life he settled in Crotona, a Greek city of Italy, and, gathering a group of wealthy men about him, founded the Brotherhood of the Pythagoreans for the purpose of studying mathematics. Pythagoras, according to some stories, was in favor of disseminating mathematical knowledge freely and was willing to lecture to any audience interested in what he had to say. But a different spirit was present among the brethren, who felt that the society should be aristocratic in nature and that the members should keep secret from the public their discoveries in arithmetic, music, astronomy, and geometry.

'Number rules the universe,' said Pythagoras. To some extent this statement was justified by the remarkable contributions of the Pythagoreans to mathematical thought, but mainly it was an expression of the deep emotion that Pythagoras, like so many other mathematicians, felt for the subject and which he constantly expressed in poetic or mystic fashion. He heard the 'music of the spheres.' He saw in the cardinal integers images of creativeness and invested them with various properties. *One* stood apart as the source of all numbers and represented reason; *two* stood for man, *three,* for woman. *Five* represented marriage, since it is formed by the union of two and three. *Four* stood for justice, since it is the product of equals. All the even numbers were regarded as soluble, therefore ephemeral, feminine, pertaining to the earth; odd numbers were indissoluble, masculine, partaking of celestial nature.

The Pythagoreans, like all secret societies, ancient and modern, had symbols, rituals, and prayers. The *tetraktys* (figure 27), the

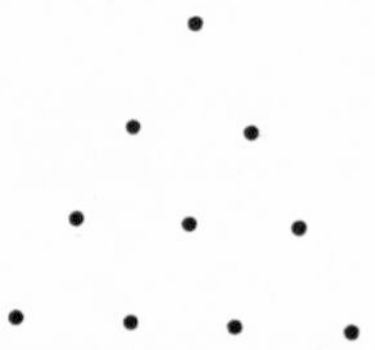

FIG. 27. Holy Tetraktys.

sacred 'fourfoldness,' was considered a totality of the reason and justice of man and woman, and of cosmic creation through the four basic elements—fire, water, air, and earth. The ceremonial of the society included the special prayer:

Bless us, divine number, thou who generatest gods and men! Oh, holy, holy tetraktys, thou that containest the root and the source of the eternally flowing creation! For the divine number begins with the profound pure unity until it comes to the holy four; then it begets the mother of all, the all-comprising, the all-bounding, the first-born, the never-swerving, the never-tiring holy ten, the keyholder of all.

Asked what a friend was, Pythagoras responded, 'One who is another I. Such are 220 and 284.' Being interpreted, this means that all the divisors of 284 (1, 2, 4, 71, and 142) add up to 220, and the divisors of 220 (1, 2, 4, 5, 10, 11, 20, 22, 44, 55, 110) add up to 284. As a result of Pythagoras' statement, such numbers are termed 'amicable' even in modern mathematics. A tale is told of a medieval prince who had imbibed Pythagorean philosophy. By means of Gematria he discovered that his name had the value 284, and hence he sent heralds throughout the land to discover a bride whose name spelled 220, believing that this would result in an ideal marriage. Legend says that Pythagoras' own life was not without romance, although he does not seem to have made his choice on the basis of amicable numbers. He married one of his pupils, Theano, and from all that is known, the marriage was a happy one even though Pythagoras was far older than his wife.

Number theory was not the only study of the Pythagoreans.

They are reputed to have made a really remarkable discovery in the theory of musical strings, namely that other conditions being equal, if one string is half as long as another, the shorter string will produce a tone an octave higher than the longer one, and also that a string two-thirds as long will produce the fifth (*sol*). It is believed that this Pythagorean discovery may have been the origin of the laws of musical harmony. At any rate, mathematicians called the sequence of lengths, ½, ⅔, 1, a *harmonic* progression. When these numbers are inverted, we obtain 2, 3/2, 1, a sequence in which successive pairs differ by ½. When any common difference exists in successive pairs of a number sequence, it is called an *arithmetic* progression. In modern mathematics the results of inverting any arithmetic progression is called a harmonic progression whether or not there is a musical analogue.

Thales, the teacher of Pythagoras, was the first man in history to insist on proof rather than intuition in geometry. Pythagoras perpetuated the notion of his teacher and firmly established logical procedures as a Greek tradition. It is said that when he discovered the proof of the famous theorem that bears his name, he sacrificed a hundred oxen to the gods. The Pythagoreans were authors of many other geometric proofs. We cannot assign credit with certainty for any of the discoveries of the Society since its secret methods prevented posterity from learning just what the master did and what the members themselves worked out. So strong was the feeling that mathematical discoveries should be carefully guarded that Hippasus, a Pythagorean, was drowned for revealing the nature of one problem considered by the brotherhood. We shall shortly examine the nature of this particular secret, for its modern applications are very important.

The story of Pythagoras has an unhappy ending. The Society became involved in politics and tried to exert a dominant influence. More democratic elements in Crotona were successful in having the government disband the group and Pythagoras died in exile. Some stories say he met a violent end. His mathematical ideas and those of the Society, however, have lived on.

We shall now consider the most classic Pythagorean contribution to mathematical thought, namely the famous theorem of Pythagoras. The tile pattern of figure 28 is of a type that must have been fairly common in the Orient. It is surmised that the Babylonians arrived at a knowledge of the famous theorem by counting tiles in just such patterns. In the figure, a right triangle (one that contains a right angle) is indicated. The sides of the right angle are commonly referred to as the *arms,* and the side opposite the right angle as the *hypotenuse.*

The Pythagorean theorem states that *the square on the hypotenuse of a right angle is equal to the sum of the squares on the arms.* In the figure, the square on the hypotenuse contains 16 tiles while the squares on the arms contain 8 each. The Babylonians may have

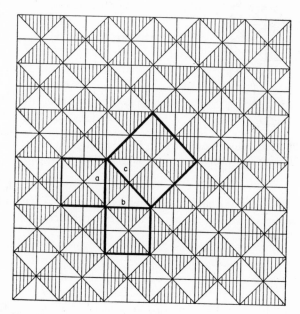

FIG. 28. Tile pattern illustrating theorem of Pythagoras.

considered such a tile formation an adequate proof. As far as we know, the first real proof of the theorem was given by Pythagoras, although the Babylonians had applied the fact and set up 'Pythagorean' numbers by 1600 B.C., and the Chinese had used it in 1000 B.C. Since the time of Pythagoras, one hundred or more different proofs have been given of the theorem that bears his name and many descriptive titles have been applied to it, such as the *Bride's Chair,* the *Franciscan's Cowl,* the *Goose's Foot,* the *Peacock's Tail.* Pupils who puzzled over the figure for the proof at one time or another saw a resemblance to these varied forms. (Figs. 29 and 30)

Leonardo da Vinci and President Garfield may be mentioned among those who have contributed original proofs.

To put the theorem of Pythagoras into modern algebraic form—which the author of the theorem could not do—let us symbolize the

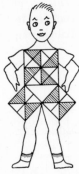

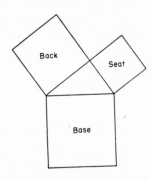

FIG. 29. A schoolboy's cartoon of the Pythagorean Theorem.

FIG. 30. Diagram of the theorem suggests the bride's chair.

lengths of arms by *a* and *b,* and hypotenuse by *c*. Then the areas of the squares involved are *aa, bb* and *cc* respectively. The modern algebraist writes

$$aa \quad \text{as} \quad a^2$$
$$bb \quad \text{as} \quad b^2$$
$$cc \quad \text{as} \quad c^2$$

but clings to geometric language and speaks of *a*-squared, *b*-squared, *c*-squared, and symbolizes the Pythagorean theorem as

$$a^2 + b^2 = c^2$$

Thus, modern algebra would write the *volume* of any cube the length of whose edge is *a* as *aaa* or a^3, read *a*-cubed. The *exponent* tells how many times the letter is to be used as a factor, that is in multiplication, and thus we are back to the basic formula of the previous chapter.

It took untold centuries for this simple exponential symbolism to be formulated and adopted. Credit for it goes to Descartes (father of modern mathematics), although he and Gauss (probably the greatest mathematician of the nineteenth century) would occasionally still write xx instead of x^2.

Suppose we are asked to find the hypotenuse of a right triangle in which the arms are 3 inches and 4 inches. We have

$$a^2 + b^2 = c^2$$
$$9 + 16 = c^2$$
$$c^2 = 25$$
i.e. $c \cdot c = 25$

and any one can guess that

$$c = 5 \text{ inches}$$

($c \cdot c$ means $c \times c$; a raised dot signifies multiplication).

Let us take next the case of an isosceles right triangle in which the arms are 1 inch and 1 inch.

How long is the hypotenuse? We have

$$1^2 + 1^2 = c^2$$
$$1 + 1 = c^2$$
$$c^2 = 2$$
or $c \cdot c = 2$

Certainly no whole number will give the value of c. One will not work, and every other whole number is too large. Neither will any common or decimal fraction satisfy the condition. We may guess $1\frac{1}{2}$, and multiply it by itself, giving $2\frac{1}{4}$. Thus $1\frac{1}{2}$ is too large. We may try 1.4, and the product by itself yields 1.96, which is too small. We may guess 1.41, and so on. No matter how well we approximate, the result will always be a little too small or a bit too large. Still, it is certainly a simple matter to draw an isosceles right triangle. Can there be before our very eyes a line whose length cannot be expressed, a line that cannot be measured by a foot-rule with fractional subdivisions of any type, however fine?

Although the Greeks did not use literal notation, exponents, or modern arithmetic, they were aware of this problem in geometric form. An inability to cope with this question was the greatest weakness of Pythagoras. 'Number rules the universe' was his belief, and here was a challenge to his faith. The numbers that he knew were ineffectual in a simple situation!

Alogon, the 'unutterable,' was the adjective applied by the Pythagoreans to the hypotenuse of an isosceles right triangle and other lines like it. Members of the Pythagorean Society were sworn not to divulge the existence of such lines to outsiders. It was for revealing this particular secret that Hippasus was assassinated. To quote Proclus (A.D. 412–85) on the Pythagorean attitude:

It is told that those who first brought out the incommensurables from concealment into the open perished in shipwreck, to a man. For the unutterable and the formless must needs be concealed. And those who uncovered and touched this image of life were instantly destroyed and shall remain forever exposed to the play of the eternal waves.

The modern algebraist with his symbols is far better off than the old geometer Pythagoras and his followers—the concrete-minded, geometric Greeks. To see wherein the superiority lies, let us return to the illustration of the right triangle with arms 3 inches and 4 inches.

In obtaining the hypotenuse, we had

$$c \cdot c = 25$$

To guess the answer, we asked 'What number multiplied by itself will yield 25?' or 'What are the two equal factors of 25?' Mathematics calls this the process of finding the *square root* of 25 and symbolizes the result as

$$\sqrt{25}$$

Hence, to be consistent, in the case of the isosceles right triangle

where $$c^2 = 2$$

or $$c \cdot c = 2$$

we should write

$$c = \sqrt{2} \text{ inches}$$

Although the layman, like Pythagoras, may feel dissatisfied on first encountering the $\sqrt{2}$, he must admit its existence in an isosceles right triangle—a very common figure in ordinary life, as are other *incommensurable* quantities. Most 'jay-walking' is not only illegal but also incommensurable. It is easy to prove that $\sqrt{2}$ is incommensurable or *irrational* (without ratio). We must show that it cannot be equal to the ratio of any two integers. Our plan is first to assume that such a ratio for $\sqrt{2}$ exists, and then to indicate that this assumption leads to a logical contradiction and must therefore be rejected. Suppose

$$\sqrt{2} = \frac{a}{b}$$

where $\frac{a}{b}$ is a fraction in lowest terms so that a and b have no common divisor. (This is possible because a fraction can always be reduced to lowest terms.) Then

$$2 = \frac{a^2}{b^2}$$

and $\quad 2b^2 = a^2$

Since 2 is a divisor of the left member it must be a divisor of the right member. Hence it is a divisor of a. If a is exactly divisible by 2, it must be 2 or 4 or 6 or 8, etc. It must be some multiple of 2. Writing this as a formula, we have

$$a = 2p$$

where p is some integer. Substituting this in the previous equation

$$2b^2 = 4p^2$$

and $\quad b^2 = 2p^2$

Hence 2 is a divisor of b. Then a and b have the common divisor 2, which contradicts the original statement that a and b have no common divisor.

If Pythagoras was troubled by incommensurables, so were later mathematicians. But as Klein, a well-known German mathematician remarked, the symbols are often more reasonable than the mathematicians who invented them. In this particular case, we have a new type of number, born from the use of the square root symbol. To quote Heinrich Hertz, discoverer of wireless waves:

One cannot escape the feeling that these mathematical formulae have an independent existence and an intelligence of their own, and that they are wiser than we are, wiser even than their discoverers, that we get more out of them than was originally put into them.

The use of algebraic symbolism remedied a situation that existed from the time of Pythagoras to that of Vieta. On other occasions the pre-Vieta mathematicians were to label many situations 'impossible' and despair of their treatment by the science of numbers. The

use of the literal notation brought about a change in the attitude of
mathematicians as a whole. The very act of expressing an 'impossible' answer in symbolic form made the 'unutterable' utterable and
stimulated a search for meanings. Mathematicians merely created
new types of number as occasion demanded, and are still doing so.
In many cases the new types can be pictured satisfactorily in concrete fashion, as in the case of the square roots we have been discussing.

Everyone has learned at some time or other how to find $\sqrt{2}$ approximately to as many decimal places as he may please—that is, to
get a better and better fractional (rational) approximation. The
Babylonians in 1600 B.C. estimated by some subtle technique, not yet
clearly understood, that

$$\sqrt{2} = 1.414213$$

Perhaps some moderns suspect that such work might terminate if
carried out to a sufficient number of decimal places. It will not—
otherwise $\sqrt{2}$ would be an ordinary decimal fraction and not a
brand new type of number. Neither can a *cyclic* repetition of figures
be obtained for $\sqrt{2}$ or other incommensurables.

When the fraction 1/7 is converted into a decimal, it becomes
$1/7 = .142,857,142,857,142,857$ . . . where the figures 142,857 are repeated over and over again forever. Certain fractions have such
repeating or recurrent decimals as their representation. Conversely,
repeating decimals can always be converted into ordinary fractions.
To see how this can be done, consider

$$x = 0.217217217\ldots\text{forever}$$

Multiplying this equation by 1000 gives

$$1000x = 217.217217\ldots\text{forever}$$

or $\qquad 1000x = 217 + 0.217217\ldots\text{forever}$

or $\qquad 1000x = 217 + x$

and $\qquad 999x = 217$

$$x = \frac{217}{999}$$

which is the fractional equivalent of the recurring decimal.

There are infinitely many irrationals with very real pictures. We need merely apply the theorem of Pythagoras to obtain a large number of these. If, for example, we have a right triangle in which the hypotenuse is 2, and one arm is 1, we have

$$a^2 + b^2 = c^2$$

$$a^2 + 1 = 4$$

We readily see that, to make this equation true,

$$a^2 = 3$$

$$a = \sqrt{3}$$

A length of $\sqrt{3}$ units can readily be constructed, and other incommensurable square roots as well, by the method used in the square root spiral (fig. 31).

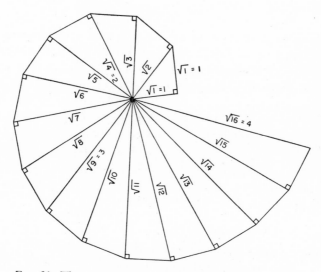

FIG. 31. The square root spiral. Repeated use of the Pythagorean theorem will give the length of any desired square root. In the diagram one arm of every right triangle is 1 unit in length. In successive triangles the hypotenuses have successive square roots as lengths.

From this discussion it might appear that irrationals are only a subdivision of square roots, that such roots are the only source of incommensurables. This is not the case. We are led to other irrationals by problems with exponents. If $x^3 = 8$, what is the value of

x? We easily guess 2. Finding one of the *three equal factors* of a number is called the process of taking the *cube root* of the number. Thus

$$\sqrt[3]{8} = 2$$

But not all numbers have integral or fractional cube roots, and hence we are led to a new species of irrational: $\sqrt[3]{2}$, $\sqrt[3]{3}$, $\sqrt[3]{4}$, etc. are of this type. It is then easy to guess what fourth, fifth, sixth, and higher roots signify, and to realize that these roots will in many cases furnish further types of irrationals. The number π is an irrational, but it is not a root of any type, or any finite algebraic combination of roots. In fact, as mentioned previously, it is transcendental or beyond algebra, which makes it *a fortiori* irrational.

Root extraction is the *inverse* process of 'raising to a power' (repeated multiplication of the same number), in the same sense that subtraction is the inverse of addition, and division of multiplication. Considering the inverse of a process has continually led to great inventions. *'Man muss immer umkehren'* (One must always invert) said the mathematician Jacobi (1804–51). By following this motto he and Abel (1802–29), a youthful Norwegian genius, created a new branch of mathematics (*the theory of elliptic functions*) out of what had previously been a series of awkward and difficult manipulations. Hence it has become a scientific 'must' to reverse mathematical operations in general to see if something novel or simpler will appear.

Having invented irrational numbers, mathematicians made rules for adding, subtracting, multiplying, and dividing them. These laws were laid down so that the usual commutative, associative, and distributive laws would hold; and in general, rules were designed to make the behavior of irrationals consistent with that of integers and fractions.

Only square roots and cube roots appeared in ancient mathematics, and more advanced irrationalities were absent. When, in the famous problem of 'doubling the cube,' a cube root did come up, it perplexed the Greeks and plagued their successors. Most cube roots cannot be constructed by the use of compasses and the unmarked straight-edge (as distinguished from the ruler, which allows measurement of length). These are the instruments to which Greek geometry had been limited by the philosopher Plato, who thought mathematics should be a mental discipline and objected to mechanical aids.

Although Pythagoras described even the simplest incommensurables as *alogon,* another Greek mathematician, Eudoxus, two centuries later, devised a scheme for handling those that appeared in Greek geometry. The art of the classic periods in Egypt and Greece, moreover, made tremendous use of incommensurable proportions. Classic art is truly a magnificent monument to the irrational. The late Jay Hambidge of Yale University made a detailed study of the dimensions that the Egyptians and Greeks used in their vases, bas reliefs, ornamentation, sculpture, and temples. He gave the name 'dynamic symmetry' to the form of composition they employed. He discovered that the Greeks were particularly fond of the proportions $1:\sqrt{2}$, $1:\sqrt{3}$, and $1:\sqrt{5}$ (especially the last). Hence we should surmise that these are the proportions occurring most frequently in nature.

Hambidge and his followers have worked out an entire theory of artistic composition for those who would continue the Greek tradition. According to this school of artists, a painting, photograph, etching, vase, monument, or other work of art should be planned so that its dimensions have an incommensurable ratio equal to some square root or combination of square roots. Thus $\sqrt{2}$, $\sqrt{3}$, $\sqrt{5}$, $\sqrt{6}$, $\sqrt{7}$, $\sqrt{8}$, etc. can all be used.

We have previously seen how to obtain a line equal in length to $\sqrt{2}$. In figure 32a we have drawn a rectangle whose sides are 1 and $\sqrt{2}$. We have also reproduced from Michel Jacobs' *Art of Composition* a sketch that fits this rectangle. In that book the author deals not only with the proportions, but also with the arrangements demanded by dynamic symmery. If one diagonal is drawn in the $1:\sqrt{2}$ rectangle (fig. 32a) and a line is drawn from one of the remaining corners of the rectangle to meet this diagonal at right angles, the point of intersection is called an *artistic center* of the rectangle. Figure 32a shows the 'principal' and 'second' points of interest formed in this way. Figure 33a shows the four points of interest formed by using both diagonals and the lines perpendicular to them from the corners. We have also reproduced Mr. Jacobs' sketch of the composition of 'Little Miss Muffet.' Notice that her face is the principal point of interest, the spider is the second point of interest, his web the third, and the tuffet the fourth. In using the theory of the centers of interest of a dynamic composition, artists do not follow the rules absolutely any more than they observe the laws of perspective rigidly. But, as in the case of perspective,

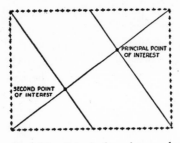

FIG. 32a. Principal and second points of interest.

FIG. 32b. 'Little Miss Muffet' in $1 : \sqrt{2}$ rectangle.

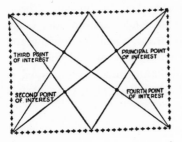

FIG. 33a. Four points of interest.

FIG. 33b. Composition of 'Little Miss Muffet.'

From Jacobs, M. *Art of Composition,* Garden City, New York, Doubleday, 1930.

they find the guiding principles useful and apply them to varied compositions with dimensions $1:\sqrt{2}$, $1:\sqrt{3}$, $1:\sqrt{5}$, etc.

After the discussion in a previous chapter on the frequent occurrence of golden section and the spiral form in nature, a logical query would seek a connection of these phenomena with the theory of dynamic symmetry. Golden section ought to fit in somewhere, and it does, for the favorite rectangle of all those used in compositions in the Greek style is the one whose proportions are in golden section. Now we are ready to reveal the exact value of the ratio in golden section and show how to obtain it. In figure 34 we first draw a 2 by 2 square. Next we connect the mid-point of one side

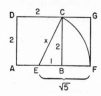

Fig. 34. Golden rectangle.

with an opposite vertex. By the Pythagorean theorem the line x is such that

$$x^2 = 1 + 4$$
$$x^2 = 5$$
$$x = \sqrt{5}$$

Next, we lay off $EF = EC = \sqrt{5}$. Then rectangle $AFGD$ is a shape with 'divine proportions.' As the psychologists Fechner and Wundt have shown, most people will unconsciously favor these dimensions in selecting pictures, cards, book covers, mirrors, parcels, etc. For some reason not yet satisfactorily formulated by either artists or psychologists, the golden rectangle holds the most aesthetic appeal.

From figure 34 we see that the ratio of golden dimensions is

$$2 : 1 + \sqrt{5}$$

Since $\sqrt{5} = 2.236$ approximately, this ratio is

$$2 : 3.236 = 0.6180 \text{ (approximately)}$$

In any of the dynamic compositions, whether the proportions $1:\sqrt{2}$, $1:\sqrt{3}$, $1:\sqrt{5}$, or the divine proportions are involved, the construction of the lines prescribed by Mr. Jacobs for obtaining a center of interest will lead to a rectangle similar in shape to the original. To make the similarity in shape apparent, we have turned the rectangle $FBCE$ around to the position indicated (fig. 35). Figure 36 shows a repetition of the center-of-interest construction with the rectangle $FBCE$. The line GH was drawn forming rectangle

GHCE similar to *FBCE* and the original rectangle. This procedure can be continued *ad infinitum*. In figure 37 we have suggested this process and have drawn in an angular spiral, formed from the large sides of the rectangles in the series, as well as a curved spiral through successive turning points of the angular spiral. The curved spiral

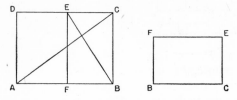
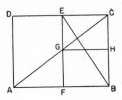

FIG. 35. Similar rectangles.   FIG. 36. Second center of interest construction.

approximates to the important logarithmic spiral of nature. Mr. Jacobs' 'center of interest' is the *center* of all the whorls of the spiral.

If we take the 'golden rectangle,' it turns out that all the successive rectangles are *squares* (fig. 38) and so present a sequence of

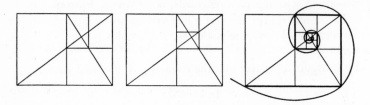

FIG. 37. Center of interest construction repeated. Angular and logarithmic spiral.

especially beautiful forms, at least according to Professor Birkhoff's theory. In this case, the angular spiral has the proportions of the familiar Greek pattern, and the logarithmic spiral is the one commonly used as ornamentation on Ionic columns.

Let us leave the irrationals for a while and return to the algebraic representation of the Pythagorean theorem, which started us on their track. The exponential notation used in stating the theorem is not only convenient shorthand for condensing repeated multiplica-

tion, but a tremendous aid in expressing concisely the huge numbers
of astronomy or the minute ones of atomic physics, of which we

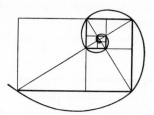

FIG. 38. Angular and logarithmic spirals from the
golden rectangle.

have had examples in the previous chapter. The speed of light is
more conveniently written as

$c = 3 \times 10^{10}$ rather than as 30,000,000,000 centimeters per
sec.

and $c^2 = 9 \times 10^{20}$ is certainly simpler than
900,000,000,000,000,000,000

and $E = mc^2 = 9 \times 10^{20}m$ is certainly more pleasing to eye and
mind than

$E = 900,000,000,000,000,000,000m$

Planck's constant of the quantum theory is

$$h = \frac{6.55}{10^{27}} \quad \text{or} \quad h = 6.55 \times 10^{-27}$$

the *negative exponent* signifying that we should operate oppositely
to the command of the multiplication sign and hence divide by 10^{27}.
   Other illustrations are:

Loschmidt number $N = 2.76 \times 10^{18}$ (number of molecules in a cubic
centimeter of gas under standard conditions)

Weight of the earth = 6×10^{24} kilograms

A light year (distance traveled by light in one year) = 6×10^{12}
miles

Distance to the nearest visible star (Proxima Centauri) = 2.5×10^{13}
miles

Candle power of the Sun = 3×10^{27}

Diameter of the uranium atom = $10^{-8} = \dfrac{1}{10^8}$ inches

Diameter of the hydrogen nucleus = $5 \times 10^{-17} = \dfrac{5}{10^{17}}$ centimeters

The frequency spectrum on page 90 indicates how the exponential notation makes possible the unification and comparison of so many things the physicist considers as 'waves.'

As the figures above show, it has been agreed on in science to express very large numbers as powers of ten, the base of our number

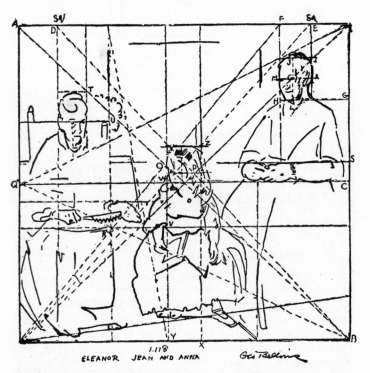

ELEANOR   JEAN AND ANNA

Fig. 39a. From Hambidge, J. *Dynamic Symmetry in Composition,* New Haven, Yale University Press, 1923.

system, multiplied by a number between 1 and 10 (numbers to the right of the decimal point indicate precision of measurement). If numbers are very small, they are written according to the same convention, using negative exponents to signify the quotient by the power of 10 instead of the product.

Astronomers, physicists, and chemists wish not only to symbolize numbers, but to do arithmetic with them. If an astronomer wishes to express the distance in miles of the furthest universe visible through the telescope, knowing that it is 140,000,000 light years away, he must perform the multiplication

$$6 \times 10^{12} \times 1.4 \times 10^8 = 8.4 \times 10^{20}$$

Or if a physicist wishes to say that the diameter of an electron is about 2,000 times as large as that of the hydrogen nucleus, his arithmetic is

$$5 \times 10^{-17} \times 2 \times 10^3 = 10^{-13}$$

Instances like these illustrate the law: *To multiply two powers with the same base, add the exponents and use the sum as the exponent*

Fig. 39b. George Bellows's International Prize Painting, 'Eleanor, Jean and Anna.' *By permission of Albright Art Gallery.*

of the common base. The inverse or *division* law involves *subtraction* of exponents.

Using the frequency spectrum, if we wish to compare the frequency of the hardest cosmic rays with infra-red rays, then the ratio of frequencies is

$$10^{23} \div 10^{14} = 10^9$$

FREQUENCY SPECTRUM

FREQUENCY

	10^{23}	
	10^{22}	- - - Cosmic rays
	10^{21}	
	10^{20}	- - - Gamma rays
	10^{19}	- - - Hard X-rays
1 Angstrom unit $= 1$ A.U. - - -	10^{18}	
		- - - Soft X-rays
	10^{17}	
	10^{16}	- - - Ultra-violet
	10^{15}	- - - Visible
	10^{14}	- - - Infra-red
	10^{13}	
	10^{12}	
	10^{11}	
	10^{10}	
	10^{9}	
	10^{8}	- - - Television
		- - - Frequency modulation
	10^{7}	- - - Short wave radio
	10^{6}	- - - Commercial radio broadcasting
	10^{5}	- - - Long radio waves
	10^{4}	
1 Kilocycle - - -	10^{3}	Audible range
	10^{2}	
	10^{1}	
1 Cycle - - -	$10^{0} = 1$	

Just what significance does this carry? To answer, we must digress.

In 1900 Professor Max Planck upset classical physics by proposing abandonment of the belief that energy was radiated as waves (that is *continuously, rhythmically,* in *all directions*) and offered instead the theory that energy was released intermittently in tiny 'packages,' which he called *quanta*. Hence his hypothesis became known as the *quantum theory*. His concept of energy explained hitherto incomprehensible physical phenomena. The size of the little package of energy or quantum, according to Planck, depends on the frequency of the radiation.

The size of any quantum is given exactly by the multiplication formula emphasized in the previous chapter:

$$z = xy$$

where in this case x = Planck's *constant* = 6.55×10^{-27}

y = frequency of radiation

z = size of quantum

The physicist often uses the symbol E for energy, h for Planck's constant, and the Greek letter γ for frequency, and writes the quantum formula as

$$E = h\gamma$$

For cosmic rays $\gamma = 10^{23}$, and for infra-red $\gamma = 10^{14}$. Symbolizing the respective energies by E_c and E_i (c for *c*osmic rays, i for *i*nfra-red),

$$E_c = 10^{23}h \qquad \text{and} \qquad E_i = 10^{14}h$$

Dividing,

$$\frac{E_c}{E_i} = 10^9$$

since h, Planck's constant, cancels out. In other words, the energy of cosmic rays is 10^9 or a billion times as great as that for heat rays. This is the sort of thing meant when we say that cosmic-ray energy is the greatest known to physical science. The frequency spectrum on page 90, in conjunction with the law of exponents for division, will give comparisons for X-rays and ultra-violet light, gamma rays and X-rays, etc.

If the law of exponents for division is applied to $a^3 \div a^3$, or $a^n \div a^n$, the answer should be a^0. But, on the other hand, $a^n \div a^n = 1$ (if a is not zero), since any number other than zero divided by itself must give 1. Hence, for consistency, mathematics defines

$$a^0 = 1$$

But a can be thought of as a variable, representing any and all numbers other than zero. Hence any base (not zero) with a zero exponent, or 'any number raised to a zero power,' as mathematicians say, is merely a synonym for 1. Thus, in the frequency spectrum table, $10^0 = 1$.

To illustrate a very important use of exponents, let us temporarily favor Leibniz's point of view and employ the base two to perform some speedy multiplications and divisions.

Powers of two

$2^0 = 1$			
$2^1 = 2$	$2^6 = 64$	$2^{11} = 2048$	$2^{16} = 65536$
$2^2 = 4$	$2^7 = 128$	$2^{12} = 4096$	$2^{17} = 131072$
$2^3 = 8$	$2^8 = 256$	$2^{13} = 8192$	$2^{18} = 262144$
$2^4 = 16$	$2^9 = 512$	$2^{14} = 16384$	$2^{19} = 524288$
$2^5 = 32$	$2^{10} = 1024$	$2^{15} = 32768$	$2^{20} = 1048576$

To find 2048·256, we see that

$$2048 = 2^{11}$$
$$256 = 2^8$$
$$\overline{\text{product} = 2^{19}}$$

by the law of exponents for multiplication. From the table, we see that

$$2^{19} = 524288$$

Next, find the quotient of 1048576 ÷ 128

$$1048576 = 2^{20}$$
$$128 = 2^7$$
$$\overline{\text{quotient} = 2^{13}}$$
$$= 8192$$

The reader will doubtless admit that this certainly is painless division. Let us work one more exercise by the 'painless' and speedy method.

$$\frac{16384 \cdot 4096}{512} = \frac{2^{14} \cdot 2^{12}}{2^9} = \frac{2^{26}}{2^9} = 2^{17} = 131072$$

Would it not be a pleasure if all arithmetic could be done so quickly and so easily? That was the gist of the question the Scotch mathematician Napier must have asked himself in 1614. Whereupon he set to work and invented *logarithms,* a device for which he merits universal blessing, since its use has simplified arithmetic for all time. Logarithms are nothing more than exponents, although Napier's original concept was somewhat different. The exponential notation that we employ was not in common use in his day, and only the sheerest of geniuses could have arrived at the concept as he did 'by climbing over the mountain to get next door.' At that it was the outcome of twenty years of thought on his part. It seems that logarithms were developed independently by a Swiss watch-maker, Jobst Bürgi, who actually did use the idea of exponents in his work. Bürgi did not publish until 1620, while Napier's work appeared in 1614.

It was the idea of the English mathematician Henry Briggs (1616) to put Napier's concept to work by the use of a table of 10's in much the manner in which we have used a table of 2's here. Since 10 is the base of our number system, its use has definite advantages, as scientific notation illustrates. An account of the meeting at which Briggs made his suggestion to Napier is recorded by the astrologer William Lilly (1602–81):

Mr. Briggs appoints a certain day when to meet in Edinburgh; but failing thereof, the lord Napier was doubtful he would not come. It happened one day as John Marr and the lord Napier were speaking of Mr. Briggs: 'Oh, John, Mr. Briggs will not now come.' At the very moment one knocks at the gate; John Marr hastens down, and it proved Mr. Briggs to his great contentment. He brings Mr. Briggs up into my lord's chamber, where almost one quarter of an hour was spent, each beholding the other with admiration before one word was spoken.

The world of science still feels this same reverence toward the invention of logarithms. The philosopher Hume evaluated Napier as 'the person, to whom the title of great man is more justly due than to any other whom his country has ever produced.' But the 'Laird of Merchiston,' stories to the contrary, probably had no notion of the true importance of his discovery. He was too busy championing the cause of John Knox and writing fanatical literature.

Napier's interests were manifold. As a member of the Scotch landed aristocracy, he was interested in improving agriculture. He also wrote on military science in preparation for the holy wars he envisioned. He anticipated three hundred years in advance those destructive devices that unfortunately came into use in World War I. The reaction of the common folk toward the genius Napier was to consider him a magician and to exercise imagination in composing suitable stories of his dark art. Even the sophisticated would grant some element of 'black magic' in the miraculous technique of logarithms.

It is evident at once that the reason why a table of 2's, like the one just given, cannot be used for all multiplications and divisions is that *not all numbers are simple integral powers of* 2. The mathematician has got around the difficulty by extending the notion of an exponent to include *fractional* and *irrational* values. Thus since

$$2 = 2^1$$

and

$$4 = 2^2$$

it is reasonable to expect that for

$$3 = 2^?$$

the exponent should have a value between 1 and 2. We assert that [1]

$$3 = 2^{1.5850} \text{ (approximately to four decimal places)}$$

Note the word *approximately*—the exponent is actually an *irrational* in this case and most others.

In the same way, since

$$4 = 2^2$$
$$8 = 2^3$$

then for,

$$5 = 2^?$$
$$6 = 2^?$$
$$7 = 2^?$$

the exponent should have a value between 2 and 3. Now

$$5 = 2^{2.3222} \text{ (approximately)}$$
$$6 = 2^{2.5853} \text{ (approximately)}$$
$$7 = 2^{2.8076} \text{ (approximately)}$$

all of which seems reasonable.

The mathematician can express every number as an approximate power of 2, and hence all multiplications, divisions, and many more complicated arithmetic processes can be performed by the use of a table of 2's, containing approximate exponents like those just listed.

Actually, as we have mentioned, a table of 10's is usually used. Every real number can be expressed as an approximate power of 10 or any other base and hence arithmetic can be made 'painless' by the use of a table of 10's, or the ordinary *logarithm table,* as it is called.

[1] Series like those of chapter 9, page 206 furnish this result.

At this point we wish to present only the concept of a logarithm and indicate that the formal-sounding word merely signifies an exponent. Instead of a logarithm table, engineers, statisticians, and other computers often use a *slide rule*. On the scales of the rule the values of the logarithms (or exponents) are measured off, and are added or subtracted to perform multiplications or divisions by sliding the scales back and forth.

It turns out, however, that while Briggs' choice of 10 as base was a boon to ordinary arithmetic, the base originally used by Napier was the best one for use in the calculus. The Napierian base is an irrational (nay, even a transcendental) number! The Pythagoreans would have frowned most disapprovingly on the widespread modern use of Napierian logarithms. And so it is that the forbidden numbers of the ancient Pythagoreans have become universally used numbers of modern science and practical life.

5

The Human Equation

> Ah, but my computations, people say,
> Reduce the year to better reckoning—nay,
> 'Tis only striking from the calendar
> Unborn tomorrow and dead yesterday.
>
> OMAR KHAYYAM

THE following is a problem from the *Lilavati* of Bhaskara:

A necklace was broken during an amorous struggle. One-third of the pearls fell to the ground, one-fifth stayed on the couch, one-sixth was found by the girl, and one-tenth recovered by her lover; six pearls remained on the string. Say of how many pearls the necklace was composed.

Solving this problem may spoil the romance somewhat but it is easy to see that if there are to be no fractional pearls, their number should be exactly divisible by 3, 5, 6, and 10. The smallest number meeting this requirement is 30, which checks, since $10+6+5+3+6=30$.

Is there any other solution? Will 60 do, or 90, or 120, etc.? None of these numbers will work, and we can keep on substituting to find suitable answers until we reach the upper bound of sensible values for the number of pearls in a necklace. But obviously guesswork is no way to solve serious problems, and definite techniques are needed for finding solutions and determining whether or not they are unique.

The early history of algebra furnishes numerous pseudo-practical or completely recreational problems. One of the oldest recreational problems is found in the Ahmes papyrus, an Egyptian mathematics text of about 1650 B.C. A more recent and human-interest version of this problem is:

A nobleman has a butt of Malmsey containing twelve measures. One of his servants, who has but six days to stay in the employ of his master, drinks one measure of wine from the barrel each day, and each time puts in a measure of water. How much of the wine is left at the end of six days?

Most students at school meet such questions in the standard algebra courses dealing with linear and quadratic (first- and second-degree [1]) algebraic equations. Eventually many become so expert at purely manipulative techniques that they forget just why they proceed as they do. For example, the method of handling quadratics becomes mechanical, and few realize that it is essentially the Greek geometric method of antiquity. The quadratic

$$x^2 + 6x = 7$$

meant to the Greeks that the area of a certain figure was 7. This figure was made up of a square with unknown side x and area x^2, and a rectangle with one side 6 and the other side equal to the unknown quantity (fig. 40).

In order to solve the problem they preferred to think of the area as made up of the square (x^2) and *two* rectangles, each with sides 3 and the unknown quantity. Now, they said, let us complete the figure to make it a square. The shaded square in the corner of figure 40 does the trick.

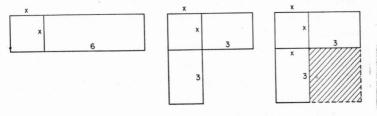

FIG. 40. Solving a quadratic by completing the square.

The area of this square is obviously 9, and since the original area was 7, the whole area is 16. If the large square has an area of 16, its side must be 4. But from the figure we see that the side is also $x + 3$. Hence, the Greeks reasoned,

$$x + 3 = 4$$
$$x \quad = 1$$

Notice that the essence of this technique is to reduce a second-degree equation to one of first degree. As the theory of equations

---

[1] The degree of an algebraic equation in one variable is that of the highest power of the variable which appears; e.g. $3x^4 - x^2 + 1 = 0$ is a fourth degree equation.

developed, attempts at solution were often based on the fundamental question of *reducibility*. Can some equations of higher degree be reduced to quadratics? If so, we have just seen that further reduction to the easiest of all types is possible.

In connection with certain famous problems, the Greeks came into contact with cubic equations. The Delian problem relates that Apollo, being angered, visited a plague on the people of Delos. They appealed to the oracle, who commanded them to double the size of the altar but to keep its shape the same. The form of the altar was that of a cube, and hence Apollo's command was to duplicate the cube, that is, to construct a cube with volume double that of the original.

Let us represent the side of the initial altar by 1 (linear unit). Then its volume was $1 \cdot 1 \cdot 1 = 1$ cubic unit. The new altar was to have a volume of 2 cubic units. Calling the length of its edge x its volume would be x^3, and

$$x^3 = 2$$

Today we can easily indicate the answer as $x = \sqrt[3]{2}$, and if we wish to use logarithms or some other method of approximation, we can obtain a rational estimate. According to the rules that Plato had formulated, however, geometers were restricted to the use of straight-edge and compasses, that is, straight lines and circles, in performing constructions. Plato feared that geometry would become child's play, unworthy of Greek intellectuals, if too great a choice of instruments were permitted, or, on the other hand, that latitude in selecting tools might complicate procedures. Therefore the problem of the Greeks was to construct, with straight-edge and compasses, a line-segment of length $\sqrt[3]{2}$ units. Modern algebra has proved that this is an impossible task, and that the only irrationals the use of circles and straight lines will produce are square roots and combinations or iterations of such roots. Thus the Greeks found the apparently simple Delian problem utterly baffling.

The trisection of an angle, another of the famous problems of antiquity, also leads to a cubic equation, but a more complicated one than that for the duplication of the cube. The problem has also been proved impossible to solve with straight-edge and compasses. Still each year produces its quota of angle-trisectors, whose efforts indicate their ignorance of mathematics. They unconsciously use some trick that is a violation of Plato's rules.

The growth of Greek geometry owed much to such classic unsolved problems, and considerable mathematics for centuries to come was to center about them. By latter-day antiquity, Greek mathematics had got away from purely geometric methods, and more emphasis was placed on algebra. Diophantus of Alexandria was the greatest algebraist of this era. His work may possibly have been influenced by Babylonian algebra. At any rate his ingenious techniques were not surpassed for over a thousand years. We know nothing, however, of Diophantus the man. We are not even sure of his dates. The latest studies place him in the first century, about the time of Nero, where previous estimates had given his time as A.D. 250. The Greek Anthology furnishes this brief biography:

God granted him youth for a sixth part of his life, and adding a twelfth part to this, He clothed his cheeks with down; He lit him the light of wedlock after a seventh part, and five years after his marriage He granted him a son. Alas! lateborn wretched child; after attaining the measure of half his father's life, cruel Fate overtook him, thus leaving to Diophantus during the last four years of his life only such consolation as the science of numbers can offer.

If x represents Diophantus' age

$$\tfrac{1}{6}x + \tfrac{1}{12}x + \tfrac{1}{7}x + 5 + \tfrac{1}{2}x + 4 = x$$

$$\tfrac{75}{84}x + 9 = x$$

$$9 = \tfrac{9}{84}x$$

$$84 = x$$

Diophantus lived to be 84 and had married at 33. His son was born when the father was 38 and lived to the age of 42.

In addition to determinate equations like the one just solved, Diophantus treated *indeterminate* questions to which many sets of answers may be possible; for example, $x + y = 10$ has as solutions $x=1$, $y=9$; $x=2$, $y=8$; $x=3$, $y=7$; etc. Such equations are still termed *Diophantine*. Superior as Diophantus' work was, he balked at procedures that held no fears for some of his Babylonian predecessors. For example, he labeled as absurd the simple equation

$$4x + 20 = 4$$

He was willing to subtract 20 from the left side of the equation, but hesitated to take 20 from the right side, since this involved the difficulty of subtracting a larger number from a smaller. Although in progressive Alexandria commerce could not have been conducted on an entirely cash basis, Diophantus was unwilling in a mathematical situation to take more than he could pay for.

Commentaries on the work of Diophantus were written by Hypatia (*c.*A.D. 410), the first woman mathematician in history. All her scientific writings are lost, but we know that in addition to writing on Diophantine algebra, she wrote on the *Conics* of Apollonius of Perga (chapter 7) and the *Almagest* of Ptolemy. She was co-author with her father Theon of commentaries on Euclid and Ptolemy. About A.D. 400 she became head of the Neoplatonic school in Alexandria, and the lectures that she delivered in this capacity attracted many distinguished men. Among them was Synesius of Cyrene, later Bishop of Ptolemais. Several of his letters to Hypatia are extant. They are full of chivalrous admiration and reverence, as well as requests for scientific advice. He wrote her, for example, to ask just how to construct an astrolabe and a hydroscope.

The novelist Charles Kingsley presented a romantic picture of Hypatia's life, but the blunt truth of the matter is that Hypatia was barbarously murdered by a fanatical mob. She was torn from her chariot, dragged to the Caesareum, a Christian church, stripped naked, slashed to death with oyster shells, and finally burned piecemeal. In the eloquent, beautiful, and brilliant high priestess of mathematics and philosophy, the bigoted could see nothing but a pagan influence on the prefect of Alexandria.

The Babylonians as well as Diophantus and Hypatia could solve some first-degree and quadratic equations, but not all of them. As the degree of the equation increases, so does the difficulty. Cubics also interested these early mathematicians, and the Babylonians even tackled some equations of fourth degree. Later, the Arabs were successful in solving especially simple types. The Persian poet, mathematician, and astronomer, Omar Khayyam (1100) classified thirteen types of cubic for which he had obtained solutions. Not until the sixteenth century, however, was a method of solution for *any* cubic equation evolved. Everyone knows that Omar Khayyam was the author of the immortal *Rubáiyát*. Few are acquainted with the fact that he was the greatest mathematician and astronomer of his time, and the most original of all the Saracen mathematicians; that he devised a calendar superior to the one we use; and that his work in the field of algebra was the greatest contribution to the subject between the fifth and fourteenth centuries.

Omar was a pure mathematician who placed very little stress on the practical; he was an algebraist in his choice of material but a geometer in method. He was influenced by Diophantus in his choice of subject matter but used none of the convenient symbolism that the Alexandrian had introduced. Instead, he reverted to the earlier, clumsy techniques of the Greeks. His greatest original contribution to mathematics was the complete classification of cubic equations, and the solution of some types. He solved some types of quartic (fourth degree) equations as well. He also considered the binomial theorem (chapter 8); his findings were not improved on until Isaac Newton took up the same problem.

The story of the discovery of the general methods for solving cubics and quartics begins in the sixteenth century, when a mathematical contest in the solving of cubics was proposed by Antonio Mario Fior of Bologna. Each contestant was to deposit a certain stake with a notary, and whoever could solve the most problems out of a collection of thirty propounded by the other was to get the stakes, thirty days being allowed for the solution of the questions proposed. Fior had learned to solve a special type of cubic from his teacher, Scipione del Ferro. His opponent in the contest was a Venetian mathematics teacher, Tartaglia, a nickname meaning 'stammerer' but nevertheless adopted by Niccolo Fontana, whose impediment was due to an injury suffered during the French sack of Brescia, his native town. Tartaglia suspected that the questions would all be cubics and so developed a formula for solving *any* cubic. He answered all the questions put to him, and in return gave Fior cubics of a type the latter could not handle. Thus Tartaglia won the contest and composed some verses to commemorate his victory.

His happiness, however, was to be short-lived. He planned to keep his method secret, but another Italian mathematician, Cardano (Cardan), professor of medicine at Milan and author of the algebraic masterpiece *Ars Magna*, wheedled it out of him. Having secured the facts, Cardano published the technique of solving a cubic in the *Ars Magna*. He gave full credit to Tartaglia but in many modern texts the method is still referred to as 'Cardan's Solution of the Cubic.'

The cubic-equation incident was only one of many that reveal Cardan as an atypical mathematician. That his career was no path of ease or virtue is set forth in his *Book of My Life,* written at the age of seventy-four, a sort of Rousseau's *Confessions;* though the book lacks the literary and philosophic qualities of the latter, it is equally lusty, in the true spirit of the Italian sixteenth-century scene. To place Cardan in the correct historic epoch, we need only state that he was a contemporary of Benvenuto Cellini.

We might go into the inspired ingenuities of Cardan's friend Tartaglia, or of his pupil Ferrari, who handled the general fourth-degree equation successfully. But it will be easier to follow the ideas of the empirical-minded Babylonians, which are still adequate for practical purposes. We postpone to a later chapter a discussion of the modern mathematical principles that determine whether or not an equation of any degree has an answer in terms of the numbers of algebra, and if so, how the solution can be found.

Since the Babylonians were incessant tabulators, it is no surprise to learn that they relied on tables to solve cubics and quartics. Have you ever used a table of squares (which, inversely, is also a table of square roots)? In it you would naturally read that $\sqrt{64} = 8$. But suppose you want the approximate value of $\sqrt{70}$. You would judge that it is a little above 8, and you might *interpolate* in the table to estimate the excess. What the Babylonians did in solving cubic equations was to use tables of $x^3 + x^2$, obviously obtained by combining tables of squares and cubes. By algebraic manipulations, any cubic can be reduced to a 'normal' form where it gives the value of $x^3 + x^2$, and then solved approximately by interpolating in the tables; for example, if

$$x^3 + x^2 = 12$$

then the tables would show a reading of 12 opposite $x = 2$. If

$$x^3 + x^2 = 10$$

the value of x will be a little below 2 and can be approximated by interpolation. The Babylonians apparently solved only exact equations of this type and thus never had to interpolate to solve cubics. They evidently decided on the answers first, using 'easy' numbers, and then constructed problems to fit these answers, presenting the equations so obtained as exercises for students. However, they used interpolative processes freely in square-root tables and astronomic tabulations.

Before we can adequately discuss other facts connected with equations of higher degree, we must settle issues that come up in connection with simpler equations, such as the algebraic ones that puzzled Diophantus. We have seen how the natural numbers—1, 2, 3, 4, 5, etc.—made their appearance just as soon as man had reached a degree of civilization where it was important for him to count. Fractions arose almost as naturally as the integers, for what could be more usual than to parcel out food or divide land? The Ahmes papyrus attests to the use of fractions among the early Egyptians. In the centuries that followed, the arithmetic of this type of number was developed simultaneously with that of the whole numbers. Next, other new numbers made their appearance, like the incommensurables of the Greeks.

If we mention a temperature of $-10°$, a change in stock quotation of -3, an electron charge of -1, or an exponent of -27, the reader's hair will hardly stand on end, for such figures are commonplaces to him. Yet the unflattering term 'negative' number has become the traditional appellation for such quantities. We have seen how puzzled the Greeks were by the length of the diagonal of a square. 'Incommensurable,' they termed it. 'Irrational,' an epithet of later origin, has an unfavorable connotation in our language. Still other novel types of number were to make their appearance on the mathematical horizon—'imaginary' is the adjective applied to one species. The nomenclature selected for new types of number is evidence of the fact that they were the result of a long, slow process of unwilling creation. Unfortunately, the terms, 'negative,' 'irrational,' and 'imaginary,' have remained to prejudice even modern minds against the truly *positive, sane, real* meaning and use of these numbers.

How did these novelties come into being? In a way typical of all mathematical discovery and expansion. In order to make the older laws of the subject consistent, or older operations complete—in short, to generalize previous knowledge—we must employ a fourth dimension, non-Euclidean geometries, new numbers. To round out arithmetic we must be able not only to subtract 3 from 5, and obtain 2, but to subtract 5 from 3, and get—well, what you will, or rather what the early algebraists willed, and consistent mathematics demands.

The difficulty that stopped the progress of Diophantus and his successors for centuries to come was a faulty concept of what a number should be. The source of his trouble was the notion that numbers should describe *magnitude* and magnitude only. But many quantities in ordinary life require a description not only of size but also of *direction* or *sense*. We walk up or down; a train travels north or south; a wind blows east or west; temperatures rise or fall; a wheel rotates in clockwise or counterclockwise direction. Directed numbers or *vectors*, as they are termed in mathematics, effectively describe quantities of this sort. Although directed quantities (e.g. the points of the compass) are capable of great variation, we shall first treat the case of two opposite directions or senses and postpone temporarily the generalization to all directions.

We shall use, as is customary,

$+15$ to describe a tail wind of 15 miles per hour

-15 to describe a head wind of 15 miles per hour

$+1$ to indicate the charge of the hydrogen nucleus

-1 to indicate the charge of any electron, as for example, the beta particles ejected from radioactive substances

The origin of the $+$ and $-$ signs should delight the hearts of the practical, for these marks were first used in warehouses by German merchants of the fifteenth century to show the excess or defect in weight of a cask in comparison with the nearest hundredweight. Having taken our directed numbers out of the warehouse, we must review their arithmetic. How shall we add, subtract, multiply, and divide these numbers? As a matter of fact, when mathematicians invent new numbers (they are manufacturing them by the hundreds these days) they are often quite arbitrary in laying down the rules for their brain-children. Men who apply mathematics may give some thought to 'practical' uses, but logical consistency is the sole criterion of pure mathematics. We shall not list the rules for operations with directed numbers since laws like 'the product of two negatives is positive' were known even to the Babylonians and are commonplace in modern thought. Instead, we shall consider some current applications.

The present atomic theory pictures the nuclei of all elements as combinations of protons, each of which carries an electric charge of $+1$, and neutrons, carrying no charge. Outside the nucleus there are as many electrons as there are protons in the nucleus. Each electron has a charge of -1. The gold atom, for example, has 79 protons and 118 neutrons in the nucleus and 79 extranuclear electrons. The number 79 is called the *atomic number* of gold. For each element the atomic number is the number of protons in the nucleus, or the number of extranuclear electrons. Normally, the atoms of all elements are electrically *neutral,* or algebraically, the nuclear and extranuclear charges balance as follows:

$$\text{for gold} \qquad (+79) + (-79) = 0$$
$$\text{for hydrogen} \quad (+1) \; + (-1) \; = 0$$
$$\text{for helium} \qquad (+2) \; + (-2) \; = 0$$

and, if n represents any atomic number, then

$$(+n) + (-n) = 0$$

An atom is *ionized,* as chemists say, when one or more of its extranuclear electrons is removed, or, in reverse, when free electrons attach themselves temporarily to an atom. If a helium atom (atomic number 2) loses 1 electron it is said to be positively ionized, since the algebra of charges is:

$$\text{nuclear} + \text{extranuclear} = (+2) + (-1) = +1$$

or, if both electrons are removed

$$(+2) + (0) = +2$$

This last example shows why the *alpha particles* that emerge from radioactive substances have an electric charge of $+2$. These particles are nothing more than helium nuclei or positive doubly ionized helium.

With certain exceptions, most substances that dissolve readily in water are spontaneously dissociated into positive and negative ions. Such solutions are called *electrolytes.* For example, salt water is an electrolyte. A molecule of table salt contains a positive sodium and a negative chlorine ion. Salt is a necessary part of our diet, but each of its non-ionized constituents is a deadly poison. Because the sodium atom loses an electron while the chlorine atom gains one, the algebra of charges in the sodium ion in salt (atomic number of sodium $= 11$) is

$$\text{nuclear} + \text{extranuclear} = (+11) + (-10) = +1$$

and for the chlorine ion ($n = 17$)

$$(+17) + (-18) = -1$$

Do directed numbers obey the *commutative* and *associative laws* of addition to which the summation of ordinary arithmetic numbers conforms? The examples we have just cited illustrate that they do. In atomic arithmetic there is this example that addition is commutative:

$$(\text{nuclear charge}) + (\text{extranuclear charge})$$

is exactly the same as

$$(\text{extranuclear charge}) + (\text{nuclear charge})$$

As for the associative law of addition, namely that

$$(a + b) + c = a + (b + c)$$

let us give an aeronautical illustration. Picture a plane with an air speed (attempted speed) of 210 m.p.h., a head wind of 20 m.p.h., being accelerated 30 m.p.h. The ground speed (net result) would be

$$(+210) + (-20) + (30)$$

which would give the same result whether we evaluate it as

$$(+190) + (+30) = +220$$

or as

$$(+210) + (+10) = +220$$

Neptunium and plutonium are two new elements of atomic numbers 93 and 94 respectively. They were discovered in the diligent search of nuclear physicists for the possible existence of elements with larger atomic numbers than that of uranium ($n = 92$). This work led to the discovery of nuclear fission, a process of which the whole world is now aware. Some of the algebra of the production of neptunium and plutonium illustrates the subtraction of directed numbers.

When Uranium 238, the most abundant component (99.3%) of natural uranium, is bombarded with neutrons having suitable speeds, capture of a neutron will occur in some uranium nuclei, producing an *isotope* or twin of ordinary uranium. This isotope is called Uranium 239, because its nucleus contains 92 protons and 147 neutrons, a total of 239 nuclear particles instead of the usual 92 protons and 146 neutrons. This kind of uranium nucleus is unstable and disintegrates rapidly, and, like other radioactive substances, emits beta rays, that is, *electrons*. The algebra of this particular nuclear change is

$$(+92) - (-1) = +93$$

because the original charge on the uranium nucleus is $+92$. If an electron is emitted, this means losing a -1 charge, signifying the algebraic subtraction of -1 from $+92$. Since there are no electrons in the nucleus, a natural inquiry would be: What is the source of the beta radiation? The physicist reminds us that a neutron contains a little more mass than a proton (see page 66). He offers the theory that one neutron breaks up into a proton and an electron, the latter being ejected from the nucleus with tremendous speed in the form of a beta ray. This process balances electrically, since

$$\text{neutron charge} = \text{proton charge} + \text{electron charge}$$
$$0 = (+1) + (-1)$$

To return to the uranium nucleus, the net effect of the beta radiation is to give the nucleus a charge of $+93$. In other words, algebra decrees that a *new* element has been formed, one with atomic number 93. Chemists called it *neptunium,* since the planet beyond Uranus in the solar system is Neptune.

Neptunium, too, is very unstable and emits beta rays as it disintegrates. (Its rate of decay is so rapid that there is practically no trace of this element in nature.) The change in charge is:

$$(+93) - (-1) = +94$$

Another new element must result with nuclear charge or atomic number of 94. This was named *plutonium* since the planet beyond Neptune is Pluto. Because plutonium undergoes fission it can be used in making atomic bombs. It exists only in exceedingly minute quantities in nature and hence is produced artificially in bomb manufacture.

Not only do directed numbers solve formerly impossible problems, but they also furnish additional solutions to others. In answer to the question: What number, when multiplied by itself will yield 9, or what is the square root of 9, we have the equation

$$x^2 = 9$$
and $$x = 3 \quad \text{or} \quad x = -3$$

A number has not only a *positive,* but also a *negative* square root. The geometric equivalent of the problem in question is: If a square has an area of 9, what is its side? Although -3 cannot be considered as an answer to this particular geometric problem, we have

seen that -3 and all negative numbers can be represented geometrically, since $+3$ may be pictured as walking 3 miles east thus:

while -3 may be thought of as 3 miles west and given geometric
representation by pointing the arrow the other way:

The classic Greek problem of finding the hypotenuse of an
isosceles right triangle with arms one unit long led to

$$x^2 = 2$$

which, taken abstractly, now has two solutions

$$x = \sqrt{2} \quad \text{or} \quad x = -\sqrt{2}$$

It is possible to walk an incommensurable distance east or west,
north or south. Thus the entire theory of equations is enriched by
the concept of directed numbers.

We have just solved some quadratic equations.

$$x^2 = 9$$

is a quadratic equation, and its roots (answers) are

$$x = 3 \quad \text{and} \quad x = -3$$

Likewise $x^2 = 2$ is a quadratic with roots $x = \sqrt{2}$ and $x = -\sqrt{2}$.
Let us reconsider the question of quadratic equations in the light
of our new knowledge. We saw that the Greeks solved the quadratic equation

$$x^2 + 6x = 7$$

by completing the square (page 97) to obtain

$$(x + 3)(x + 3) = 16 \quad \text{or}$$

$$(x + 3)^2 = 16$$

Now let us consider this equation abstractly without regard to the
diagram. It says that $x + 3$, when multiplied by itself, yields 16 as
a result. Hence

$$x + 3 = 4 \quad \text{or} \quad x + 3 = -4$$

since either $+4$ or -4, when squared, will equal 16. To solve

$$x + 3 = 4$$

we subtract 3 from both sides and obtain

$$x = 1$$

To solve

$$x + 3 = -4$$

we subtract 3 from both sides and obtain

$$x = -7$$

Thus, this quadratic has two roots. The Greeks recognized only one root, for they were limited by the geometric figure.

Every quadratic, as mentioned, has two roots (answers), and we see that the method of completing the square will solve it. This process may yield negative answers. Again, consider

$$x^2 + 2x = 4$$

Figure 41 shows the completing of the square by the addition of a square with side 1, yielding a large square with side

$$x + 1$$

The area of the large square is equal to the original area (4) plus the square added (1). Hence its area is 5, and its side is $\sqrt{5}$. The

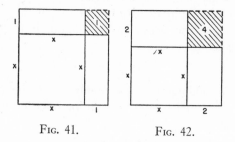

FIG. 41.   FIG. 42.

side of the square in the figure is thus incommensurable with the unit used and is represented by an *irrational* number. Figure 41 says

$$(x + 1)^2 = 5$$

Let us now disregard the figure and treat the equation as an abstract quadratic. Since 5 has both a positive and a negative square root,

$$x + 1 = +\sqrt{5} \qquad \text{or} \qquad x + 1 = -\sqrt{5}$$

and subtracting 1 from both sides in each equation, we have

$$x = \sqrt{5} - 1 \qquad \text{or} \qquad x = -\sqrt{5} - 1$$

Here we have an illustration of a quadratic with irrational roots, one of which, in this case, is also negative.

If we were to consider the quadratic

$$x^2 + 4x = -3$$

we could make the diagram indicated in fig. 42, but it would now merely be a scheme to help us, for no figure used by surveyor or carpenter would have an area of -3. This quadratic, naturally, would never have been considered by the Greeks. Still, the scheme of completing the square tells us to add a square of area 4, and obtain a large square with side $x + 2$. Then, in the abstract sense,

$$(x + 2)^2 = -3 + 4$$
$$(x + 2)^2 = 1$$

Hence

$$x + 2 = +1 \qquad\qquad x + 2 = -1$$
$$x = -1 \qquad\qquad\qquad x = -3$$

and we find that both roots are negative.

We have used a figure to assist us, but actually the solution of the quadratic is in no way dependent on a figure. In the equation just treated, namely

$$x^2 + 4x = -3$$

we are merely adding the same number, 4, to both sides of an equation. This complies perfectly with the rules for operation with any equation. Thus

$$x^2 + 4x + 4 = -3 + 4$$

Figure 42 merely helps us to decide what quantity should be added and tells us how to express the left side of the equation as a *square*, in this case

$$(x + 2)^2$$

Occasionally both roots of a quadratic come out the same. Consider

$$x^2 + 2x = -1$$

From figure 41

$$(x + 1)^2 = -1 + 1$$

$$(x + 1)^2 = 0$$

$$x + 1 = +0 \qquad\qquad x + 1 = -0$$

$$x = -1 \qquad\qquad x = -1$$

Since $+0 = -0 = 0$, both roots are the same.

It may seem that in carrying the theory of quadratic equations beyond the Greek stage, we are forcing an impractical issue, but we have seen that negative numbers have very definite significance in modern times. If we are permitted to use negative numbers indiscriminately in quadratic equations, we may sooner or later encounter the quadratic

$$x^2 = -1$$

Translated into ordinary language, this asks: What number, multiplied by itself, will give the answer -1? No type of number that we have encountered thus far will meet this requirement. A positive number will not do, since a positive number multiplied by itself will yield a positive product. A negative number will not serve for a similar reason, since a negative number multiplied by itself will yield a positive product. As a result, the roots of

$$x^2 = -1, \; x^2 = -2, \text{ etc.}$$

were termed 'fictitious,' 'impossible,' and finally, 'imaginary.' There is something ironic in the fact that the sixteenth-century mathematicians who applied these epithets were the very men who had frowned on their predecessors' unsophisticated use of 'absurd,' 'false,' and the like for negative numbers.

Mathematicians, with their love of generality, insisted that there should be no exception to the possibility of solving quadratic equations. Proceeding by algebraic formalism, the answers to the quadratics

$$x^2 = -1 \qquad \text{and} \qquad x^2 = -7$$

should be

$$x = \pm \sqrt{-1} \qquad \text{and} \qquad x = \pm \sqrt{-7}, \text{ respectively}$$

Hence mathematicians decided to endow these symbols with meaning. In order that all quadratics might be solvable, it became necessary to create a new type of number, just as it had been necessary to create negative numbers in order to make all first-degree equations capable of solution, and irrational numbers to express lengths exactly. Unfortunately the name 'imaginary' has clung to these numbers in spite of the fact that a very real use has been found for them. In relativity, for example, the separation or 'space-time interval between two real events may be $\sqrt{-1}$ units or $\sqrt{-2}$ or any 'imaginary.'

These imaginary quantities, by which is meant even roots of negative numbers, were mere abstractions at first, invented to satisfy the mathematician's ideal of a perfection that tolerates no exception to any rule. Subsequently they developed into entities of paramount importance in modern physics. It is a commonplace that physics deals with quantities like forces, velocities, and accelerations, which are all directed numbers or vectors. We have seen how positive and negative numbers will take care of opposite directions like north and south, east and west, and up and down. Still, if we wanted to describe simultaneously all the vectors represented in figure 43, positive and negative numbers would not suffice. If we described arrows OA and OB (east and west) as $+4$ and -4, how would we describe the others? It turns out that 'imaginary' numbers are just the thing.

The mathematician makes use of these numbers as follows. He uses the symbol i as the imaginary unit, putting

$$i = \sqrt{-1}$$

All other imaginaries can be expressed in terms of i. Thus there are $2i$, $3i$, $4i$, $5i$, $-2i$, $-3i$, $i\sqrt{5}$, $i\sqrt{2}$, $-i\sqrt{3}$, etc. Then there are the so-called *complex numbers*, which are sums of 'reals' and 'imaginaries' like $-1+2i$, $\sqrt{2}-3i$, and $-5+i\sqrt[3]{4}$.

If in figure 43 we take east and west as 'real' directions, and north and south as 'imaginary' directions, all vectors can be represented by complex numbers (which include real numbers and pure imaginaries as special cases). For this reason Professor Arnold Dresden renames the classic imaginaries 'normal' numbers. 'Normal' is often synonymous with *perpendicular* in mathematics. Imaginary numbers are normal because their direction is perpendicular to that of ordinary numbers. 'Normal' is thus a doubly good term, first, because it has a much healthier sound than 'imaginary,' and second, because it is geometrically descriptive.

We shall now illustrate how vectors, that is *complex numbers,* are applicable in mechanics. Suppose that a plank is floating down a stream which flows at the rate of 3 feet per second (fig. 44). A

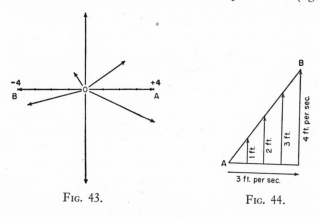

FIG. 43.   FIG. 44.

man whom we are observing walks across the plank at the rate of 4 feet per second. Let us watch his path. While he walks 4 feet across the plank, the plank has been carried 3 feet downstream so that we see him describe the path *AB*. By the Pythagorean theorem we can find the length of *AB*, for

$$x^2 = 9 + 16 = 25$$
$$x = 5$$

In other words, his total progress in 1 second is 5 feet in the direction indicated. We usually say that the *resultant* velocity is 5 feet per second. The direction of this resultant can be found by protractor to be 53° approximately (or more accurately by the trigonometry of the next chapter). Thus, to an observer on the bank, the man would appear to move 5 feet per second in a direction at an angle of 53° with the stream.

His motion could be described either as

$$3 + 4i$$

meaning 3 downstream and 4 normal or as

$$(5, 53°)$$

Similarly, in fig. 45 the other vectors have the alternative representations

$$OR = -2 + 2i \quad \text{or} \quad (\sqrt{8},\ 135°)$$

$$OS = -3 - 5i \quad \text{or} \quad (\sqrt{34},\ 239°)$$

$$OT = +2 - 5i \quad \text{or} \quad (\sqrt{29},\ 292°)$$

The angular direction of vectors is customarily obtained by measuring the angle counterclockwise from 'east.'

Velocities are not the only vectors of science. Forces, accelerations, and many other physical entities have both magnitude and direction and are susceptible to representation by complex numbers.

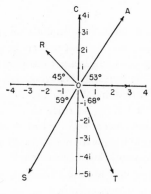

FIG. 45.

Hence it is not surprising to learn that the advanced theory of complex numbers was one of the keynotes of the nineteenth-century mathematical renaissance. Further applications of complex numbers will be made easier by our study of trigonometry, which will furnish an abstract tool to replace the protractor in finding the angular directions of vectors.

6

Ascent Without Rockets

> Yet we, who are borne on one dark grain of dust
> Around one indistinguishable spark
> Of star-dust, lost in one lost feather of light
> Can by the strength of our own thought, ascend
> Through universe after universe.
>
> ALFRED NOYES

CEPHEUS was king of Ethiopia, the legends say, and Cassiopeia was his beautiful wife. Humility was not one of the queen's virtues, and she boasted that she was as handsome as any goddess. This enraged the sea nymphs and, as a result, Neptune, god of the sea, threatened to destroy the kingdom of Ethiopia unless Princess Andromeda was offered as a human sacrifice to a sea monster. To save their land, the king and queen were forced to chain their daughter to a rocky cliff. Before the monster Cetus could harm her, however, out of the sky flew Perseus. This fearless youth, born in Argos, had become a flier by borrowing Mercury's magic sandals. First he had slain the snaky-haired witches known as the Gorgons, carrying away with him the head of one of them, Medusa, which had the power of petrifying all who gazed upon it. He fell in love with Andromeda on sight and rescued her by distracting Cetus and getting him to focus on Medusa's head. Having turned the sea beast to stone he removed Andromeda's fetters and married her amidst all the pomp and circumstance of a royal wedding festival.

Starry memorials to the Ethiopian royal family illuminate the northern and northeastern skies on autumn nights. Cassiopeia is represented by a choice constellation, the *chair* or great *W*, at the end of a line from the Big Dipper through the North Star. Cepheus (see fig. 46) resembles a church steeple with summit directed toward Polaris (the North Star), which appears a dull star to the naked eye. Andromeda's head rests on Pegasus, the flying horse of Perseus, whose celestial form resembles that of a graceful dancer more than that of a fighter.

Such was the mythical astronomy of the ancients. It still assists the amateur stargazer in identifying heavenly bodies. Between 8 and 10 p.m. of October nights Cepheus is visible to the north and fairly high in the sky in mid-northern latitudes. The twentieth-century scientific story of this constellation may seem even less credible than the ancient version, for in the eyes, or the crown jewels, or the gleaming scepter of the king of Ethiopia can be read the secret of the *size of the universe*. The flickering of certain stars

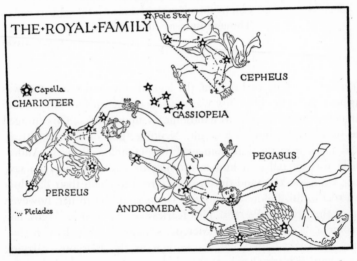

Fig. 46. From Beet, E. A. *Guide to the Sky,* Cambridge, at the University Press, 1933.

in Cepheus contains the mathematical key to stellar distances, however great, and makes possible the cartography of the heavens.

That mathematics in general and astronomy in particular deal with *variables* is part of their essence. That apparent brightness varies from star to star is a commonplace. But it is not generally known that many individual stars fluctuate in brilliance from day to day, hour to hour. For certain stars of this kind the astronomers use the name *Cepheid variable,* since the discovery of the phenomenon we shall now describe was due to the observation of a particular star in the constellation of Cepheus. This star was δ Cephei (read Delta of Cepheus), the name signifying that it is approximately the fourth brightest star in the particular constellation (δ or delta is the fourth letter of the Greek alphabet).

This star was found to perform periodic oscillations in brilliance, waxing from dull to bright to dull over and over again in regular cycles (fig. 47). Later observations revealed that the length and breadth of the heavens were populated with stars behaving this way. For some Cepheids the cycle is run through daily. Others wax and

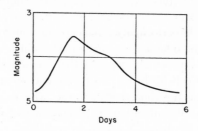

Fig. 47. Variation in brightness of δ Cephei.

wane more slowly, the lengthiest period observed to date being about 32 days. The star δ Cephei, requiring 5⅓ days for a performance, is an average Cepheid.

In 1912 Henrietta S. Leavitt, a worker at the Harvard Observatory, made a minute telescopic study of about 25 Cepheid variables, all about equally distant from the Earth, since they were located in the same star cluster, the Lesser Magellanic Cloud, so named because Magellan observed this group of stars on his historic journey around the earth. Because distance was constant for the Cepheids in question, any difference in brilliance from star to star was intrinsic and not caused by a variation in remoteness. Thus these stars could be compared for luminosity as if they were electric light bulbs in the same room, or suns in a row with our own, or rather suns at the standard distance used in astronomy—about 2×10^{14} miles, called 10 parsecs (a parsec $= 2 \times 10^{13}$ miles).

Miss Leavitt discovered that the brighter Cepheids oscillated more slowly than the less brilliant ones. Just what turns the lights on and off in the Cepheids and regulates the time the process takes has not been completely explained to date, but the theory of Professor Shapley of Harvard ascribes the behavior to 'pulsation.' Cepheids are considered rather 'young' stars, condensed from nebulae and still in the process of condensation. It is believed that they have reached a period in their life history when the gravitational forces working toward condensation are practically balanced by the internal forces tending to disrupt them. This is pictured as the cause of the pulsation. A Cepheid is visualized as a sort of gigantic inflated balloon from which air is released until it reduces somewhat in size, when it is reinflated until its original volume is regained. Then, according to the Shapley theory, the whole procedure is duplicated again and again, the time from start to finish being the the same for each performance. Balloons of different sizes with different means of inflation and deflation would lead to different time intervals for the trick. So it is that the varied masses and temperatures of Cepheids bring about different pulsation periods.

Miss Leavitt was not concerned with the 'why' of the pulsations. She merely observed some additional Cepheids and then fitted her total data with a mathematical formula indicating the dependence of intrinsic brightness on period. Professor Shapley then made studies of Cepheids throughout the heavens and a general *period-luminosity law* was the result. Astronomers at the Harvard Observatory have by now examined the behavior of close to 600 Cepheid variables. Having obtained periods directly through telescopic observation, they compute intrinsic brilliance indirectly by the Leavitt-Shapley formula. This luminosity or actual sun power is not directly discernible either by the naked eye or the telescope, since suns that outshine ours a millionfold may, because of their remoteness, leave but faint impressions on photographic plates attached to the most powerful telescopes. But the Period-Luminosity Law furnishes a scale that rates our Sun and the Cepheids side by side. For example, if a star winks in the same manner and with the same period 5⅓ days, as δ Cephei, it is known from the formula that it has 700 sun power. This means that if its distance were the same as the Sun's (93,000,000 miles), it would shine 700 times as brightly as the Sun.

Once the true sun power is assigned, it is an easy matter to figure by means of the 'inverse square law' the distance responsible for the apparent brightness. To understand this law let us explain that if two variables, x and y, are so related that

$$y = \frac{k}{x^2}$$

where k is some constant, y is said to vary *inversely* as the square of x. In the theory of light, the inverse square law is: *Intensity of illumination varies inversely as the square of the distance from the source of light.* If x is a particular distance and y the intensity at this distance, then we have just stated that

$$y = \frac{k}{x^2}$$

For a different distance X and associated intensity Y

$$Y = \frac{k}{X^2}$$

Dividing these two equations, we obtain the proportion

$$\frac{y}{Y} = \frac{X^2}{x^2}$$

If $x = 1$ foot and $X = 2$ feet

$$\frac{y}{Y} = \frac{4}{1} \qquad \text{or} \qquad Y = \tfrac{1}{4}y$$

In other words, if distance is doubled, intensity becomes one-fourth as great. In the same way, if distance is trebled, intensity is one-ninth as great. Figure 48 shows that this is so and indicates the experimental basis of the inverse square law for light.

We have just seen that it is possible by the Period-Luminosity Law to get an intrinsic or standard brightness rating for stars,

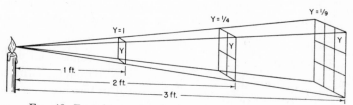

Fig. 48. Experiment showing inverse square law for light.

which means that this law gives the value of y when $x = 2 \times 10^{14}$ miles (i.e. $x = 10$ parsecs). The apparent brightness Y, obtained by telescopic photography, corresponds to the actual (unknown) distance X. Then

$$\frac{X^2}{100 \text{ parsecs}} = \frac{\text{standard brightness (known)}}{\text{apparent brightness (known)}}$$

X^2, and then X, the distance to the star, can be figured from this equation.

In this way distances are obtained not only for Cepheids but also for the different groups of stars throughout the heavens of which these variables are members. Thus ω Centauri (omega of the Centaur) is a star cluster with thousands of stars but at least 76 Cepheids whose periods have been observed. The luminosities of these Cepheids were determined by the Period-Luminosity Law. Then their distances were found as just explained. Thus the range of distances of the stars in the cluster became known, since astronomic theory places all of them 'close' together. The average distance is 20,000 light years, which means that the photographs taken today picture the cluster as it was 20,000 years ago. In summary, then, Cepheid study is one tool whereby we

> Can by the strength of our own thought, ascend
> Through universe after universe.

Mathematics is forever and again a study of different *functions*. When we remark that 'Price control is a function of the state,' or 'Mrs. Smith's bridge parties are boring functions,' the term function is not being used in a mathematical sense. But if we say that the weight of an object is a function of its physical and chemical composition, that health is a function of nutrition, that Hitler wrote that the justification of the use of the most brutal weapons is always a function of fanatical belief, that Mr. Brown's treatment of his employees is a function of his moods which, in turn, are functions of the activity of the stock market, then we are being mathematical.

If, when the value of one variable is known, a second can be found, the second is called a function of the first. Or one variable can be a function of several others, or several can be a function of one, or several can depend on several others, as we can conjecture from ordinary experience.

Functions or relationships must be subdivided into smaller groups. We have already seen a few of the algebraic and geometric species of function, and more of these will come up in surveying the heavens, but even in the single instance we have just considered, new elements are apparent.

In the first place the astronomers had to know the distances to some 'near-by' Cepheids. This was necessary in setting up the Period-Luminosity Law. This law gives a formula for intrinsic or standard brightness when period is known. Originally, when Miss Leavitt and others at the Harvard Observatory established the Cepheid relationship, all that could be determined by observation was apparent brightness. How was standard brightness of δ Cephei, for example, determined? The distance to some near-by Cepheid whose period is the same as that of δ Cephei, namely 5⅓ days, was found by use of the functions we shall next examine. Then application of the inverse square law gave standard brightness, since

$$\frac{\text{standard brightness (unknown)}}{\text{apparent brightness (known)}} = \frac{(\text{distance})^2 \, (\text{known})}{100 \text{ parsecs}}$$

The matter of obtaining distances to near-by Cepheids is a large-scale surveying job and some refinement of elementary geometric methods is called for. How this generalization took place will be the major theme of the present chapter.

In the second place, the Cepheid oscillations are just one instance of a general characteristic of cosmic phenomena—their *periodicity*. There is the succession of night and day, the regular change of seasons, the cycling of planets in their orbits, the recurrent changes in tides, and so on. There are the man-made alternating current oscillations, business cycles, etc. Periodicity is of such frequent occurrence that it demands an idealization through pure mathematics, and hence the mathematician has had to create *abstract periodic functions*.

By a strange coincidence the functions which the mathematician originally designed for the first task mentioned, that of surveying when distances are astronomic in magnitude, have the very qualities needed to handle periodicity as well. Such is the essence of *trigonometry* (trigonon—triangle, metron—measure), the branch of mathematics treating the measurement of triangles. It was first scientifically formulated by Hipparchus (180 B.C.–125 B.C.), a leading astronomer of antiquity, to assist him in his back-breaking job of charting upward of 1000 stars without the aid of a telescope. From his day to the present time, trigonometry has been the special hand-maiden of the astronomer, at the same time expanding its services to apply to all fields where practical geometry was the original, cruder tool, as well as to those situations arising out of the inevitable periodicity in nature's and man's affairs.

Although Hipparchus, Father of Trigonometry, represented the spirit of Alexandrian science at its height, he did not live in Alexan-

dria, but instead made most of his observations at Rhodes. The charting of stars was not the only result of Hipparchus' stargazing. It was
he who first discovered that the Sun's apparent annual orbit is 'eccentric' (meaning that it does not have one center but two—in other
words it is not a circle). Although he did not describe the path as
an ellipse in the manner of Kepler, the seventeenth-century astronomer, he did arrive at the conclusion that the Sun is nearer the

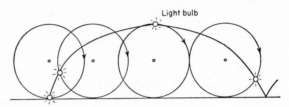

Fɪɢ. 49. The cycloid.

Earth at certain times of the year than others. He could not, however, bring himself to commit the heresy of asserting positively that
a heavenly body could describe a path less perfect than a circle.
When he discovered that not only the Sun but also the Moon and
the planets behave in the same 'eccentric' fashion, it behooved him
to develop some explanation of this phenomenon. To do so he
assumed that the planets do not move in unvarying circular arcs
in their motion about the Earth, but instead describe minor circles
as they go round. A light attached to the rim of a wagon wheel in
motion will give a tangible description of this sort of motion.
Mathematicians term such a path a *cycloid* (see fig. 49). For an
accurate picture of the Hipparchian theory of planetary motion we
must imagine a wheel moving not on level ground but, instead, in
such a way that its hub progresses in a large circular path like that
of the apparent planetary orbit. Mathematics describes the path of
a point on the rim of such a wheel as an *epicycloid*. Figure 50 suggests such a wheel motion and also shows the sort of path a planet
would thereby be assumed to follow.

Hipparchus' epicyclic theory was popularized by Ptolemy, whose
name is commonly attached to it. The Hipparchian cosmology of
epicycles is thus termed the *Ptolemaic theory,* and as such, domi-
nated scientific thought until the day of Copernicus. Of course, this
theory was not incorrect, as is the common notion, but merely
cumbrous, becoming more and more so as additional observations

entailed more and more corrections. It was not poor practical science, but merely inadequate abstraction of the common properties of planetary motion. It is an interesting fact that the Hipparchian (Ptolemaic) theory was actually taught in the early days at Harvard and Yale as an alternative theory to the Copernican. A familiar story records that Alfonso X of Castile (1244–84), who was deeply interested in astronomy, pondered long and deeply on the

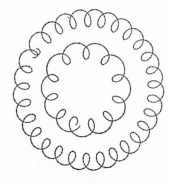

Fig. 50. Apparent epicyclic orbits of Jupiter and Saturn, the Earth supposedly fixed at the center, with the Sun revolving in a small circle. A loop is made by each planet each year (adapted from Proctor 'Old and New Astronomy' in Duncan, J. C. *Astronomy,* New York, Harper, 1935).

complicated epicycles of Hipparchus, until he was finally led to remark that, had he been consulted at the time of creation, he could have suggested a much better and simpler plan for the universe. Latter-day discussions of the theory led Walt Whitman to write:

When I heard the learn'd astronomer;
When the proofs, the figures were ranged in columns before me;
When I was shown the charts and the diagrams, to add, divide and measure them;
When I, sitting, heard the astronomer, where he lectured with much applause in the lecture room,
How soon, unaccountable, I became tired and sick;
Till rising, and gliding out, I wander'd off by myself,
In the mystical moist night-air, and from time to time,
Look'd up in perfect silence at the stars.[1]

Hipparchus is generally believed to have discovered the *precession* of the equinoxes, although research may ultimately give priority to some Babylonian astronomer. The phenomenon may be described as follows. Even the most amateur of stargazers today can

[1] Whitman, Walt, *Leaves of Grass,* Garden City, N. Y., Doubleday & Co., 1926.

tell you how to locate the *pole star,* that is, the star in the 'celestial sphere' to which our own North Pole points. In spite of Shakespeare's description,

> . . . constant as the northern star
> Of whose true-fix'd and resting quality
> There is no fellow in the firmament

the pole star does not stay the same from age to age. About four thousand years ago the star known as *Alpha Draconis* was the pole star; about twelve thousand years hence the pole star will be *Alpha Lyrae;* about twenty-six thousand years hence the pole star will once again be the one we know. This periodic circling is caused by the slow conical rotation of the axis of the Earth (fig. 51). Its cause

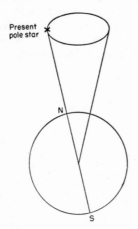

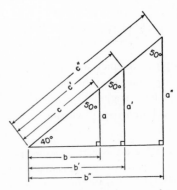

FIG. 51. Precession of the equinoxes.

FIG. 52. Set of right triangles with 40° angle.

is the gravitational tug of the Sun and Moon on the equatorial bulge of the Earth. This effect can be pictured by thinking of an ordinary top spinning so that the upper end of its axis describes a circle, while the lower end on the ground does not move. The conical spinning of the Earth displaces the points on the Earth's orbit at which the equinoxes occur. Hence the term precession.

As for trigonometry, what Hipparchus did was based on the use of similar triangles, which are defined as those that agree in corresponding angles and in which corresponding sides have equal ratios. In a study of geometry it is proved that if either condition is

known—equal angles or sides with equal ratios—the additional condition will also hold, and the triangles will be similar.

In figure 52 we have drawn a series of right triangles all containing the same 40° angle. Since the sum of the angles of every
triangle is 180°, the remaining angle in each triangle will be 50°.
Hence all the triangles are similar. Therefore corresponding sides
have equal ratios, and

$$\frac{a}{a'} = \frac{b}{b'}$$

or, alternating the terms,

$$\frac{a}{b} = \frac{a'}{b'}$$

Similarly $\qquad \frac{a}{c} = \frac{a'}{c'} \qquad$ and $\qquad \frac{b}{c} = \frac{b'}{c'} \quad$ etc.

In other words, if triangles are similar, *the ratio of a particular pair
of sides is constant* from triangle to triangle.

This is a simple fact but one for the surveyor or astronomer to
rejoice over. The ratio of two sides of a triangle in his scale drawing
will be the same as the corresponding ratio for the triangular piece
of land or sky he is measuring. Moreover, if he encounters a triangle of the same shape tomorrow or next week or next year, the
ratio will still be the same. Then why draw a new picture each
time? Why not measure the ratios of sides in today's picture and
keep the results on file for next time? That was just what Hipparchus did in the course of his survey of the heavens. By agreeing
to use right triangles his tabulation was simplified, since only one
acute angle need be named to characterize the situation; if the
angle is 32°, say, it is understood that the remaining angles of the
triangle are 90° and 58°.

Tradition has given names to the ratios of sides in a right tri-
angle, that is to $\frac{a}{c}, \frac{b}{c},$ and $\frac{a}{b}$. The ratio $\frac{a}{c}$, that is, the ratio the side
opposite the given angle bears to the *hypotenuse* of the right tri-
angle, is called the *sine* of the given angle. The ratio that the side
adjacent to the given angle bears to the hypotenuse is called the
cosine of the given angle. The ratio that the side opposite the given
angle bears to the side adjacent to it is called the *tangent* of the
given angle. In figure 52

$$\text{sine } 40° = \frac{\text{side opposite}}{\text{hypotenuse}} = \frac{a}{c} = \frac{a'}{c'} = \frac{a''}{c''}$$

$$\text{cosine } 40° = \frac{\text{side adjacent}}{\text{hypotenuse}} = \frac{b}{c} = \frac{b'}{c'} = \frac{b''}{c''}$$

$$\text{tangent } 40° = \frac{\text{side opposite}}{\text{side adjacent}} = \frac{a}{b} = \frac{a'}{b'} = \frac{a''}{b''}$$

The derivation of our term 'sine' from the original Hindu is of philological interest. About A.D. 500 Aryabhata used the term *jiva* (chord). Notice, in figure 53, that if the radius of the circle is 1 unit, the half-chord *DB* represents *sine* α. Classic trigonometry usually treats the ratios in connection with a unit circle, and hence

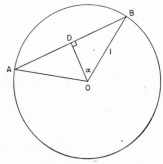

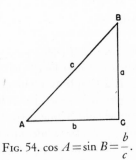

FIG. 53. Sine means half-chord.   FIG. 54. $\cos A = \sin B = \dfrac{b}{c}$.

the Hindu term. The Arabs translated the Hindu *jiva* as *gib,* which, because of similarity in sound to the word for 'fold' or 'bay' in their language, was confused with it and translated into Latin as *sinus* (fold), which later became *sine*.

There are names for the inverted ratios $(\frac{c}{a}, \frac{c}{b}, \frac{b}{a})$ also, but since we can get along without these ratios, we shall not burden the reader with their names. In the work that follows we shall use the abbreviations: *sin, cos,* and *tan*.

To explain the 'co' in *cosine* consider figure 54. In this diagram

$$\sin A = \frac{a}{c}$$

$$\sin B = \frac{b}{c}$$

$$\cos A = \frac{b}{c}$$

We see that

$$\cos A = \sin B$$

Since the sum of the angles of any triangle is always 180°, the sum of the two acute angles in a right triangle will always be 90°. Two angles whose sum is 90° are termed *complementary* angles, for one 'completes' the other in the sense of forming a 90° total. Hence angles A and B are complementary, and $\dfrac{b}{c}$ *is the sine of the complement of A.* Hence $\dfrac{b}{c}$ was called cosine, an abbreviation of the Latin *complementi sinus.*

Although the original meanings of the trigonometric ratios is connected with right triangles, they can be employed in problems involving any type of triangle. The first use of these ratios was merely in work with triangles, but the constant generalization of mathematical facts has brought about the application of trigonometry to many fields outside of surveying and astronomy.

The preparation of a table like that on page 128 would be possible by the use of large precise scale drawings. Ancient mathematicians used instead theoretical calculations with sides of polygons. In the latter days of trigonometry the calculus afforded a superior way of computing the values of the trigonometric ratios correct to any desired number of decimal places (for most angles, the ratios are *incommensurable*), and the tables of today derive from this source.

Let us next examine a few illustrations of how to survey the universe with a pencil—and a trigonometric table.

To find the height of a cloudbank at night, (see fig. 55) a search-light at C is directed vertically upward to the bottom of the cloud at B. At point A, some distance from C the angle of elevation of B is found by means of a *clinometer* (a special protractor) or some other instrument.

Fig. 55.

Suppose the distance AC is 500 feet and the angle of elevation is 83°, what is the height of the cloud?

$$\tan 83° = \frac{BC}{500}$$

$$8.1443 = \frac{BC}{500}$$

$$(8.1443)(500) = BC$$

$$4072 \text{ (to nearest foot)} = BC$$

Values of the Trigonometric Functions

Angle	Sin	Cos	Tan	Angle	Sin	Cos	Tan
1°	.0175	.9998	.0175	46°	.7193	.6947	1.0355
2°	.0349	.9994	.0349	47°	.7314	.6820	1.0724
3°	.0523	.9986	.0524	48°	.7431	.6691	1.1106
4°	.0698	.9976	.0699	49°	.7547	.6561	1.1504
5°	.0872	.9962	.0875	50°	.7660	.6428	1.1918
6°	.1045	.9945	.1051	51°	.7771	.6293	1.2349
7°	.1219	.9925	.1228	52°	.7880	.6157	1.2799
8°	.1392	.9903	.1405	53°	.7986	.6018	1.3270
9°	.1564	.9877	.1584	54°	.8090	.5878	1.3764
10°	.1736	.9848	.1763	55°	.8192	.5736	1.4281
11°	.1908	.9816	.1944	56°	.8290	.5592	1.4826
12°	.2079	.9781	.2126	57°	.8387	.5446	1.5399
13°	.2250	.9744	.2309	58°	.8480	.5299	1.6003
14°	.2419	.9703	.2493	59°	.8572	.5150	1.6643
15°	.2588	.9659	.2679	60°	.8660	.5000	1.7321
16°	.2756	.9613	.2867	61°	.8746	.4848	1.8040
17°	.2924	.9563	.3057	62°	.8829	.4695	1.8807
18°	.3090	.9511	.3249	63°	.8910	.4540	1.9626
19°	.3256	.9455	.3443	64°	.8988	.4384	2.0503
20°	.3420	.9397	.3640	65°	.9063	.4226	2.1445
21°	.3584	.9336	.3839	66°	.9135	.4067	2.2460
22°	.3746	.9272	.4040	67°	.9205	.3907	2.3559
23°	.3907	.9205	.4245	68°	.9272	.3746	2.4751
24°	.4067	.9135	.4452	69°	.9336	.3584	2.6051
25°	.4226	.9063	.4663	70°	.9397	.3420	2.7475
26°	.4384	.8988	.4877	71°	.9455	.3256	2.9042
27°	.4540	.8910	.5095	72°	.9511	.3090	3.0777
28°	.4695	.8829	.5317	73°	.9563	.2924	3.2709
29°	.4848	.8746	.5543	74°	.9613	.2756	3.4874
30°	.5000	.8660	.5774	75°	.9659	.2588	3.7321
31°	.5150	.8572	.6009	76°	.9703	.2419	4.0108
32°	.5299	.8480	.6249	77°	.9744	.2250	4.3315
33°	.5446	.8387	.6494	78°	.9781	.2079	4.7046
34°	.5592	.8290	.6745	79°	.9816	.1908	5.1446
35°	.5736	.8192	.7002	80°	.9848	.1736	5.6713
36°	.5878	.8090	.7265	81°	.9877	.1564	6.3138
37°	.6018	.7986	.7536	82°	.9903	.1392	7.1154
38°	.6157	.7880	.7813	83°	.9925	.1219	8.1443
39°	.6293	.7771	.8098	84°	.9945	.1045	9.5144
40°	.6428	.7660	.8391	85°	.9962	.0872	11.4301
41°	.6561	.7547	.8693	86°	.9976	.0698	14.3007
42°	.6691	.7431	.9004	87°	.9986	.0523	19.0811
43°	.6820	.7314	.9325	88°	.9994	.0349	28.6363
44°	.6947	.7193	.9657	89°	.9998	.0175	57.2900
45°	.7071	.7071	1.0000	90°	1.0000	.0000	

Suppose that, standing on the same spot, our observer later reported 'ceiling 2400 feet.' What angle of elevation must he have recorded before making this reading? Obviously

$$\tan A = \tfrac{2400}{500} = \tfrac{24}{5} = 4.8000$$

Consulting the tangent column of the tables, we find that the number closest to this is 4.7046, and hence the angle of elevation was approximately 78°.

To find the vectorial directions on page 114 of the previous chapter, it is only necessary to use the tangent column of the tables and then to find the acute angles in figure 45 by trigonometry, and the directions themselves by suitable additions and subtractions. The tangent ratios involved in figure 45 of the previous chapter are

$$\tfrac{4}{3} = 1.3333, \ \tfrac{2}{2} = 1, \ \tfrac{5}{3} = 1.6667, \ \tfrac{5}{2} = 2.5000$$

and the corresponding acute angles are

$$53°, \ 45°, \ 59°, \ 68°$$

A pair of vectors may readily be added when they are in standard complex form. Thus, the sum or *resultant* of $4 - 2i$ and $-5 - 6i$ is $-1 - 8i$, found by adding 'real' and 'imaginary' parts separately. Just what does an addition of vectors mean in a physical sense? To

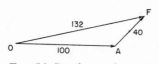

Fig. 56. Resultant of an air speed of 100 m.p.h. and a southwest wind of 40 m.p.h.

illustrate, suppose a plane is heading east with air speed of 100 miles per hour and a 40 mile per hour wind is blowing from the southwest. The plane behaves as if it first proceeded 100 miles east in still air, *then* was pushed 40 miles northeast, all in 1 hour (see fig. 56). If a scale drawing is made, as in the diagram, it will show that the resultant speed is about 132 miles per hour and that the plane will drift 13° north of its easterly heading.

Any two vectors can be added by a drawing like that in figure 56, where one vector is imagined to follow the other in its action.

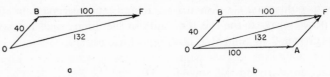

FIG. 57. The commutative law of addition holds for vectors. Note that the resultant is the same as in figure 56 if we consider the 40 m.p.h. wind as acting first and the air speed second. In diagram b we have fused the two orders of addition. The quadrilateral thus formed is called a *parallelogram of vectors*.

If we wish to translate these vectors into complex form, we can use figure 58 and obtain

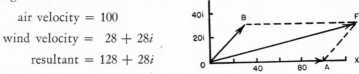

air velocity = 100

wind velocity = $28 + 28i$

resultant = $128 + 28i$

FIG. 58. Vectors as complex numbers.

If we do not wish to depend on the accuracy of a scale drawing we can apply trigonometry to some of the work: Thus, for the wind,

$$\frac{\text{horizontal component}}{40} = \cos 45° = 0.7071$$

and hence

horizontal component = $40 \times 0.7071 = 28.28$
$$= 28 \text{ (approximately)}$$

Similarly,

vertical component = $40 \sin 45° = 40 \times 0.7071 = 28$

To return to the source of our present discussion, the determination of the distance from the Earth to a near-by star is a matter of simple trigonometry. When this is done for a Cepheid variable, it is the initial step in the survey of the entire heavens. Remote Cepheids are then located by the double application of period-luminosity and inverse square laws. The *parallax* of the star must first be determined. To understand the idea of parallax, perform the following experiment: Hold a pencil at arm's length in front of you and sight it against a distant wall, first with one eye closed and then with the other closed. You will find that the pencil seems to shift its position on the distant wall. Repeat the experiment, holding the pencil nearer to the eye. The shift on the distant wall will seem even greater than before. If, now, you think of the pencil as a star, and of your eyes as two points on opposite sides of the Earth's annual orbit around the Sun (fig. 59), and the distant wall as the location of distant stars, then it is obvious that the star observed will seem to shift its position relative to the very remote stars if observations are made from different positions in the Earth's orbit. Moreover, the nearer the star, the greater this shift will be. To obtain the shift in position of a star, it is customary to perform

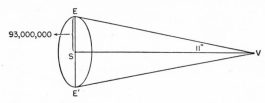

Fig. 59. Obtaining distance of Vega from its parallax.

telescopic photography of its situation in the heavens at a certain time and then six months later, when the Earth is diametrically opposite in its orbit (fig. 59); the angle between the first line of sight and the line of sight six months later is measured. Half of this angle is termed the *parallax* of the star. It is actually the shift in direction that would take place if the star were observed from a position on the Earth and then from one on the Sun. The parallax of Vega, for example, is found to be 0.11", that is, 0.11 of a 'second' where a second is $\frac{1}{3600}$th degree. Hence, in figure 59, we have

$$\tan 0.11'' = \frac{93,000,000}{x}$$

By using more precise trigonometric tables than those presented here, we should find

$$\tan 0.11'' = .00000055 \text{ (approximately)}$$

and

$$x = \frac{93,000,000}{.00000055} = 1.7 \times 10^{14} \text{ miles}$$

Our discussion thus far has dealt merely with the elementary phases of *plane* trigonometry. Strange as it may seem, not even this small unit of the subject existed for many centuries. Greek influence against the practical was strong. On the other hand, *spherical* trigonometry, that is, the facts governing the solution of triangles drawn on a spherical surface, developed early. Trigonometry, it must be remembered, was initially used in astronomy and not in pure mathematics. The astronomers were not interested merely in the flat triangles of surveying but in the large curved triangles of the celestial sphere.

The trigonometry of the right triangle, which we have described, is capable of generalization in many important ways. We have alluded to two of these—namely, the solution of the spherical triangle and the general plane triangle. The properties of the trigonometric ratios have important uses in other branches of mathematics as well as in astronomy and physics. We shall generalize the meaning of the trigonometric ratios in the next chapter in order to indicate their use in describing periodic phenomena.

7

Father of Modern Mathematics and His Legacy

> It is impossible not to feel stirred at the thought of the emotions of men at certain historic moments of adventure and discovery—Columbus when he first saw the Western shore, Pizarro when he stared at the Pacific Ocean, Franklin when the electric spark came from the string of his kite, Galileo when he first turned his telescope to the heavens. Such moments are also granted to students in the abstract regions of thought, and high among them must be placed the morning when Descartes lay in bed and invented the method of coordinate geometry.
>
> WHITEHEAD

RENÉ DESCARTES (1596–1650) has been called the 'father of modern mathematics.' He was creative in other fields as well: philosophy, physics, cosmology, chemistry, physiology, and psychology. His outstanding contribution to pure science was *analytic geometry*. In this subject he wedded algebra and geometry, and very few mathematicians since the seventeenth century have attempted to rend the two asunder. Calculus was the illustrious offspring of this happy union. In fact, the mathematical family which Descartes' analytic geometry initiated became exceedingly prolific in latter days.

The progenitor of modern mathematics came of a noble family. His father was in comfortable circumstances and expected his son to lead the life of a French gentleman. René was a delicate child and did not start his formal schooling until the age of eight. At the Jesuit college at La Flèche the rector Father Charlet observed the boy's physical frailty and advised him to lie in bed as late as he pleased in the mornings. It was thus that Descartes formed the life-long habit of spending his mornings in bed whenever he wished to think.

At an early age he entered the army, a strange thing for a man to do who expressed his personal philosophy in the words, 'I desire only tranquillity and repose.' Be that as it may, there was a brief

interval of tranquillity and repose during the wars of William the
Silent, and at this time Descartes invented analytic geometry.
According to one story, he was indulging his habit of lying in bed
one morning when his eye chanced on a fly crawling on the ceiling
in his room. He set himself the problem of describing the path
of the fly in mathematical language. Another story has it that the
idea of analytic geometry came to Descartes in a dream.

At the age of twenty-five Descartes left the army for good. Later,
in 1628, he retired to Holland for twenty years of thinking about
philosophy and mathematics. He did not neglect other scientific
studies, and much of his time was given to the preparation of an
imposing treatise, *Le Monde*. This book presented a scientific ra-
tionalization of the Book of Genesis and gave Descartes' physical
doctrine of the universe. He determined to preserve all his work
for posthumous publication as his legacy to science, but his friends
persuaded him in 1637 to release his masterpiece—*Discours de la
Méthode pour bien conduire sa raison et chercher la vérité dans les
sciences.* In an appendix of this work, entitled 'La Géométrie,'
analytic geometry was given to the world.

In 1649 Descartes decided to vary his existence and accepted an
invitation to the court of Queen Christina of Sweden. This head-
strong, masculine girl, whose tyrannic behavior is historical, was
Descartes' undoing. The poor philosopher, who could not endure the
harsh climate or the difficult routine set by Christina, fell ill and
died of pneumonia at the age of fifty-four.

Words are an easy form of penance. The eccentric tyrant wrote
to a friend:

The greatest of philosophers has just died. If I were superstitious, I
should weep like a child over his death, and I should bitterly repent
having drawn this bright star from its course. His death depresses me;
it will always fill me with justified but useless regret.

Let us now examine Descartes' mathematical estate. In doing so,
we note that he was the first to put graphic methods to serious use.
He was no journalist bent on exploiting man's weakness for pictures nor was he concerned with clarification of statistical data.
His objective was to give concrete representation to the abstractions
of algebra, and conversely to increase the generality of geometry by
furnishing analytic (algebraic) formulation of its facts.

To the layman, a curve is a curve. A corkscrew or a camel's

hump are merely deviations from the straight and narrow. Not so to the mathematician. Figure 60 illustrates the form assumed by a perfectly flexible cord when you hold the two ends and let the rest of the cord hang loose. To the reader this curve may seem much like the arch of a bridge, the George Washington Bridge in New

FIG. 60. The catenary.

York City, for example. The mathematician judges differently. In the case of the bridge the formula or equation is algebraic; for the cord it is *transcendental*—which implies that the latter is mathematically more sophisticated, since its expression transcends or defies elementary algebra.

The bridge curve is termed a *parabola;* the cord is a *catenary.* The following are also approximately parabolic: the path of a baseball (or cannon ball of less pleasant association), the orbit of a comet, the cross section of an automobile headlight. The catenary is the curve formed by a string of pearls or by dewdrops suspended on a spider's web. The mathematician Jacob Bernoulli termed it the 'sail-curve' because it is the cross section of a sail filled with wind. The dome of the cathedral at Florence (work of Brunelleschi) has a catenary as its cross section, although the great Italian architect lived long before mathematicians revealed the special properties of the catenary.

The mathematician is not interested in curves for their shape or beauty however, but rather because many of them are the graphic expression of mathematical functions embodying nature's laws. Some of the curves that have been of great use in this connection are the conic sections. We mention them first because the formulas defining them put them in the most elementary class. If a right circular *cone* (hourglass figure like two ice cream cones placed end to end) whose curved surface extends indefinitely up and down is cut by a plane, the curve of intersection is called a conic section or merely a *conic.* In figure 61 we have illustrated the cone and the five typical conics: circle, ellipse, parabola, hyperbola (a curve of two branches), and two intersecting straight lines.

The geometry of the conics was worked out in perfect form by Apollonius (260?-200?B.C.). Without this work of the Greek geometer, the great astronomer Kepler would never have been able

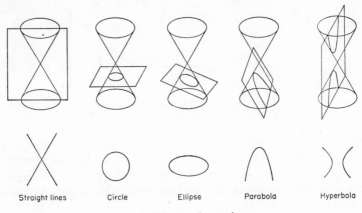

| Straight lines | Circle | Ellipse | Parabola | Hyperbola |

FIG. 61. The conic sections.

to discover the laws of planetary motion (1609). One of Kepler's law states that the path of each planet is an ellipse. Without Kepler's laws, Newton would probably have been unable to formulate his theory of universal gravitation. Hence the work of Apollonius deserves more prominence than historians have accorded it.

Since nature's fondness for the ellipse gets regular publicity through diagrams like that in figure 62, it might be well to discuss

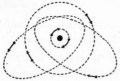

FIG. 62. Rutherford-Bohr model of an atom of carbon (12). The nucleus (heavy central dot) contains 6 protons and 6 neutrons. There are 6 extranuclear electrons.

this conic first. A definition of the ellipse that is more suitable for algebraic handling than its description as a particular cross section of a cone is: An ellipse is the *path of a point in a plane the sum of whose distances from two fixed points is constant*. Each fixed point is called a *focus* of the ellipse. Figures 63 and 64 show how to draw an ellipse mechanically from this description. According to Kepler's laws, the Sun is at one focus of each planetary orbit. The paths of the planets are almost circular. In that case, the foci of

Fig. 63. The ends of a string are attached to the foci *A* and *B*. *A* moving pencil *P*, which holds this string taut, will describe an ellipse.

Fig. 64. This is probably an easier way to draw an ellipse. A loop of fixed length is allowed to slide around the foci while the tracing pencil holds it taut, tracing the curve. Because the length between the foci will always be the same, what remains of the cord (sum of distances) is also constant.

the ellipse are close together, and the position of the Sun is almost central.

One geometric property of the ellipse is illustrated in certain whispering galleries. The law of reflection of light, sound, etc. states: *The angle of incidence must equal the angle of reflection.* By the angle of incidence is meant the angle that the incident ray *AP* (fig.

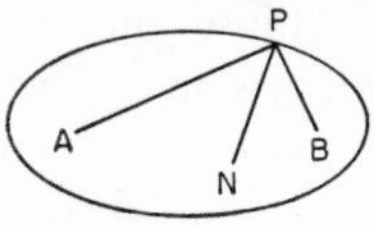

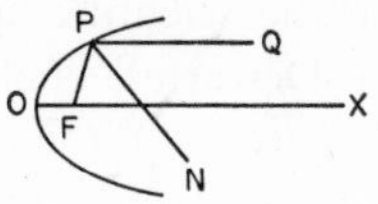

Fig. 65. Reflection from elliptic surface.

Fig. 66. Reflection from parabolic surface.

65) makes with the *normal NP* (perpendicular) to the surface. By the angle of reflection is meant the angle that the reflected ray *BP* makes with the normal. If *A* and *B* are foci of the ellipse in fig. 65, angle *APN* must always equal angle *BPN* no matter what position on the ellipse is occupied by point *P*. If a sound wave issues from focus *A* and strikes *any point* of the curve, it will be reflected to focus *B*. This means that a sound emitted at *A* will be heard distinctly at *B*, even when the distance between *A* and *B* is considerable.

A cross section of the dome of the famous Taj Mahal is elliptical. Shah Jehan built this edifice at Agra, India, in 1650, to preserve the memory of his favorite wife, Mumtaj Mahal. In prewar tours, honeymooning couples who visited this most famous monument to romance were supposed to separate, one standing at either focus of the ellipsoidal structure. The young man at one focus was told to whisper 'To the memory of an undying love.' The message was conveyed distinctly to his bride at the other focus more than fifty feet away, but was inaudible to any one standing elsewhere.

A similar property of the parabola brings about the use of *parabolic reflectors* in our giant telescopes. The parabola has a single focus, F (see fig. 66). By a geometric property of this curve, angle FPN = angle NPQ, where PN is the normal at P, and PQ is a line parallel to the axis OFX of the parabola. This fact is true whatever the position of P on the parabola. Therefore, by the law of reflection, if rays parallel to the axis hit a parabolic surface, they will all be reflected to the focus. Reversing the situation, if a light is placed at the focus, a parallel beam will be sent out from the parabolic surface. The former fact causes the parallel rays from a star to converge and give a sharp image of the star at the focus of a parabolic reflecting telescope. The latter fact explains the use of a parabolic surface when a strong light is needed, as in the automobile headlight, where the powerful parallel beams illuminate the road ahead.

Such are the scientific applications of ellipse and parabola. One purpose of Descartes' analytic geometry was to study the mathematical properties of these curves, and many others, through the medium of the *graph*. Descartes' plan for picturing curves was quite a simple one. His scheme was similar to that of an engineer laying out a suburb. Imagine a lattice of streets and avenues as planned in figure 67. Streets run north and south, avenues east and west. There is one main street, and one main avenue. These are called *axes,* and their point of intersection is called the *origin.* Streets east of Main Street receive positive numbers, those west, negative. Avenues north of Main Avenue are positive, those south are negative.

When Mr. Smith states that he lives on Street 3 and Avenue 5, you will be able to locate his home. The numbers 3 and 5 are called the *co-ordinates* of the house and are indicated thus: (3, 5). Suppose that Mr. Smith decided to preserve some of the mathematical classics against the contingency of a book-burning episode. He could bury them on his grounds, easily ascertain the co-ordinates, as, say (3.3, 5.2), and transmit these co-ordinates to posterity in cipher form. We have indicated some other points in figure 67. The point Q with co-ordinates $(-2, 3)$, R $(-4, -1)$, S $(3, -4)$, T $(4, 0)$, and V $(0, -3)$ are shown in the diagram.

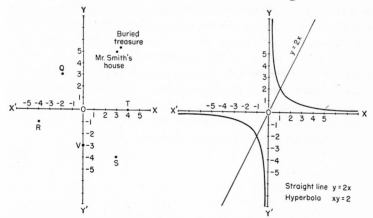

FIG. 67. Cartesian co-ordinate system.   FIG. 68.

Since there are two co-ordinates for each point, and these vary from point to point, the network scheme (usually called a *Cartesian co-ordinate system*) can be used to picture a relationship between two variables. Consider, for example, the equations for direct and inverse variation,

$$\frac{y}{x} = k \quad \text{and} \quad xy = k, \text{ respectively}$$

If we choose k = 2, these become

$$y = 2x \quad \text{and} \quad xy = 2$$

Choosing any values we like for x, we can figure the corresponding values of y, which will yield for

$y = 2x$	x	-4	-2	-1	0	$+1$	$+2$	$+4$	
	y	-8	-4	-2	0	$+2$	$+4$	$+8$	
$xy = 2$	x	-8	-4	-2	-1	$+1$	$+2$	$+4$	$+8$
	y	$-\frac{1}{4}$	$-\frac{1}{2}$	-1	-2	$+2$	$+1$	$+\frac{1}{2}$	$+\frac{1}{4}$

(Notice that $x = 0$ is not given in the latter case, since division by 0 is impossible.)

These functions are plotted in figure 68. The first is evidently a straight line passing through the origin of co-ordinates. The second can be proved by Cartesian methods to be a hyperbola—that is a section of a cone formed by cutting both parts of the hourglass but avoiding its vertex. Whatever the value of k, it can be proved that the pictures of direct and inverse variation will be a line and hyperbola respectively. Just as the handling of the ellipse was eased by redefinition, the same is true of the hyperbola. The former curve required a constant *sum;* the latter demands a constant *difference*: *A hyperbola is the path of a point in a plane, the difference of whose distances from two fixed points (the foci) is constant.*

This definition of a hyperbola is used in LORAN (LONG RANGE NAVIGATION), a special use of radar. The *foci* are two stations on shore a number of miles apart. The 'master' station sends out a

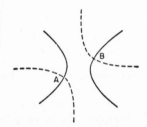

FIG. 69. LORAN locates position by the intersection of two hyperbolas.

pulse, which the 'slave' station receives immediately (the interval is too tiny to be measured); then the second station automatically sends out its own pulse. On a ship with LORAN equipment both pulses are received and the difference between times of arrival is indicated on a 'scope' (screen). Next the difference in distance is automatically figured as 186,000 (the speed of electromagnetic waves) multiplied by this interval. Then the ship's position is on the hyperbola so defined. This is plotted. If signals from another pair of stations are received, another hyperbola (see fig. 69) is plotted, and the intersection of the two curves marks the ship's position. Two hyperbolas may intersect in more than one point, in fact, in as many as four. Since 'dead-reckoning' gives some idea of the ship's locality, the proper point of intersection can be selected.

There are two opposite routines in Cartesian geometry. The first is to go from *formula* to *picture*. We should like to know whether the picture will be a straight line, circular arc, or some other type of curve. In reverse, we should like to know what type of formula to assign to a straight line, circle, or any other curve. The first problem involves translating abstract algebra into concrete geometric pictures; the second is a case of furnishing a geometric situation with its algebraic equivalent.

It is often easy enough to go from equation to picture. We merely assign values to x and find the corresponding values of y. But suppose the formula, or equation of the curve, as it is usually called, is given by

$$x^2 + y^2 = 9$$
$$\text{If we let } x = 1 \text{ then}$$
$$1 + y^2 = 9$$
$$y^2 = 8$$
$$y = \pm\sqrt{8}$$

Here we have two points $(1, \sqrt{8})$ and $(1, -\sqrt{8})$. The coordinates involve irrationals and are not much fun to plot. For this reason, generalities rather than point-to-point plotting is eventually essential in analytic geometry. We shall see that such rules will tell at once that this equation represents a circle with center at the origin and radius 3. Other analytic generalities state: Every *first-degree* equation represents a *straight line,* and, conversely, every straight line picture has a first-degree formula. Every *second-degree* equation represents some *conic,* and conversely.

Again, suppose the equation of a curve is

$$x^4 + y^5 - x^3y^2 + 1 = 0$$
$$\text{Let } x = 1$$
Then
$$1 + y^5 - y^2 + 1 = 0$$

which gives us an equation of the fifth degree to solve. In a later chapter, we shall see that, in general, an equation of the fifth degree cannot be solved in terms of the numbers with which the reader is familiar—integers, fractions, and roots. Only approximate results can be obtained. Here we see that the graphing of equations is closely connected with the theory of solving equations. In fact, although we shall not go more deeply into the question here, graphs are often used as nomograms to accomplish approximate solutions.

While we are on the topic of graphing equations, it is appropriate that we consider the generalization of the trigonometric ratios, for this involves the use of the graph. If we are to work with sines, cosines, and tangents of angles in any sort of plane triangle, we must give meaning to these ratios in the case of obtuse angles, for the general triangle, in contrast to the right triangle, may contain

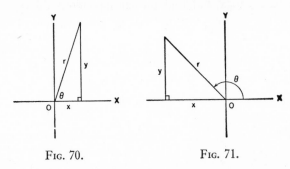

FIG. 70.   FIG. 71.

an obtuse angle. The ratios as we defined them applied only to acute angles in a right triangle. How shall we define them for the more general case?

If, moreover, trigonometry is to be applied to science, we must not limit ourselves to acute and obtuse angles. Wheels cannot stop rotations at 180°. How, then, shall we define the sine of an angle of 200° or one of 375°?

The definition is easily suggested by the customary one for an acute angle. In figure 70

$$\sin \theta = \frac{y}{r}$$

$$\cos \theta = \frac{x}{r}$$

$$\tan \theta = \frac{y}{x}$$

by the old definitions.

Now let θ grow until it becomes an obtuse angle (fig. 71). Mathematical convenience suggests that we still define the ratios as

$$\sin \theta = \frac{y}{r}$$

$$\cos \theta = \frac{x}{r}$$

$$\tan \theta = \frac{y}{x}$$

These same definitions prove satisfactory whatever the size of θ. It makes facts simpler if we choose $r=1$. (Remember that the ratios depend on the angles and not on the sides of a triangle.) In this case

$$\sin \theta = \frac{y}{1} = y$$

$$\cos \theta = \frac{x}{1} = x$$

$$\tan \theta = \frac{y}{x}$$

It is interesting to make a study of how the values of the ratios change as the angle grows larger. To do this, imagine yourself making a trip on the Ferris wheel in an amusement park. To add to the thrills as you go round, try to estimate your vertical distance from the horizontal axis of the wheel. This will be the sine of the angle through which you have rotated.

To use more technical language—since $\sin \theta = y$ when $r=1$, all we need to do is watch the y-co-ordinate of a point as it moves

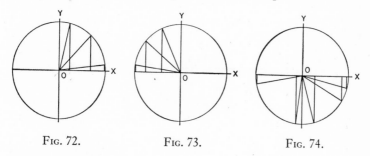

FIG. 72.   FIG. 73.   FIG. 74.

around a circle of radius 1. In figure 72 we have indicated a growth in angle from 0° to 90°. Notice that the y-co-ordinate grows larger until it reaches the value 1. When there is a 0° angle, the y-co-ordinate is 0. Hence sin $0° = 0$, and as the angle goes from $0°$ to $90°$, the sine increases from 0 to 1, a fact the tables on page 128 will verify.

Now that we have gone one-fourth the way round our Ferris wheel, our angle passes the $90°$ mark (fig. 73). The carriage in which we are seated has been rising up to the $90°$ point, and now it starts to drop. The y-co-ordinate, in other words the sine, is decreasing. In fact, as the angle goes from $90°$ to $180°$ the sine decreases from 1 to 0.

Something very interesting occurs after the carriage passes the $180°$ mark. It is now below the horizontal axis of the wheel and hence its distance from this axis is negative. In figure 74 the y-co-ordinate is *negative,* and sin θ is negative as θ changes from $180°$ to $360°$. The Ferris wheel can make you experience a negative number. We can now understand why general trigonometry could not progress until algebra had developed to a point where directed numbers were no longer considered absurd.

A study of figure 74 shows that the sine changes from 0 to -1 as the angle goes from $180°$ to $270°$, and from -1 to 0 as the angle goes from $270°$ to $360°$. We see, too, that if the angle continues beyond $360°$, all the values will be repeated once more.

$$\sin 400° = \sin 40°$$
$$\sin 450° = \sin 90° \text{ etc.}$$

If the various values of the sine are tabulated and graphed, we obtain the picture in figure 75. The same pattern, the portion of

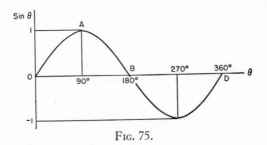

FIG. 75.

the curve from $0°$ to $360°$, is repeated forever. We say that the *sinusoid* is *periodic,* and that sin θ is a *periodic function* and is likely to be associated with scientific applications that involve identical repetition or periodicity.

As an illustration, consider the principle of the electric dynamo or generator. In 1831 Michael Faraday, one of the greatest physicists of all time, discovered that an electric current can be generated by moving a coil of wire between the poles of a magnet. Figure 76 omits the magnet but indicates the magnetic field and a coil of wire which is rotated in this field. The strength of the electromotive

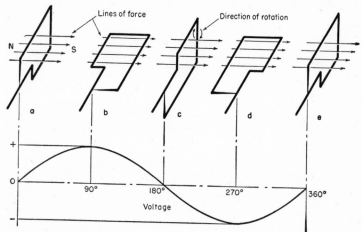

FIG. 76. Coil rotating in a magnetic field generates an alternating voltage.

force or voltage induced in the coil varies with its position as indicated in the graph. It can be proved that this graph is a sine curve. The diagram indicates that the voltage is zero when the plane of the coil is vertical and the wires in it are moving parallel to the lines of force, cutting none of them. As the coil moves, the voltage varies, increasing to a maximum when the plane of the coil is parallel to the lines of force while the wires in it are moving perpendicular to these lines. Then the voltage decreases again, reaching zero when the plane of the coil is once more vertical. The cycle is then repeated with the voltage in the opposite direction. The sine graph pictures an *alternating voltage,* which is the kind supplied to most homes. An alternating voltage produces an *alternating current* whose graph is a different sine curve. In ordinary electric lighting circuits, the alternation of current is so rapid that it is not noticeable. There are usually 60 cycles a second, that is, the rotating wires revolve 60 times in 1 second. We say that the *frequency* is 60 or the *period* of the sine curve is 1/60th of a second.

To take another example of the use of the sine curve, consider the phenomenon of sound. Sound is transmitted in a material medium like air by means of oscillations of the particles in the medium. To study such vibrations in detail, we may attach a phonograph needle to the end of one prong of a vibrating tuning fork (fig. 77) and run a piece of smoked glass under it, taking care that we move the glass in a straight line at a constant speed. If the fork

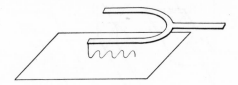

FIG. 77. Vibrations of a tuning fork record a sine curve.

were not vibrating we should merely obtain a straight line trace on the glass. But, when a tuning fork is emitting sound, the vibrations form a record which proves to be a sine curve. This sine curve will have greater height or *amplitude* if a fork is struck harder to produce a louder sound. A sound from a tuning fork of higher *pitch* would have a sine curve with shorter period or 'wave length.' Instead of giving the period to describe the pitch we may mention the frequency. If the period is 1/260th of a second, it means that in one second there will be 260 oscillations of the needle or repetitions of the sine curve; that is, the frequency is 260.

Not all sounds have so simple a picture as that of the tuning fork. The back and forth vibration of the needle which describes the sine curve is called a *simple harmonic motion*. An instrument called a *phonodeik* or *harmonic analyzer* shows that sounds which are not simple harmonic motions are composites of such motions—that is, *sums of sine curves*. A tone that has the quality of a violin note of frequency 500 can be obtained by striking simultaneously three tuning forks with frequencies 500, 1000, and 1500 and amplitudes in the ratio of 6 : 2 : 1 (see fig. 78). The tone of lowest pitch (smallest frequency) is called the *fundamental* and the other frequencies are called *overtones*. In this case 1000 is called the *second* harmonic because its frequency is twice that of the fundamental. We notice, in passing, that the frequency 1000 is an octave higher than 500. Doubling any frequency will raise the tone one octave.

The frequency 1500 is called the *third* harmonic. This illustration concerns a synthesis of tones. The natural situation is the reverse. A violin tone is produced and the phonodeik analyzes it to reveal the component sine curves, that is, the various harmonics and their relative strengths.

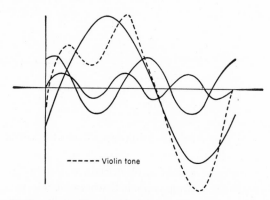

Fig. 78. Synthesis of tuning fork notes to produce violin tone.

It is agreed in musical theory that it is the relative amplitude of overtones that gives quality to a sound. The second harmonic is found to add clearness. The third adds a throaty or nasal quality, like that heard in clarinet notes. The fourth harmonic, being two octaves above the fundamental, adds shrillness. The fifth harmonic adds a horn-like quality, etc.

The mathematical techniques of harmonic analysis are used not only to break down sounds into their component sinusoids, but are employed extensively by the electrical engineer in the study of alternating currents, by the mechanical engineer in the investigation of valve motion, and by those scientists who specialize in the study of tides. In a large class of other phenomena that are roughly periodic, such as weather, sun spots, river flow, and atmospheric strays in radio reception, modifications of harmonic analysis are being used.

All of this originated with the French physicist and mathematician Fourier, who lived during the Napoleonic era. He showed that any well-determined graph, subject to a few restrictions unimportant in science, can be resolved into a series of sine curves. It is a remarkable fact that you might scribble a curve thus:

and it would nevertheless have a sine equation. Of course, three or four sine curves might be too few. You might need a hundred for a good approximation. Since a graph represents a function, Fourier's discovery meant that all the relationships of science are expressible in terms of sines. In a sense then trigonometry is at the basis of all scientific formulation. The idea of periodicity dominates portions of pure mathematics as well as applied science. There is the theory of *elliptic functions,* for example, which is a sort of higher trigonometry. Mathematicians and physicists alike hardly associate the importance of the trigonometric ratios with their initial elementary use in the fields of surveying and astronomy, since these ratios have led to more far-reaching results in later generalizations.

We now return to other questions in Cartesian geometry. We have got an inkling of the sort of problem involved in going from formula to graph. Let us see to what the reverse leads, for going from graph to formula is the second basic problem of analytic geometry. In the table below, from which we could graph the relation between weight and volume of iron, we can guess quite readily the formula

Volume (cubic cms.)	Weight (grams)	
1	7.8	$W = 7.8V$
2	15.6	
3	23.4	
4	31.2	

The reader might find it much more difficult to guess the relationship involved in the next table.

x	y
0	0
1	4
2	14
3	36
4	76
5	140

In this case, it is $y = x^3 + 3x$

Let us analyze the process of *abstracting a formula from a graph or table*. It is similar to other processes of abstraction that we have studied. The abstraction called *three* is something that all groups of a certain type have in common. In analytic geometry we search for something that all the points on a certain graph have in common. This common feature takes the form of a relationship between the co-ordinates, called the *equation of the curve*.

Suppose that we wish to find the equation of a circle with radius 5. Let us place the circle so that its center will lie at the origin (fig. 79). We have indicated three different sample points, Q, R, S,

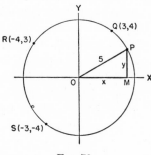

Fig. 79.

on this circle and have marked their co-ordinates. We shall now assist the reader to abstract a common property of these points, and all other points on the circle.

The definition of a circle as a plane curve, all points of which are the same distance from a fixed point called the center, requires in this case that all points of the curve be at a distance 5 from the origin. For the co-ordinates of Q (3,4) we note that

$$3^2 + 4^2 = 9 + 16 = 25$$

For the co-ordinates of R (-4,3) we note that

$$(-4)^2 + 3^2 = 16 + 9 = 25$$

For the co-ordinates of S $(-3, -4)$ we note that

$$(-3)^2 + (-4)^2 = 9 + 16 = 25$$

In fact, if P is any point on the circle with any co-ordinates (x, y), then OMP is a right triangle, and by the Pythagorean theorem

$$x^2 + y^2 = 5^2$$
$$x^2 + y^2 = 25$$

Then $x^2 + y^2 = 25$ is the equation of the circle, since it gives a relationship true for the co-ordinates of all points. That some co-ordinates may be negative does not matter, since they are squared in the relationship and hence yield a positive result.

We can, in fact, write the equation of a circle of any radius at all by replacing 5 by r. The equation $x^2 + y^2 = r^2$ is the symbolic representation of all circles with centers at the origin. In the procedure of using any point on a circle and *abstract* co-ordinates (x, y), we advance from arithmetic to algebra and our thoughts have more generality and hence greater power. In going from a particular radius 5 to any radius, a similar advance is made.

We shall not burden the reader, at present, with any more of the technical aspects of analytic geometry. We have derived the equation of the circle as a sample of how this subject achieves the generality by which one equation will describe an infinite number of curves of a specific type, and will content ourselves merely with the thought that derivation of the equations for other important types of curve is a basic issue of Cartesian geometry.

Not all curves are amenable to representation through a rectangular network. If we tried to give the abstract equivalent in such a scheme of the innocent-looking logarithmic spiral, which is such a favorite of nature, we should have a very hard time making things clear to the lay reader. To handle such curves more easily we sometimes lay out our imaginary suburb on a different plan. One way is to zigzag all our streets—somewhat in the fashion that Broadway cuts 42nd Street (see fig. 80). Another is to have a layout whose avenues are concentric circles and whose streets are lines radiating from the center of the circles (fig. 81). Until surrealism hits the city planners, such a scheme will probably not be adopted. Still the Paris boulevards suggest the circular scheme, and the layout of Washington illustrates a radial arrangement of streets.

In the latter scheme, called a *polar co-ordinate system,* the co-ordinates of a point (avenue and street) would be the *distance from the origin* and the *angle* formed with Main Street. In figure 81 we have indicated origin and initial line, point P with co-ordinates (2, 30°) and Q with co-ordinates (4, 120°). In this scheme, the equation of the famous logarithmic spiral of nature and art takes the simple

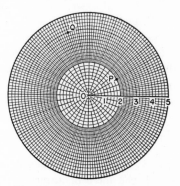

FIG. 80. Oblique co-ordinate system.

FIG. 81. Polar co-ordinate system.

form $r = a^\theta$ or $\theta =$ logarithm r, where a is the logarithmic base. Mathematicians have other city layouts to which they can resort to simplify the algebraic representation of other important curves.

Before presenting further facts of analytic geometry, it would be well to indicate how and why it is such a powerful tool. We have seen previously how the use of symbolism has a magic effect in clarifying thought that verbiage has previously muddled. So it was with Descartes' application of algebra to geometric problems. By the use of algebra, straight lines, circles, and other curves can be indicated by their equations. Algebraic work can be done with these equations, without any need for pictures. When the algebra is complete, the final results can be put into the geometric picture. But in the interim, it is not necessary to draw in the extra lines, circles, and other curves indicated by the algebraic work. Thus thought is not obstructed by confused diagrams.

Moreover there is a further and greater advantage in analytic geometry. In Greek geometry it was necessary to start with a concrete picture. The Greeks were limited to such curves as they could picture—line, circle, and other conic sections. We have seen how algebraic symbolism gave life to new numbers, by writing them first and finding a meaning for them afterward. The same stunt can be done with algebraic geometry. Write down any equation you like and then find out what its picture looks like and what it is good for. Will it be useful as a reflector—like the ellipse or parabola? Will it describe the motion of some natural object? Will it trisect an angle, and so on? Since we are at liberty to consider any equation whatsoever, infinitely more curves can be discovered and studied by the method of Descartes than by the geometry of the Greeks.

Cartesian geometry, moreover, can be extended to equations with three, four, five, or any number of letters. Naturally scientific formulas cannot be restricted to two variable quantities. The Newtonian formula for gravitational attraction contains four:

$$F = G \frac{Mm}{d^2}$$

where m, M are the masses of the two bodies, d their distance apart and F the force of attraction. G is not a variable, but a constant depending on the units of mass and distance used. To handle equations involving three variables, we can picture a three-dimensional network. Just as the two-dimensional co-ordinate system uses a network of squares, the three-dimensional can be imagined as an array of cubes. As for four-, five-, or any-dimensional co-ordinate systems, we need not picture them—the algebraic work will take care of all the facts and the geometric counterparts are superfluous. An algebraist does not balk at handling equations involving many different letters. On the other hand, a Greek geometer was decidedly limited by what he could see. By way of comment, let us remark that we have just introduced a *fourth dimension,* about which the layman is always curious. As we can see, the algebraist can create a fourth dimension merely by a stroke of his pen. Although he will not try to visualize the result, geometric language is a great convenience. To say that a relationship like

$$x^2 + y^2 + z^2 + w^2 = 9$$

is a *hypersphere* with radius 3 is so much easier than to state that four quantities vary in value but are related in such a way that the sum of the squares of corresponding values is always 9.

We have said nothing about three-dimensional 'space' or four-dimensional 'space' etc. The nature of 'space' is a question for physicists, philosophers, and psychologists. We shall have more to say about it when we discuss relativity. Pure mathematics, including analytic geometry, deals with abstractions and Descartes' 'spaces' are just networks within which 'points' can be fixed by giving 2 or 3 or 4 or 5, etc. numbers called *co-ordinates*. The results of this abstraction have amazingly numerous concrete applications. Within pure mathematics itself, the techniques of analytic geometry have proved to be equally fruitful.

8

Science and the Sweepstakes

> It is remarkable that a science which began with the consideration of games of chance should have become the most important object of human knowledge.
>
> LAPLACE

WE COME now to what may be termed the most curious chapter in the whole of mathematics, to a subject that is simultaneously closest to and most remote from the scientist's heart. On the one hand it will help to arrange insurance schemes, improve manufacturing, develop atomic theory, predict genetic phenomena, and crystallize hypotheses. On the other hand it is meat for the professional gambler, whether his game be dice or poker, whether he play a local pinball machine or the Monte Carlo roulette wheel. The same theory that will decide whether an experimental serum is effective against polio will indicate why no 'system' can prevent the eventual ruin of a gambler. The vital and the trivial have something in common in the element of *chance*.

In the simplest of all games of chance, what is the likelihood of obtaining heads when a coin of homogeneous construction is tossed? Obviously the chances are 1 in 2, since there is one favorable chance out of two total possibilities, both of which are equally likely because the coin is uniform. We say that the *probability* of obtaining heads is $\frac{1}{2}$. This suggests that if we were to toss a coin a great number of times—1000 or even 10,0000—we might reasonably expect that it would turn up heads approximately half the time. Again, suppose that we toss a single, perfectly symmetric die. What is the probability of throwing three or four? By analogous reasoning, the answer is $\frac{2}{6}$ or $\frac{1}{3}$.

Then, in general, the probability p of some occurrence may be 'defined' [1] as follows: In a complete set of *equally likely, mutually*

---

[1] Modern mathematicians avoid this classic definition. The use of the phrase 'equally likely' in the definition is the bone of contention, for if we attempt to explain its meaning we find it necessary to define 'likelihood' or chance, which are synonyms for probability. Thus we are back to our starting point and involved in a vicious circle.

exclusive events, the *probability* that some one of a subset of events will occur is the ratio

$$p = \frac{\text{number of events in subset}}{\text{number of events in the complete set}}$$

Let us apply this definition to the probability of obtaining a 7 or 11 in a throw with 2 homogeneously constructed dice. We can picture all possible throws:

$$1–1, \ 1–2, \ 1–3, \ 1–4, \ 1–5, \ 1–6$$
$$2–1, \ 2–2, \ 2–3, \ 2–4, \ 2–5, \ 2–6$$
$$3–1, \ 3–2, \ \text{etc.}$$
$$4–1, \ 4–2, \ \text{etc.}$$
$$5–1, \ 5–2, \ \text{etc.}$$
$$6–1, \ 6–2, \ \text{etc.}$$

Evidently there are 36 in all. In the favorable subset there are 1-6, 2-5, 3-4, 4-3, 5-2, 6-1, 5-6, and 6-5. Thus there are only 8 chances in 36 of obtaining the desired result. The probability is therefore $\frac{8}{36}$ or $\frac{2}{9}$. We are aware that the lucky throws will not necessarily appear twice if dice are rolled 9 times. We would expect, however, that in many throws approximately $\frac{2}{9}$ will be favorable.

Note that probabilities vary between 0 and 1 in value. The probability of obtaining 13 with 2 dice is $0/36 = 0$, and the probability of any number between 2 and 12 inclusive is $36/36 = 1$. A probability of 0 represents the *impossibility* of an event, while a probability of 1 stands for *certainty*.

In a lottery, if a million tickets are sold and you hold just one, the probability that you will obtain the grand prize is $\frac{1}{1,000,000}$. If the grand prize is \$100,000, we say that your mathematical *expectation* is $\frac{1}{1,000,000}$ of \$100,000, that is, \$.10. In a sense, this is the true value of your ticket, for it represents the amount you would get if the \$100,000 were divided equally among the 1,000,000 ticket-holders.

In this connection we must mention the 'wager' by which Pascal computed the value of a religious life. Pascal, who originated the theory of probability among other great contributions to mathematics, felt that the sort of reasoning he had employed to solve the gambling problems of his friend the Chevalier de Méré might assume a more moral tone if applied to questions of theology. 'The value of eternal happiness must be infinite,' said Pascal. If you grant this, he reasoned, it pays to be religious. For if eternal happiness is like the prize in a lottery, and even if the probability of your winning by leading a religious life is very small (like that of the ticket-holder in the lottery), your mathematical expectation (or the value of your ticket in this eternal lottery) is still infinite, for any fraction of infinity is infinite. Let us eschew 'infinite' quantities for the present but picture the probability as $\frac{1}{1,000,000,000}$ and the prize as $1,000,000,000,000,000,000,000,000. Then the expectation would be $1,000,000,000,000,000, which is very large, even though the probability is very small.

While we are on the topic of the eternal life, we might also examine affairs on this side of eternity. By consulting a mortality table you can find the 'probability' that you will still be alive at any particular age. Such a table shows that approximately 749 out of 100,000 typical American ten-year-olds will die before the age of eleven. But can we call the ratio $\frac{749}{100,000} = \frac{750}{100,000} = \frac{3}{400}$ (approximately) a probability? If so what are the 100,000 or 400 'equally likely' factors and which are the 749 or 3 factors 'favorable' to the death of ten-year-olds? Are they diseases, accidents, crimes, economic conditions, sanitation controls, etc.? Life may be a game of chance but it is evidently impossible to decide on 'equally likely' events.

If probability is to be applied practically, there is need for modification of the classic definition. In the case of cards, lotteries, unbiased coins or dice, and in all situations bearing a close resemblance to games of chance, the possibilities are known in advance. Hence our original definition, which is substantially the same as that given by two prime contributors to probability theory—Bernoulli (*c*.1700) and Laplace (*c*.1800)—is termed the *a priori* concept of probability. In life insurance and many other applied fields, a measure resulting from experience is required—an *empirical* or *statistical* probability. Mortality-table ratios and other vital statistics are of this sort. A department store can afford to double a layette gratis on the advent of twins, since the empirical probability of double births is slight. The fundamental assumption is that in a long series of trials repeated under essentially stable conditions, the relative frequency of some occurrence will tend to a definite *limit*. By this is meant that the proportion of 'successes' will fluctuate only slightly after a sufficiently large number of trials. If, for instance, records of 100,000 individuals of a certain age in the United States at the present time show a death rate of 0.1%, the assumption is that examining the records of 5,000 more or even 20,000 more people of the same type will make but little difference in this percentage. This kind of thinking appears to be less exact than that involved in coin-tossing, but if we realize that the perfect coin or entirely symmetric die exists in the mind only, then we are faced with empirical probabilities even in games of chance. After a particular coin is tossed 10,000 times, the empirical probability may turn out to be closer to 0.56, say, than to the *a priori* 0.50.

To return to an instance where the classic concept of probability is useful, we cite an example given by the statistician R. A. Fisher. It concerns a lady who claims that by tasting a cup of tea she can tell whether the milk was poured into the tea or the tea into the milk. We shall describe an experiment designed to test the theory that this is a whimsical notion on the part of the woman and that she actually has no ability to discriminate.

The procedure will illustrate the fact that the theory of probability is at the basis of *inductive* reasoning. This scientific method may be described as consisting of three steps: the formulation of a *hypothesis,* the deduction of consequences from this hypothesis, and the determination whether the consequences agree with observed facts. It is in the last stage that probability plays a fundamental role in deciding whether a hypothesis is true or false with a given degree of practical certainty.

How shall we formulate our tea-tasting hypothesis? If we assume that the woman in question can never err, a single failure on her part would disprove the hypothesis, but even hundreds or thousands of successful repetitions of an experiment could not prove the hypothesis but merely add to the likelihood that it is true. We cannot propose the theory that she possesses *some* talent of the type claimed because such a statement is too vague. Therefore we select a negative hypothesis, namely that the lady does not have the tea-tasting ability she describes. We can then perform an experiment to test this theory. Take eight cups of tea, four of which are prepared by pouring the milk into the tea, and the other four vice versa, the order of mixing being the only known difference in the cups. The lady is to be told this fact and then the cups are to be presented to her in random order. After tasting them she is to divide them into equal groups of four, according to her verdict on how they were prepared.

We shall judge her ability objectively, taking into account that chance alone might possibly explain her success. There are actually 70 different ways in which the cups could be divided into equal groups. We shall indicate a little later in our story just how this figure is computed. Only 1 of the 70 methods of division is correct. Then if the cups are divided at random, as in a game of chance, all 70 groupings are equally likely and the probability of effecting a correct division is $\frac{1}{70}$. This means that even if a lady has no tea-tasting faculty, she can be expected to get the cups correctly classified approximately 1 time in 70, if the experiment is repeated many times.

Along with the computation of the number 70, we shall presently carry out arithmetic to show that in random groupings of the cups, 16 of the 70 possible divisions would have 3 right and 1 wrong in each group of cups, and 16 groupings would have 3 wrong and 1 right in each set, while in 36 divisions there would be 2 right and 2 wrong. The related probabilities are $\frac{16}{70}, \frac{16}{70}$, and $\frac{36}{70}$, respectively.

Taking as our hypothesis the lack of tea-tasting ability of the lady, suppose it should happen that on sipping from the 8 cups, she gets every one of them classified correctly. Common sense would lead us to decide in favor of the lady and against our own hypothesis. In other words, we can make one of two decisions—either reject our hypothesis or else let it stand because we think the event is one of those 'once in seventy' chance occurrences where the woman accidently guesses right in spite of no particular ability. Ordinarily we would surely follow the first course because the alternative seems to attribute altogether too much to chance.

Suppose on the other hand that the woman divides the cups so that she gets 3 right and 1 wrong in each set of cups. On the basis of chance alone, she could accomplish this or an even better result, that is, obtain either 3 or 4 right in each group $16 + 1 = 17$ times in 70 or roughly 1 time in 4. Should we credit the lady with discrimination and reject our hypothesis that she does not have the talent claimed? We could not fairly do so because we cannot deny that even if she has not an iota of discrimination in the matter, chance alone would enable her to get 3 or 4 cups in each group correct once in 4 times in a continued series of experiments.

In much statistical work, 5 per cent or 5 in 100 is considered a level of practical certainty for rejecting a hypothesis. In an experiment like the one described, if the woman were to do something that could occur by chance alone only 5 (or fewer) times in 100 experiments, we would judge in her favor and reject our own hypothesis of whimsicality. We did this when the probability was 1 in 70 or 1.4 per cent because this figure is less than 5 per cent. In the second case, we did not give credence to the woman's claim; that is, we did not reject our own hypothesis because the level was $\frac{17}{70} = 24$ per cent, which was far greater than the critical 5 per cent standard.

Naturally a single trial with 8 cups of tea cannot be expected to yield conclusive evidence. The lady must be asked to repeat the experiment, or else in planning it we must increase the number of cups in each category. It does not necessarily follow that conclusiveness will be arrived at, for we cannot eliminate the possibility of explaining results by chance alone in any finite experiment. By making the number of cups sufficiently large, however, we can raise the level of practical certainty arbitrarily high by requiring the correct designation of a large enough number of cups. For example, if the experiment consisted of 16 cups and if the lady were to get 7 correct and 1 wrong in each set, the probability figures would indicate that our right to reject our 'null' hypothesis—that is, to declare in her favor—would be more firmly supported than when she designated all the cups correctly in the 8-cup experiment.

To test the more serious hypotheses involved in scientific thought, some facility in the arithmetic of *a priori* probabilities is required. Even for the simple case of the teacups, we must select a few easier instances in order to get a start. Suppose, for example, that Mr. Brown wishes to travel from Chicago to England. At the time set for his departure he has a choice of boats on Cunard, French, Holland-America lines, or transoceanic plane. To get from Chicago to New York he has the option of speed by plane, comfort by railroad, or economy by bus. In how many different ways could he travel from Chicago to England?

Let us say that he started by plane. Then

> plane—Cunard
> plane—French
> plane—Holland-America
> plane—Transoceanic Plane

would be four varieties of trip. Starting by train would yield four more.

> train—Cunard
> train—French, etc.

and setting out by bus would yield another four. Thus, there are three groups of four arrangements or twelve different trips in all.

Suppose that a set of two-light signals is to be formed using the colors red, green, yellow. Starting with red we could have

> red—red
> red—green
> red—yellow.

Starting with green

> green—green
> green—red
> green—yellow.

Starting with yellow, there would be three more. Thus there are three groups of three each, or nine in all.

These two problems reveal a method of handling all such questions. In each case we had to make a choice for the first place in the arrangement. In how many ways can the first thing be done? In the case of the trip abroad, there were three choices for the first place—plane, train, or bus—thus yielding three groups of arrangements. The next question was: In how many ways can the second thing be done? In our first problem there were four ways of crossing the Atlantic, yielding us the number of arrangements in each group. Three groups multiplied by four arrangements in each group gives a total of twelve arrangements, or *permutations,* as they are customarily termed.

In our second illustration there was a choice of three colors for the first light, giving three groups of arrangements. For the second place there was also a choice of three, yielding three signals in each group. Three groups of three gave a total of nine.

It is not hard to see that, in general, if the first thing can be done in *m* ways, there will be *m* groups; that if the second thing can be done in *n* ways there will be *n* arrangements in each group so that the total number of arrangements will be *mn*. Here we have the fundamental principle of permutations: *If an act can be performed in any one of* m *ways, and when it has been done in any one of these ways, a second act can be performed in any one of* n *ways, then the number of ways of performing the two acts in succession is* mn.

Let us answer a question that we have already worked out in detail: How many different events can result when a pair of dice are rolled (that is, not different numerically but different as far as position and arrangement of the faces of the dice are concerned)? We now reason that since the first die can turn up in 6 ways, and the second one in 6 ways, the answer is $6 \times 6 = 36$.

If Gertrude Stein had wished to arrange a chart consisting of varied syllables like ba, ca, da, fe, ge, he, ji, ki, li, etc., how many 2 letter syllables could she have formed consisting of 1 consonant and 1 vowel of the Latin alphabet? Since there are 21 consonants and 5 vowels, the answer is $21 \times 5 = 105$.

The fundamental principle of permutations can be extended to include the arrangement of more than two things; for example: If 6 people in a theater party have consecutive seats in the same row, in how many different ways can they arrange themselves? Since the first to arrive has a choice of 6 seats, the second a choice of 5, the third a choice of 4, and so on, the answer is $6 \times 5 \times 4 \times 3 \times 2 \times 1 = 720$, offering an unexpectedly large number of social complications.

The product $6 \times 5 \times 4 \times 3 \times 2 \times 1$ used in this illustration is called *factorial* 6 and is symbolized by 6!. By factorial 6 we mean the product of the first six consecutive integers. By 4! we mean $1 \times 2 \times 3 \times 4$. By *n*! we mean the product of the first *n* consecutive integers. If we arrange any 6 entities—letters, numbers, cards, colors, people, using all of them—the number of arrangements possible will be 6!. For there will always be 6 choices for the first, 5 for the second, 4 for the third, etc. Similarly, if we arrange *n* things using all of them, the number of arrangements possible will be *n*!.

When the arrangement is not purely random, this formula cannot be used, and it is wise to return to the original principle of permutations. Suppose that in the theater party of 6 people, the arrangement was to be such that ladies and gentlemen alternate; how many different seating plans would be possible? There would be 6 ways of choosing   fill the   but only 3 ways of filling the second place, for if a gentleman fills the end seat, a lady must occupy the second place, or if a lady fills the end seat, a gentleman must occupy the second place. In either case, there will be a choice of only 3. There will be a choice of only 2 for the third place (since there will be only 2 ladies or 2 gentlemen from whom to make the selection depending whether a lady or a gentleman occupies the end seat). Thus we shall have $6 \times 3 \times 2 \times 2 \times 1 \times 1 = 72$ arrangements, only one-tenth as many as in the case of random seating!

To return now to the original question of the teacups: If this were a mere matter of arrangement, we could reason that there are 8 possible choices for the first 'tea, then milk' cup, 7 for the second, 6 for the third, 5 for the fourth. The remaining cups must then be pronounced 'milk, then tea,' as there are exactly 4 cups of each type. Hence there remains only 1 choice after the fourth cup. There would be

$$8 \times 7 \times 6 \times 5 \times 1 = 1680 \text{ permutations.}$$

But arrangement does not count in this case. If we name the cups T1, T2, T3 . . . T8, the lady's judgment will be the same whether she picks for the first set the cups T2, T4, T5, T7 in the order named or selects them in the order T4, T7, T5, T2 or T5, T4, T7, T2 or in any of the 4! ways in which these particular 4 cups can be arranged. In this way 4! or 24 permutations collapse into 1 grouping or *combination*. For our purposes, then, the number 1680 is 24 times too large and the answer is $1680 \div 24 = 70$ different groupings, which is the number quoted above.

In the case of getting 3 right and 1 wrong in each set of cups, it would be possible to select the wrong one in each set in 4 ways because there are 4 different cups of the 'tea, then milk' variety which the lady could pronounce 'milk, then tea,' and 4 other cups in which she could err in reverse. Then by the fundamental principle, there would be $4 \times 4 = 16$ ways of getting 1 wrong in each set. By similar reasoning there would be 16 different ways of getting 1 right in each set.

In the matter of getting 2 right and 2 wrong in each set, we might reason that in the first set it would be possible to make the first correct selection in 4 ways and the second in 3, giving $4 \times 3 =$

12 different ways. Again, arrangement does not matter. T1 T2 is the same choice, for example, as T2 T1. Then the answer 12 will be just twice as large as it should be, and the number of selections is 6. For the sake of clarification we picture the 6 selections. If T1, T2, T3, T4 are the 'tea, then milk' cups, we can get 1 of the following pairs correct (and the remaining 2 wrong): T1 T2, T1 T3, T1 T4, T2 T3, T2 T4, T3 T4.

Likewise we have 6 different ways of getting 2 correct among the 'milk, then tea' cups. Then there are $6 \times 6 = 36$ ways of getting 2 right in each set, which was the figure originally given.

Mathematicians mechanize the procedures with permutations and combinations, tabulate values of factorials, and use approximations for huge factorials, which is obviously necessary if we visualize the value of factorial 10,000, for instance. It is interesting to notice, in this connection, that some of the mathematicians who originally considered permutations and combinations had as difficult a time picturing possibilities as any layman might experience.

Rabbi Ben Ezra (c.1140), well known to us through Browning's poem, was one of the first mathematicians to consider the arithmetic of arrangements. The Moors in Spain were hospitable to Jewish scholars, and research in mathematics and medicine flourished before the days of the Inquisition. Astronomy, in the form of astrology, held interest for Arab and Hebrew mystics of the twelfth century because they believed that human destiny could be read in the heavens. The conjunction or meeting of two heavenly bodies at the same place in the sky was considered to exert a special influence on mundane events, the significance varying with the individual stars. A conjunction of three planets was considered to have a more potent influence than that of two, etc. A dreaded conjunction was that of all the seven 'planetary bodies' then known to man. These were the Sun, the Moon, Mercury, Venus, Mars, Jupiter, and Saturn. By Hindu tradition this event was expected to recur every 26,000 years and produce the end of the world. Whether Ben Ezra held to such extreme views we do not know, but he figured quite correctly, by an original method, that the number of possible conjunctions of two or more of these planetary bodies is 120.

We can check this number by the same type of reasoning used with the teacup combinations. For binary conjunctions, there are 7 choices for the first planet and 6 for the second. Since a conjunction of Sun, Moon is the same as a conjunction of Moon, Sun, the value

$7 \times 6 = 42$ must be divided by 2 to give 21, for it is a matter of grouping, not arrangement. Thus there are 21 *binary* conjunctions. For groups of 3 we should ～～～ ～ ～～ ～ ～～ which are 6 times too many if we want only groupings. Hence there are 35 possible conjunctions of planets involving 3 of them. Continuing in the same fashion,

$$21 + 35 + 35 + 21 + 7 + 1 = 120$$

Ben Ezra was a relatively early worker in the field of permutations and combinations, if we consider only Western culture, but questions equivalent to the arrangements of two or three coins were treated long before his day in the *I-king,* one of the oldest Chinese mathematical classics, whose probable date was about 1150 B.C. (as many years before Christ as Ben Ezra lived in this era). In this appear the 'two principles': the male, *yang,* — and the female, *ying,* — —. From these were formed the *Sz 'Siang* or 'four figures,'

the 4 permutations possible with 2 forms choosing 2 at a time, repetition being allowed. This question is the equivalent of tossing 2 coins. The Chinese also formed the *Pa-kua,* or 8 trigrams, the 8 permutations of the male and female forms taken 3 at a time, repetition being allowed. This is equivalent to tossing 3 coins, for the first coin can fall in 2 ways, the second in 2, the third in 2, and the total possibilities are $2 \times 2 \times 2 = 8$. Symbolically they are

HHH   TTT   HHT   HTH

THH   TTH   THT   HTT

The probabilities of all heads, all tails, 2 heads and 1 tail, 2 tails and 1 head for 3 homogeneous coins are thus $\frac{1}{8}$, $\frac{1}{8}$, $\frac{3}{8}$, and $\frac{3}{8}$, respectively.

The *Pa-kua* were invested with various symbolic properties by the Chinese and have been used from the time of invention to the present day for purposes of divination. They are found today on the compasses used by Chinese diviners, and on amulets, charms, fans, vases, and many other objects that come from China and India. Figure 82 shows the *Pa-kua* or eight trigrams, the meaning and direction connected with each in the *I-king*. Three males stood for heaven, three females for earth, a female followed by two males for steam, a female between two males for fire, etc.

The same subject matter, which the *I-king* treated more than

3000 years ago, proves to be important in modern physics. If the trigrams are not connected with the elements in the mystic manner that the ancients indicated, they are involved in the more recent theories that explain physical phenomena. It does not matter whether we speak of *yang* or *ying,* heads or tails, or any two-sided

The Pa-Kua or Eight Trigrams

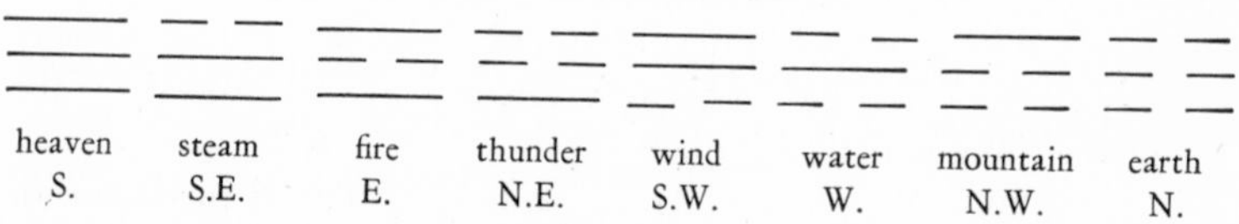

heaven	steam	fire	thunder	wind	water	mountain	earth
S.	S.E.	E.	N.E.	S.W.	W.	N.W.	N.

FIG. 82

question. The mathematics will be the same. Take the question of the distribution of the molecules of a gas. These, like the coins we have considered, are all supposed to be similar. As a uniform coin, when tossed, is just as likely to fall heads as tails, a gas molecule, because it enjoys great freedom of motion, is pictured in science as just as likely to be in the right-hand side as in the left-hand side of the containing vessel. For this reason, whenever we discuss a theoretical point of coin-tossing, there is an analogous question in molecular motion.

We list symbolically the various events possible in coin-tossing.

1 coin H T
2 coins HH HT TH TT
3 coins HHH HHT HTH THH TTH THT HTT TTT

If we use the exponential symbolism, we can put $HH = H^2$, $HHT = H^2T$, etc. Thus:

1 coin H T
2 coins H^2 HT TH T^2
3 coins H^3 H^2T TH^2 TH^2 T^2H T^2H HT^2 T^3

As far as games of chance are concerned $HT = TH$, $HHT = HTH$, etc., for the person making a wager on the coins is not interested in the arrangement but in the actual number of heads or tails. Therefore:

1 coin H T
2 coins H^2 $2HT$ T^2
3 coins H^3 $3H^2T$ $3HT^2$ T^3

These are readily recognized as the terms of the algebraic ex-

$$(H + T)^2$$
$$(H + T)^3$$

It might seem reasonable to generalize that the situation for four coins is symbolized by the terms of $(H+T)^4$ or for any number n of coins by $(H+T)^n$. This fact can actually be proved by the method of 'mathematical induction.'

In connection with this work in probability Pascal made use of the arithmetic triangle:

```
                    1
                1       1
            1       2       1
        1       3       3       1
    1       4       6       4       1
1       5      10      10       5       1
                  etc.
```

in which the numbers in any row after the first two are obtained from those in the preceding row by copying the terminal l's and adding together the successive pairs of numbers from left to right to give the new row. Thus to get the fourth row, we put a 1 at each end, and, looking at the third row, say $1+2=3$, $2+1=3$ to get the other numbers; for the fifth row, we have a 1 at each end and, to obtain the other numbers put $1+3=4$, $3+3=6$, $3+1=4$. The arithmetical triangle will prove useful to those who wish to figure the chances in coin-tossing and are unacquainted with the binomial theorem, since the successive lines of the triangle furnish the binomial coefficients. The first line gives $(H+T)^0$, the second line gives the coefficients for $(H+T)^1$, the third for $(H+T)^2$, the fourth for $(H+T)^3$, etc. Using the fifth line we can write $(H+T)^4 = H^4 + 4H^3T + 6H^2T^2 + 4HT^3 + T^4$ and get the probabilities for tossing 4 coins. The expansion shows 1 case of 4 heads, 4 cases of 3 heads and 1 tail, 6 cases of 2 heads and 2 tails, etc., out of a total of 16 possible events.

We list the probabilities for *three* coins and in figure 83 represent the facts graphically, the number of heads being plotted on the X-axis and the probabilities on the Y-axis:

No. of heads	Probability
0	$\frac{1}{8}$
1	$\frac{3}{8}$
2	$\frac{3}{8}$
3	$\frac{1}{8}$

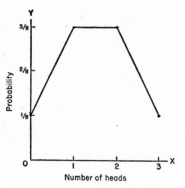

FIG. 83. Probability polygon for tossing 3 coins.

If we were to toss 3 coins (of uniform structure) 800 times, we might expect to obtain all heads or all tails approximately ⅛ of the time, 2 heads and 1 tail, or 2 tails and 1 head ⅜ of the time. The table below gives the expected frequencies, which are graphed in figure 84. Notice that this figure is an exact replica of the previous one (fig. 83), except that it reads frequencies instead of probabili-

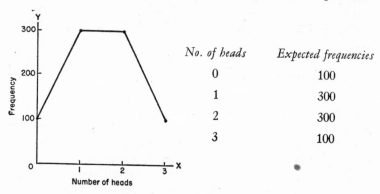

No. of heads	Expected frequencies
0	100
1	300
2	300
3	100

FIG. 84. Frequency polygon for tossing 3 coins.

ties. The former graph is called a *probability polygon,* the latter a *frequency polygon.*

What does this mean as far as gas molecules are concerned? Namely that if we had only 3 molecules in a vessel (naturally an impossible situation), and if we took 800 random snapshots of their ~~motion, then approximately~~ 100 times they would all be crowded into the left-hand side of the vessel, approximately ~~100 times they~~ would all be assembled on the right, but 600 times they would be distributed on both sides. The last situation is most likely.

Figure 85 shows the form of either the probability polygon or the frequency polygon for the tossing of 8 coins. Figure 86 shows the frequencies expected when 8 coins are tossed 768 times, as well as

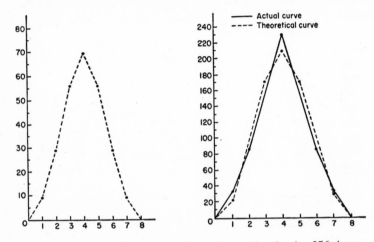

FIG. 85. Theoretical frequency polygon for tossing 8 coins 256 times.

FIG. 86. Theoretical and actual frequencies in 768 trials with 8 coins.

the actual frequencies obtained when such an experiment was performed by a group of the author's students. Considering that this experiment was not carried out under the most ideal conditions, the closeness of fit of the *a priori* and *a posteriori* curves is remarkable. If 7680 trials had been made, mathematics as well as common sense would lead us to expect closer agreement between theoretical and actual polygons.

Figure 87 gives the shape of the probability or frequency polygon for 20 coins. Note the resemblance of this polygon to a smooth curve. As the number of coins becomes greater and greater this resemblance to a smooth curve becomes more marked. In fact, the probability polygon is said to approach a certain curve as a *limit*. This bell-shaped curve is called the *normal probability curve*, or the

Gaussian law, since Gauss (*c.*1820) made such a thorough study of its properties. Its form is illustrated in figure 88. Such a curve will give the probabilities when a very large number (theoretically an unlimited number) of coins is tossed, or when a very large number of molecules is considered. If the readings on the Y-axis are altered in appropriate fashion, the curve will also furnish the expected frequencies when coins are tossed a large number of times.

If we consider the hypothetical case of 100 molecules in a vessel, only once in every 500,000,000,000,000,000,000,000,000,000 snapshots should it occur that all molecules are huddled in one side of the

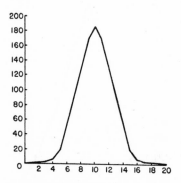

Fig. 87. Probability polygon of $(H+T)^{20}$.

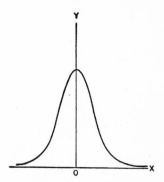

Fig. 88. Normal curve.

vessel. The probability that they will be evenly distributed, 50 on each side, is 10,000,000,000,000,000 times as great as the probability that there will be 90 on the right and 10 on the left. Actually the number of gas molecules in a vessel is not 100, but a number so enormous that the normal probability curve can give the facts to a very high degree of accuracy. It shows why no one has ever suffocated because all the molecules of oxygen happened to be in the other half of the room at once. Such a tragedy is possible, but not probable. The probability is so slight that in theory the whole history of the human race from the day of the missing link to that of the last man would not give sufficient time for it to happen even once.

As in the case of molecular motion, there is a similarity between the game of coins and some of the more worth-while games of life. If there are other phenomena like that of coin-tossing or molecular

motion subject to purely chance factors, in which the probability of
that is, not too close to 0 or 1, the
well by a normal curve, providing a large number of cases is
studied.

Thus in many situations where data are compiled in connection
with manufacturing or anthropometry or educational tests, we may
expect to find approximations to the normal law. In figures 89 and

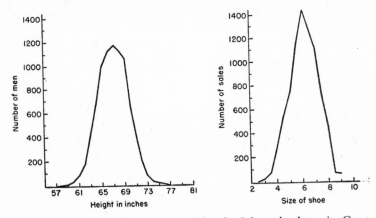

Fig. 89. Frequency polygon for heights of adult males born in Great
Britain in 1883.

Fig. 90. Frequency polygon for sales of women's shoes (from Schlauch,
W. S., *General Mathematics for Students of Business*, New York, Appleton-
Century-Crofts, 1936).

90 we have given data and graphs from biology and economics to
illustrate this point. It seems a common-sense matter that such
measurements should contain few low scores, few high scores, and
many with middle value. We naturally expect few very short men,
few very tall men, and many of average height.

These features alone do not, however, guarantee close agreement
with an ideal Gaussian distribution. If there are too many 'average'
men in a group, the frequency polygon will be too peaked to approximate normality. Or there is often a tendency to *skewness*. A
skewed curve like that in figure 91 might offer a good approximation for a frequency distribution of the ages of men at marriage,
since there is a decided tendency to marry in youth rather than

later on. If the skewness becomes very marked as in a distribution of deaths from diphtheria, almost all of which occur at a very early

Fig. 91. Skewed distribution.

age, a J-shaped curve like the first one in figure 92 becomes a suitable approximation. The other J-curve in the figure is typical of a supply curve in economics, with frequencies concentrated at the

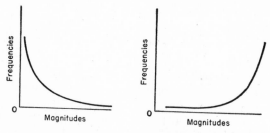

Fig. 92. J-shaped distributions.

high prices. A complete departure from normality is the U-shaped distribution pictured in figure 93. An instance of such a distribution occurs in weather data on the frequency of cloudiness over a period

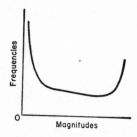

Fig. 93. U-shaped distribution.

of time. There are many clear days and many days in which the sky is completely overcast, but relatively few partly cloudy days.

There are many other types of frequency curves. In the early years of statistical theory, the normal distribution was thought to be

of almost universal occurrence in natural data. Any departure there-
... . T...... develop-
ments showed this assumption to be
ability theory, normal distributions are the exception rather than
the rule. Although we no longer expect to find so many approximations to the normal curve in nature, the Gaussian distribution is
still of great importance in the theory of probability. We cannot
disregard it any more than we can omit the right angle in geometry
just because nature seldom has angles exactly equal to 90°. One
instance where the normal curve still holds sway is in *large sample
theory*.

If we wish to find the average height of the American man, or
the average distance from the earth of all the stars in the universe,
it would be impossible to obtain an answer, because it is impracticable to measure every American, and impossible to observe every
star. Yet we have all seen such figures published. Instead of handling
all of a group, the statistician contents himself with a representative
sample. The theory of the normal curve will in this instance furnish
an estimate of the error he may commit by handling a sample instead of the entire group. It will also give the error involved in
comparing the means (averages) of samples, instead of total popula-
tions, providing the latter are normal. Are boys more intelligent,
on the average, than girls, or is this an error of sampling? Are well-
nourished children more law-abiding than undernourished, or is
this accidental in the groups investigated?

While we are on the subject of sampling theory we must mention
one of its important modern uses in the problem of maintaining
manufactured products at a uniform and acceptable quality level.
In recent years many books have been written on the subject of
quality control, as this specialized aspect of statisics has been
named. There is an American Society for Quality Control, comparable to other national professional societies. Figure 94 illustrates
a quality control chart. We have assumed that electric resistors are
being manufactured to have a resistance of 1000 ohms. A random
sampling scheme has been set up. Perhaps 1 coil will be picked
from every 100 produced, or 1 coil every 15 minutes. The resistance
of each coil is measured and the process is continued until a sample
of the size originally agreed on is obtained. Then the mean
('average') resistance of the sample is computed and plotted on the
chart. Then another sample of the same size is obtained, the mean

computed and plotted, and the process is repeated until 25 or 30 sample means, say, have been obtained. Then the mean of all these sample averages is figured. The middle line in the chart corresponds to this value. Statistical theory says that the sample means will fluctuate normally about the 'grand mean' and estimates the range of this normal fluctuation. The control bands in the quality control chart give the normal barriers. It will be observed from the figure that the manufacturing process in question appears to be under control. Now suppose some defect in the machinery occurs and causes a little more wire to be put into each coil. A dot on the

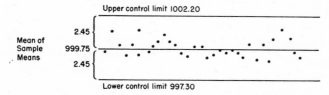

Fig. 94. Quality control chart for means of samples of electric resistors.

control chart will appear above the upper control limit and at once some cause for the trouble will be sought. Even if nothing were wrong, there is a slight chance of a dot appearing outside the control bands, a 1 per cent or 5 per cent chance, according to the level selected for the bands, but the engineer will take this 1 per cent or 5 per cent risk of looking for trouble when there is none, just to be certain some defect that might exist does not go undetected.

Where industrial variables are not normally distributed and in many other statistical situations, non-normal distributions come into play. To give an instance where tabulation of a particular non-normal distribution can be consulted to solve a statistical problem, we consider a hypothesis in regard to clairvoyance. Many people believe that there are psychic phenomena associated with dreams, apparitions, strange coincidences, and the like that cannot be explained by laws of nature known at the present time. In World War II some parents claimed to have 'premonitions' of the deaths of their sons. It is a very likely conjecture that many mothers, fathers, and sweethearts had anxiety dreams concerning boys in combat. Suppose then, that hypothetical data like the figures in the table below were actually available for all fathers of men who

Table A

Father's Dream Content

		Son's death	Not of son's death	Totals
	Died	130	10,000	10,130
Son's fate	Lived	870	90,000	90,870
	Total	1000	100,000	101,000

If there were no connection or relation between father's dream and son's fate, we would expect the percentage of deaths in each column to be approximately the same and equal to that in the group as a whole, that is, to be practically identical whether or not the father had a 'telepathic' nightmare. If, however, the proportion of deaths listed in the first column is *significantly* larger than in the second, some explanation would be in order. With the hypothetical figures in the table, deaths listed in the first column form 13 per cent of the total deaths and those in the second column 10 per cent. We must now decide whether this difference in percentage is significant or a mere sampling error,—that is a chance difference bound to occur because we are considering only one particular battle and one small group of fathers and sons.

Before deciding whether we have an instance of clairvoyance we must set up a mathematical model to correspond with our 'null' hypothesis, which we take to be the *absence* of telepathy. If the figures in the original table agree fairly well with the model, we shall accept our null hypothesis. If they diverge markedly, we shall reject the null hypothesis and admit that clairvoyance may be one possible explanation.

If we had data for all battle casualties and anxiety dreams of parents in World War II, we should have close estimates of the empirical probability for such dreams. But we have only a crude estimate on the basis of a single (hypothetical) battle. The death rate of this battle is equal to $\frac{10,130}{101,000} = 10.03\%$. Hence the model of expected frequencies in the following table is found by taking

10.03% of 1,000 and 10,000 to get the expected numbers of deaths for the first and second columns respectively.

Table B

Father's Dream Content

	Son's death	Not of son's death	Totals
Expected no. of deaths	100	10,030	10,130
Expected number alive	900	89,970	90,870
Total	1000	100,000	101,000

The deviations of the observed from the model frequencies would be

$$+30 \qquad -30$$
$$-30 \qquad +30$$

It is the magnitude of a deviation that is important and not whether it is positive or negative, since sampling errors can reasonably occur in either direction. Hence very often in statistical work deviations are squared so as to do away with their sign. Deviations of $+30$ or -30 count equally in the squared value, $+900$. Then since large deviations are natural when the frequencies themselves are large and small deviations when frequencies are small, it seems sensible to balance these facts and *weight* the squared deviations by dividing by the expected frequencies. Squaring, weighting, and totalling deviations, we have

$$\frac{900}{100} + \frac{900}{900} + \frac{900}{10,030} + \frac{900}{89,970} = 10.09$$

The total 10.09 is a measure called 'chi-square' (χ^2) since it was so named by its creator, the twentieth-century statistician Karl Pearson. It is clear that if χ^2 were equal to zero, there would be perfect agreement between observed and model data, but is the value 10.09 to be considered small, medium, or large as values of chi-square go? Theoretical statistics gives the answer that χ^2 in our example must be considered too large to be a result of chance alone, and hence we must reject the null hypothesis, thus tending to give some credence to a clairvoyance theory. On the other hand, had the first column of hypothetical figures in Table A shown 110 deaths in a thousand, a repetition of our procedure would have given deviations of $+10$ or -10 with

$$\chi^2 = 1.12$$

and a statistician would consider that this value might reasonably occur in random sampling. There would be no reason to suspect telepathy or any other special phenomenon.

For questions of this particular type, $\chi^2 = 3.84$ represents the 5 per cent level of risk and $\chi^2 = 6.64$ the 1 per cent level. The mathematical theory in back of this numerical judgment is somewhat advanced, but we can give experimental justification as follows: In developing some phase of probability theory we may set up situations resembling coin-tossing or dice-rolling in order to fix *a priori* probabilities. The matter in question is one of sampling from a population with a fixed probability of occurrence of some event. To make the situation resemble the telepathy question, set the *a priori* probability at 0.1 and prepare a sack of 1000 marbles, 100 of which are black and 900 white. Then draw 100 marbles one at a time, replacing each marble and mixing the sack after each drawing. A tally must be kept of the number of black and white drawn and then χ^2 must be computed taking 10 and 90 as the expected frequencies of black and white marbles respectively. The whole procedure should be repeated again and again so that χ^2 will be obtained for many samples of 100.

Experience shows that if the values of χ^2 were tabulated or graphed, they would approximate the ideal theoretical distribution of figure 95. Repeated sampling of 100 marbles from 1000 would be a tedious task, but an easy rainy-day pastime is to sample 20 marbles from a bag of 100 containing half black and half white marbles, that is, with an *a priori* probability of $\frac{1}{2}$. Again, frequencies of black and white can be tallied for each sample and χ^2 computed. Figure 96 shows results that were actually obtained in one experiment of this kind, where samples were drawn 400 different times. Its resemblance to the theoretical χ^2 distribution is evident.

The shaded area in the theoretical χ^2 distribution of figure 95 represents 95 per cent of the samples for this χ^2 distribution and indicates why 3.84 gives a 5 per cent level of significance. Only 5 times in 100 can a sample be expected, on the basis of chance alone, to give such a large value of χ^2. The χ^2 distribution tapers and we must go all the way to $\chi^2 = 6.64$ to include 99 per cent of the samples, that is, reach the 1 per cent level of significance.

With our discussion of χ^2 we shall conclude the 'sample' of statistics here presented. The last example, as well as some of those that preceded it, indicated the twofold nature of the science of sta-

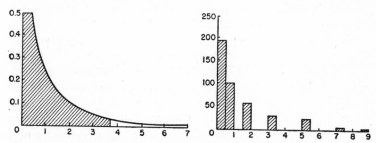

FIG. 95. Theoretical frequency distribution of chi-square.

FIG. 96. Distribution of 400 sample values of chi-square (from Snedecor, George W., *Statistical Methods,* Iowa State College Press, 1940).

tistics—the preliminary practical aspect of tabulation, computation, graphing, and the subsequent theoretical use of the theory of probability. The science itself is rather a young one as mathematical subjects go, for the portion that deals with practical, computational uses in everyday life dates from the last century, and the subject as a whole is less than three hundred years in age.

By 1700 there was considerable tabulation but the term statistics is not properly used for such work. In fact, this name was created in 1749 by the German Achenwall, who referred to the enumerators somewhat contemptuously as 'table-statisticians.' Achenwall meant the word to be used for the process of *interpreting* numerical facts. Today we use the term colloquially in all senses—for enumeration, for interpretation, and for probability theory. Tabulation came first in the natural order of things. Next, probability theory arose—quite accidentally—because mathematicians became intrigued by gamblers' problems. Lastly the two divisions of the subject were mated and the theory was used for the interpretation of numerical data.

There are not more than half a dozen problems in mathematical literature before 1600 that show any notion of a theory of probability. The early Chinese had some interest in permutations, as we have seen, but they did not link this work with problems of chance.

In fact the Chinese writer Yuan Yuan, who lived some time between 200 B.C. and A.D. 100, frowned on vital statistics, criticizing an
older writer, Sun-Tze, as follows:

Many unnecessary details appear in his works on mathematics, such as
a certain absurd problem, which surely cannot be attributed to him, on
the probability that an expected child will turn out to be a boy or a girl.[2]

The very first reference to a theory of probability in a European
work is a statement in a commentary (Venice, 1477) on Dante's
Divine Comedy. The question dealt with is the number of different
throws that can be made with three dice. Shortly afterward, Cardan
wrote a sort of gambler's handbook.

The first real work on probability was done in the seventeenth
century by Pascal and Fermat, who were mathematicians of the
first rank and are worthy of detailed attention. Blaise Pascal (1623–
62) was a child genius. At the age of sixteen he wrote a brilliant
essay on conic sections, the subject matter of which is studied in
advanced mathematics courses today. When Descartes examined
the manuscript, he believed it to be the work of the elder Pascal,
who was also a mathematician. It was hard for Descartes to believe that a boy of sixteen could produce anything so original. The
treatment of conics by Pascal belongs to the field of *projective geometry*. He proved a beautiful, now famous, proposition around the
figure of the 'mystic hexagram,' and from it derived over 400 other
propositions.

At the age of nineteen he invented and made the first calculating
machine in history, presented it to the king, and constructed a duplicate for the royal chancellor. By this step alone he anticipated modern statistical needs. At an early age, too, he became interested in
the work of Torricelli on atmospheric pressure, experimented with
the barometer, and soon established a reputation as a physicist.

As for the theory of probability, he developed this jointly with
Fermat in a most interesting correspondence initiated by a gambling problem of the Chevalier de Méré. Pascal wrote to Fermat:
'Monsieur de Méré is very bright, but he is no mathematician, and
that, as you know, is a very grave defect.' Pascal went on to describe the problem that caused the Chevalier 'to declaim loudly that

[2] Walker, Helen M., *Studies in the History of the Statistical Method,* Baltimore, Williams & Wilkins, 1929.

mathematical theorems are not always true and mathematics is self-contradictory.'

The question had originated in this way. De Méré's gambling friends would toss a single die 4 times in succession. One of the players would bet that 6 would appear at least once in the 4 throws, while his opponent would bet against it. De Méré had discovered that chance appeared to favor the man betting in favor of the appearance of a 6.

De Méré found this out empirically by tabulating the results of many games, but we can figure it out by the fundamental principle of permutations. Since there are 6 possibilities each time the die is cast, then in 4 throws there would be $6 \times 6 \times 6 \times 6 = 1296$ equally likely events. Five of these would be unfavorable each time, namely the occurrence of anything from 1 to 5. So failure for a 6 to appear could occur in $5 \times 5 \times 5 \times 5 = 625$ different ways. Since $1296 - 625 = 671$, a 6 would appear once or oftener in 671 games out of 1296, so that the odds are 671 to 625 in favor of having a 6 turn up.

The Chevalier and his friends tired of this game and decided to vary it by tossing a pair of dice 24 times and betting on double 6, or 12. De Méré was astounded to find that this time the odds were reversed, favoring the player betting *against* the appearance of a 12. If we figure this case, there are 6 possible outcomes with the first die and 6 with the second and hence $6 \times 6 = 36$ equally likely events each time. In 24 trials there would be $(36)^{24}$ equally likely possibilities and $(35)^{24}$ of these would be unfavorable to a 12. To avoid arithmetic we can use logarithms to find that the probability in question, $\frac{(35)^{24}}{(36)^{24}} = 0.5096$ (approximately) or about 0.51. This means that 51 times in 100 games, on the average, the man betting against appearance of a 12 would win, and his opponent would win only 49 times in 100. It was Pascal's task to indicate the mathematics of the situation, and in the process of doing so, he generalized the particular procedure and created the theory of probability.

Pascal belonged to a fairly large class of mathematicians who mixed mysticism and scientific activity. He caught his particular germ early when he came under the influence of the Jansenist philosophy and decided eventually that his mission in life was to blast the Jesuits. At thirty-one he turned his back on the world and retired to a solitary life at Port Royal. Here he produced two literary classics, the *Pensées* and the *Lettres Provinciales*. Although they are reputed to be masterpieces of invective and controversial skill, the scientific world does not give them a high evaluation and regrets that Pascal did not devote the remaining eight years of his all too brief life to the same activities to which he gave his childhood genius.

Only once during his retirement did Pascal yield to the 'sinful' temptation to do a little mathematics. He can be forgiven this slight lapse from grace, since the temptress was the 'Helen of Geometry.' We are merely referring to a single beautiful curve called the *cycloid* (see fig. 49). It is the path that a point on the rim of a wheel describes as the wheel rolls along a straight line. Cycloidal arches are frequently used in highway viaducts, for mechanics shows them to be superior to all others. Pascal was one of many whom this 'Helen' fascinated. It was Fermat who in the first place introduced 'her' to Pascal. The Dutch physicists, Huygens, Leibniz's teacher, paid his tribute too by using this curve in the construction of pendulum clocks. He discovered that it is the *tautochrone;* this means that when turned upside down like a bowl, objects placed on it will always take the same amount of time to slide to the lowest point. The Bernoulli brothers, Jacob and John, made the discovery that this curve is also the *brachistochrone,* that is, it furnishes the swiftest sort of slide. If you want to construct the most thrilling chute-the-chutes for an amusement park, remember the cycloid!

Sir Christopher Wren, architect of St. Paul's cathedral, experienced the traditional fascination and 'straightened Helen out,' so to speak, by finding a formula for cycloidal length. He also located the center of gravity of the curve. But we are talking about Pascal. He stated that one night he was lying awake tortured by a toothache. To take his mind off the excruciating pain, he started to think about the cycloid. The pain stopped forthwith! Was not this a sign from Heaven to continue? He did so for a week and then returned to his self-assigned routine of penance! Toothache was not his only ailment. After the age of seventeen his life was a long history of physical suffering, probably psychosomatic, coupled with a self-inflicted masochistic moral torture.

The life of Pierre de Fermat (1601–65) presents a happier, if less dramatic picture. His days were singularly uneventful as far as worldly matters were concerned, but exceptionally active in respect to things mathematical. His entire working life of thirty-four years was spent in the service of the state, first as a commissioner of requests at Toulouse, and later as King's councilor in the local parliament. Since parliamentary councilors were expected to remain socially aloof lest they be corrupted by bribery, Fermat had much lonesome leisure to divert. He did so by inventing new mathematics.

Fermat holds a record for being a 'co-inventor.' Not only did he originate the theory of probability in conjunction with Pascal, but he also conceived the idea of analytic geometry simultaneously with Descartes and gave Newton a very powerful hint on the methods of the differential calculus. Fermat stands alone, however, in his greatest work, in the field of 'higher arithmetic' or 'theory of numbers.'

One of the strangest things about Fermat was his lack of interest in publishing his work. If he had released his ideas when he conceived them, he might have been credited with being the originator of all three sciences—analytic geometry, calculus, and probability theory. Instead, he indulged in correspondence with other mathematicians, and it is through his letters that his great capacity for original thought was finally recognized.

Fermat's failure to publish in one instance has strangely enough been both a matter of chagrin and a source of inspiration for all mathematicians since his time. 'Fermat's last theorem' is as famous as the problems of antiquity. Its subject matter is easy to explain. Work with the Pythagorean theorem and its converse soon led to numerically associated facts like

$$5^2 = 3^2 + 4^2, \ 10^2 = 6^2 + 8^2, \ 15^2 = 9^2 + 12^2, \text{ etc.}$$
$$13^2 = 5^2 + 12^2, \ 26^2 = 10^2 + 24^2, \text{ etc.}$$
$$25^2 = 7^2 + 24^2, \ 50^2 = 14^2 + 48^2, \text{ etc.}$$

The Pythagorean statements show that there are many *squares which are equal to the sum of two other squares.* In fact it can be proved that there are an infinite number of such squares, that is, an infinite number of differently shaped *right triangles with integral sides.* (The Pythagorean sets 3,4,5 and 6,8,10, etc. belong to *similar* right triangles.)

Fermat made a marginal note opposite a discussion of this question in Bachet's *Diophantus,* to the following effect: 'On the contrary, it is impossible to separate a cube into two cubes, a fourth power into two powers of the same degree: I have discovered a truly marvelous demonstration which this margin is too narrow to contain.'

If only Fermat had published this marvelous proof! No one since his time has been able to produce a demonstration, even though volumes of work on number theory have been produced and greater minds than Fermat's have tackled the problem. Gauss, leading mathematician of the nineteenth century, was one of them. He was also one of those who doubted that Fermat ever had a proof—that is, a correct one—for Fermat made other assertions and marginal notes that later turned out to be incorrect. Be that as it may, mathematicians are still hopeful. They have given proofs for many cases, but not for all. In 1908 the German Professor Paul Wolfskehl left 100,000 marks for the first person who would give a complete proof of 'Fermat's last theorem.' The years have been rolling by rapidly since that time without any discovery of a proof, and what a handsome prize it might have been, with all the accumulated compound interest, if World War I had not put an end to the value of the mark!

So it was that with Pascal, Fermat, and others who contributed to the science of statistics, such work was merely incidental in broader scientific activity. Shortly after the correspondence between Pascal and Fermat, Huygens took time off from his more serious pursuits in mathematics and physics to write a small tract on certain card and dice games. This was the first printed work on games of chance.

The Swiss mathematician, Jacob Bernoulli, was the next contributor to probability theory. He was one of a famous family who produced eight mathematicians in three generations, who in turn produced a huge number of distinguished descendants well known in the fields of law, literature, science, administration, and the arts. 'Bernoulli's theorem' is a foundation stone of probability. It states that 'it is practically certain that in a sufficiently long series of independent trials with constant probability, the relative frequency of an event will differ from that probability by less than any specified number, no matter how small.' This is, in a sense, the basis of the definition of *empirical probability*, for, even with the classic concept of probability, it permits the use of the relative frequency of an event in a large number of trials as an approximation of its *a priori* probability. Bernoulli's *Ars Conjectandi* (1713) was a great treatise on probability, but, again, only one phase of his mathematical interests. Like his mathematical contemporaries, he had been fond of the 'Helen of Geometry' but was more intrigued by the famous logarithmic spiral of nature whose swirls exhibit a sort of eternal recurrence as well as other interesting properties. He ordered this spiral to be engraved on his tombstone with the inscription *Eadem mutata resurgo* (Though changed I shall arise the same).

De Moivre was the next worker in the field of probability. His life among the gamblers of a London coffeehouse led him to write the *Doctrine of Chances,* which was virtually a gambler's manual. Perhaps his conscience was uneasy about the source of his material. Like Pascal, he felt that the doctrines of probability must apply in situations more sanctified than games of chance. He wrote:

. . . these Laws serve to wise, useful and beneficent purposes, to preserve the steadfast order of the Universe, propagate the several Species of Beings, and furnish to the sentient kind such degrees of happiness as are suited to their State . . . Yet there are Writers . . . who insinuate as if the Doctrine of Probabilities could have no place in any serious Enquiry.

De Moivre must be credited with one truly great discovery, which has served 'wise, useful and beneficent purposes.' In 1733 he presented privately to a few friends a brief paper of seven pages, in which he formulated the concept of the normal curve. De Moivre himself never dreamed that this little supplement to his previous work would have any influence outside the sphere of coffeehouses and gambling dens, the moral tone of the quotation from him notwithstanding. He would never have believed that the law he had discovered would influence twentieth-century economists, psychologists, biologists, and manufacturers. Since De Moivre's paper, the *Approximatio ad Summam Terminorum Binomii* $(a + b)^n$ *in Seriem expansi,* was only recently discovered by Karl Pearson, a leading English statistician of the twentieth century, it has been the custom to credit Laplace with the discovery of the normal law.

One more anecdote before we leave De Moivre. He was a mathematician to the very end, predicting the day of his death in precise fashion. He discovered, when he began to fail, that it was necessary for him to sleep some ten minutes longer each day than the preceding one, and figured that the day after he had slept some twenty-three and three-quarter hours he would die in his sleep.

With Pierre-Simon Laplace's *Théorie analytique des probabilités*

(1812), modern probability theory was really launched. Even so, this epochal treatise, the greatest single work ever written on the subject of probability, was off the main road of his interests and was carried out by him merely as a convenient tool for mathematical astronomy. His *Mécanique céleste* was by far the greater masterpiece. Most of the subject matter of probability that Laplace presented is usually studied from secondary sources, for Laplace's style is aptly characterized by the man who said, 'I never come across one of Laplace's "Thus it plainly appears" without feeling sure that I have hours of hard work before me to fill up the chasm and find out and show how it plainly appears.'

Gauss, 'Prince of Mathematicians,' continued Laplace's work, applying probability theory to astronomical work. Again, this portion of his mathematical activity was only a minute fraction of the whole. To Laplace and Gauss is due much of the theory of the normal curve. To them it was known as the 'curve of error,' and they used it to represent the distribution of errors in astronomical experiments.

After Gauss's day mathematicians seem to have dropped a subject that had always been a sort of stepchild. Russian mathematicians like Tchebycheff, Markoff, and Liapounoff made notable contributions to its development, but on the whole the neglected brainchild was fostered by non-mathematicians—sociologists, biologists, physicists, astronomers, anthropologists, and psychologists. Among these was Quetelet (1796–1874), a teacher of mathematics and science, who inspired the building of the royal observatory at Brussels, of which he became director. His statistical work consisted of planning a census in 1829, of stirring up statistical activity all over Europe, and most important of all, of writing on moral statistics. He made a study of the influence of such factors as sex, age, education, climate, and seasons on criminal tendencies. He was shocked at the accuracy with which he could predict the number, type, and time of crimes from year to year. He could not help forming the inference that better social and economic conditions would avert many, if not most of these annual tragedies. Although this seems a commonplace fact to us, it was Quetelet's figures and formulas that first gave a proof for what could easily be a conjecture of any humanitarian. Thus, for the first time, figures were not mere figures, but a source of sociological theory.

Florence Nightingale was a great admirer of Quetelet. Astounded by the facts his statistical techniques revealed, she felt that the same

methods would furnish the answers to many questions which occurred to her and other workers for humane causes. One of her
biographers calls her the 'Passionate Statistician,' while another tells
us that she, akin to Pascal, regarded the study of statistics as a religious duty.

Sir Francis Galton (1822–1911), cousin of Darwin, and like him
a student of heredity, followed in Quetelet's path. For him the laws
of heredity became a purely statistical matter. He tabulated and

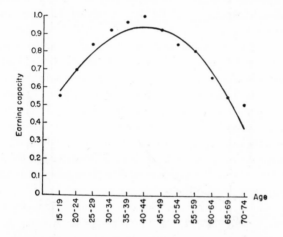

FIG. 97. Correlation between age and earning
capacity (data from U. S. Bureau of Labor
Statistics, Bulletin 37).

studied the facts of heredity for sweet peas, moths, hounds, and
human beings. He, more than anyone else, influenced American
anthropologists and biologists and so introduced statistics as a subject of study in the United States.

With Galton the emphasis in statistical techniques shifted from
the normal curve to what is usually called *correlation* in modern
texts. This term need intimidate no one who has drawn a trend
curve like the one in figure 97, which indicates the relationship
between age and earning capacity. Galton was seeking for all sorts
of relationships connected with heredity. How did the height of a
man depend on the height of his father? As an answer to this particular question, Galton found that the sons of tall fathers are not in
general as tall as the fathers, but tend to step back or regress toward

the height of the average man. So a terminology of 'regression co-efficients' was used in correlation theory.

Since Galton's time millions of questions have been asked concerning the dependence of one quantity on another. When manufacturing is active, is employment generally high? How does the death rate vary with the development of systems of public health? Will the children who are the most intelligent be the most profi-

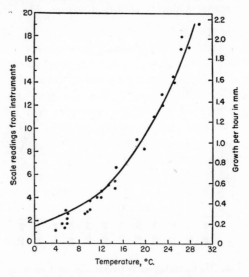

Fig. 98. Relation of rate of growth to temperature in rootlets of peas (from Thompson, D' A. W. *On Growth and Form,* New York, Macmillan, 1942).

cient in mathematics? Will rocks containing sodium also be rich in iron? If the mathematician can obtain an approximate formula in such cases, he can determine a most likely value for the weight of a star of known candle power, approximately how many people will be re-employed when a new industry is started, how much the death rate will decrease when a department of health is established in a small town, and so on.

The basic idea is to obtain the experimental figures and draw in a trend curve, as we have done in figures 97 and 98. This can be estimated very crudely by common sense, but the mathematician has a theory of curve-fitting that will tell whether a straight line or some other curve will best fit the data, and that will also furnish the technique of obtaining the equations of such lines or curves. The principle of *least squares,* evolved by Legendre, Laplace, and Gauss and based on the facts connected with the normal curve, was originally the basis of all work in curve-fitting. Later, the Scandinavian school of statisticians—Thiele, Gram, and Charlier—developed another species of curve-fitting. More recently Pearson originated still another theory, which text-books commonly refer to as the method of *moments.*

To continue the story of statistics up to the present day would make it too lengthy, for the science is growing at a very rapid rate. The manifoldness of its applications in practical life furnishes a stimulus to discovery; and statistical history always repeats itself, for games of chance seem destined to form the abstract framework of mathematical theories. In 1928 the mathematician John von Neumann wrote a paper on the strategy of poker. It is not known whether this piece of creative mathematics affected the bluffing or betting of modern de Mérés, but it has been the object of serious study by the scholars of Project Rand, who have applied it to problems of military strategy. Von Neumann, along with the economist Morgenstern, enlarged the initial ideas and came forth not long ago with a full-blown *Theory of Games,* which is a masterpiece of current mathematical thought.

The simplest of all games is the one man game, solitaire or Robinson Crusoe on a desert island. This is probability theory all over again, the player against the *a priori* probabilities of the cards or man against the empirical probabilities of nature. Poker and war and economic exchange, however, are not simple games of chance, but affairs of strategy, and this is where the von Neumann-Morgenstern creation makes its point of departure from probability theory.

Take the case of two planes in combat, or the arrival at a price in an economic exchange relation between buyer and seller. These are approximated by the picture of a duel. We may picture the opponents as having pistols containing only one bullet. They stand back to back, walk away from one another, and turn on the signal, when either one or both may fire or else start walking toward one another and fire at closer range. There is a conflict of choices in the situation. If a dueler fires immediately, his chances of a hit are least. They will improve with each pace forward. Also, to fire and miss would be to give his opponent practically certain success, since the rules we picture permit the latter to fire at close range. Still, to hold fire involves the risk of being shot before having an opportunity to shoot. There are two *maxima* to reconcile: whether to have the first shot or a better shot. Project Rand has shown how, given the distance separating the duelers and a numerical measure of their skill, the von Neumann theory will solve this problem— that is, indicate how to compute the definite moment for firing which has optimum strategical value.

As we remarked before, this model has its counterpart in a number of military situations involving encounters of tanks or planes, and it now seems as if the more advanced phases of the theory of games may make the strategy of future wars a matter of pure mathematics, assisted by high speed electronic calculating machines. One can only hope that the science of games will be applied so successfully to the strategy of maintaining peace that the military aspects would become a mere parlor pastime, a sort of highbrow poker.

9

The Distaff Side

The eternal feminine draws us skyward.
GOETHE

This can be no ordinary occasion in the affairs of the French Academy. The large lecture room is too well filled; for once a few pert hats and alluring veils take their place among the bald heads and gray beards. Suddenly a wave of silence spreads from the floor to the gallery. Monsieur le Président, dignified by his solemn carriage and long white beard, wearing conspicuously the badge of the Legion of Honor, is proceeding slowly toward the front of the hall. His age and height contrast sharply with that of the frail, sensitive-looking woman whom he is escorting. She is dressed soberly, but there is animation in the eyes which gaze now here—now there—as if to search for friends in the audience. The members on the dais exchange greetings with the President and the lady. She is given the seat of honor, and the presiding officer faces the audience and prepares to make his address.

And what are Madame Kovalevsky's thoughts during this address? At first she listens nervously to the foreign tongue lest she miss her cue. Then, more relaxed, she smiles at kindly Poincaré at the end of the table, and recalls the conference she has had with this greatest of all contemporary French mathematicians. She sighs and wishes her husband were alive to witness this moment. Now Monsieur le Président is describing at length—at great length—the nature of the Prix Bordin; how it has been awarded only ten times in the past thirty years; how as a result of Madame Kovalevsky's unusual performance the Academy has raised the prize from three to five thousand francs. It is so difficult to understand him—why must she always accustom herself to strange tongues—first German—then Swedish—now French?

Then suddenly the applause of the audience tells her that it is her turn to speak. In a few brief words, with quavering voice, she expresses her thanks for the honor which has been conferred on her.

It is over. She makes her way quickly toward the relatives who have come from Russia for this great occasion. She promises to call on them later in the day at the hotel where they are stopping. Then she returns to the prominent scientists and scholars who are waiting to deliver personal congratulations.

And when all the ceremonial is finally ended, there is Maxim waiting—patient, genial, and ever admiring. The academic surroundings make him momentarily ill-at-ease but he takes her hand, bows, and the use of their native tongue enables him to make his congratulations less impersonal and more emotional.

'What will you do here in Paris, Sonya?' he queries.

'Why study and work, of course,' she responds in Russian. 'I have never had so fine an opportunity since my days at Berlin with Weierstrass.' She speaks with enthusiasm of her plans to remain in Paris and omit the spring term of teaching at Stockholm. Her glance seems far away, and presently she appears unaware of Maxim's presence.

*   *   *

Two years have elapsed. Sonya Kovalevsky is at Genoa for the holiday between semesters. The Mediterranean skies, the friendly sun, the glistening sand, make academic questions seem remote. But a problem more puzzling than any mathematical issue troubles her mind and harries her emotionally. Shall she be judicious, she asks herself, and return to the Life Professorship, a position which no other woman has ever held? Or shall she be impetuous and accept Maxim's offer of marriage?

Undeterred by her aloofness, Maxim has followed her to the Riviera. When sentimental pleas fail, he tries practical arguments, explaining how anxious he is to provide for her and her young daughter.

Finally it is the twenty-sixth of January, but Sonya is still undecided. As she prepares to take the long, ugly journey back to Stockholm, she cannot restrain her sadness.

'This will be my last parting from Maxim,' she thinks. 'I shall arrange for my resignation from the University.'

At this point the fates step in. Perhaps they fear that she actually will break her faith with science; perhaps they wish to relieve her of making a painful choice. They give her no chance to make a misstep, for, a few days after her return to Stockholm, the mathematical world awakens one morning to find that one of its favorites has departed—Sonya Kovalevsky has passed suddenly and painlessly from this confused realm of driving work and mortal woe—to the happy sphere of peaceful rest and immortal fame.

*   *   *

If our picture of Sonya Kovalevsky is a romantic one, we must give the praise or blame to her close personal friend and biographer, Anne Charlotte Leffler, to whom mathematical historians are greatly indebted. If it were not for this Swedish writer's story, we should have no intimate picture of the most glamorous woman mathematician who ever lived—Sonya Kovalevsky (1850–91). Mathematical history contains few feminine names. The facts concerning women mathematicians like Hypatia may be apocryphal, and the work of others has been undistinguished; but there can be no doubt about Sonya Kovalevsky—her mathematical work belongs in the very first rank.

The name of Lise Meitner certainly belongs in the group of leading mathematical physicists of the present day. Hermann Weyl, distinguished mathematician of our day, has written an eloquent tribute to Emmy Noether (1882–1935), whom he considers to have surpassed even Kovalevsky in mathematical talent. We have no argument with him; but we quote one of his statements that tells the whole story of the woman mathematician. He says of Noether, 'her life would have been that of an ordinary woman had it not happened that just about that time it became possible in Germany for a girl to enter on a scientific career without meeting any too marked resistance.'

When society approves wholeheartedly of scientific careers for women, there will be many women mathematicians. Except where dictatorship reduced the role of woman once more to that of household drudge and rearer of cannon fodder, women today are playing a more prominent part in the field of mathematics. It is significant that Emmy Noether had to flee to our own country to escape Nazi persecution—to a refuge at Bryn Mawr and Princeton—for she was a triple offender, being an intellectual woman, a Jewess, and a liberal.

Emmy Noether had the advantage of the liberal German bourgeois surroundings possible before Hitler's day. In addition, she came from a mathematical family; her father Max Noether was himself a mathematician and her brother Fritz was an applied mathematician (he found refuge in the Research Institute for Mathematics and Mechanics in Tomsk, Siberia). Sonya Kovalevsky had the advantage of prosperous parents and the liberal beliefs of the young Russian men and women with whom she associated. She was the daughter of General Ivan Sergyevitch Krukovsky. The family circle and friends, among whom the writer Dostoevsky was included, are pictured charmingly in Sonya Kovalevsky's own literary account of her childhood, *The Sisters Rajevsky*.

Anne Charlotte Leffler tells us how Sonya and her sister Anyuta were part of a young people's movement to promote the emancipation of women in Russia. It was customary for one of the girls to contract a marriage of convenience to enable her to leave the country and study at a foreign university. Then her whole retinue of friends could also make their escape—on the pretext of visiting the 'married' friend in France or Germany. At eighteen Sonya contracted just such a nominal marriage with Vladimir Kovalevsky.

Vladimir escorted her to Heidelberg where she studied mathematics and he geology. He soon left for Jena and she for Berlin. There she was befriended by Weierstrass, the greatest worker in the field of mathematical *analysis* of the nineteenth century. Since Sonya, as a woman, could not be admitted to university lectures, Weierstrass gave her private lessons. She studied with him for four years and in 1874 she took her doctorate (*in absentia,* because she was a woman) at the University of Göttingen. Her thesis on partial differential equations revealed her great mathematical talent.

After the strain of all the years of study, Sonya felt a natural desire for a change of scene and activity. She returned to her family in Russia and became a part of the gay social whirl at St. Petersburg. She met Vladimir Kovalevsky again; this time he wooed and won Sonya in earnest, and they lived happily together. Their first and only child was born in 1878. Vladimir became Professor of Paleontology at the University of Moscow, and all went well until he became involved in shady speculations that eventually resulted in his disgrace and suicide.

Sonya found herself once more in a foreign country, this time on no intellectual lark, but faced with a serious problem—that of earning a living for herself and her little daughter. Once again kind Weierstrass came to her assistance. Through Mittag-Leffler, another of Weierstrass's distinguished students, she secured a position as lecturer at the University of Stockholm. The advanced attitude of the Swedish toward women worked to her advantage. In 1889 Mittag-Leffler succeeded in obtaining a life professorship for her.

During her years in Stockholm Sonya Kovalevsky did her best work. Weierstrass, always her friend, carried on an inspirational mathematical correspondence with her; the great teacher advised from afar when he could not be present in person. His distinguished pupil wrote a paper on the refraction of light in a crystalline medium and followed this by the memoir that won the Prix Bordin of the French Academy, *On the Rotation of a Solid Body about a Fixed Point.*

A great friendship existed between Sonya and the sister of Mittag-Leffler, Anne Charlotte. The woman mathematician and the woman writer were kindred spirits; they shared the same views on women's rights; there was even a similarity in their personal lives, for both had contracted early marriages that ended unhappily, then seemed to find 'true love' at forty, and at the height of fame and happiness met sudden and unexpected death. Anne Charlotte married the Duke of Cajanello, a man much younger than herself. Sonya's love affair, like her mathematical work, was cut short by her untimely death from influenza. Sonya and Anne Charlotte had promised each other that whoever survived the other would be the biographer of the deceased friend. Anne Charlotte survived Sonya just long enough to write her story and bear the Duke of Cajanello his first child.

As for the mathematics of Sonya Kovalevsky, we must say that she was, above all, the disciple of Weierstrass and hence a worker in the field of analysis. She applied the techniques of analysis to questions in physics. Her work and Weierstrass's are beyond the scope of this book, but we can at least present the fundamental concept at the root of the work of the illustrious teacher and his favorite pupil. The notion to be discussed is that of *series*. When we have studied this idea we shall be closer to Sonya Kovalevsky's true nature than any presentation of biographical facts can bring us.

Let us shift the scene half a century forward in time and select an illustration of this concept from the work of Lise Meitner, foremost living successor of Kovalevsky. This twentieth-century mathematical physicist shares the honor with several others for the initial discovery of uranium fission. In 1939 she helped to launch the procedures that culminated a few years later in the production of the atom bomb.

Fission of the Uranium 235 atom is accomplished by the entrance into its nucleus of a neutron (a basic nuclear particle that is electrically neutral—see page 66). This causes the U235 nucleus to fly apart with tremendous release of energy. One of the by-products is the release of some of the atom's own neutrons, the number ranging from 1 to 3. Let us call the average figure 2 and picture a hypothetical situation where fission of a single nucleus initiates a chain reaction. We shall imagine that each neutron released by fission enters another U235 nucleus and that this in turn splits apart, releasing 2 new neutrons. Fission of a single atom thus produces 2 neutrons which will cause 2 new fissions. Each of these will produce 2 neutrons and the result will be 4 new fissions, the process being repeated until all U235 nuclei in a pile have been broken down. Then the number of atoms undergoing fission at a particular instant would be described by some term in the sequence 1, 2, 4, 8, 16, 32, 64, 128, 256 . . . Since the interval between fissions would be about a millionth of a second, an examination of these numbers shows that there would be $2^{60,000,000}$ atoms splitting at the end of a minute.

The eventual hugeness of numbers in the sequence 1, 2, 4, 8, etc. is a shock to most people. At first glance a great many might be willing to join a Christmas Club saving plan of 1 cent the first week, 2 cents the second week, 4 cents the third week, and so on, never realizing that the last payment would be 2^{51} cents (more than 22 trillion dollars) and the sum total to be put aside about 45 trillion dollars! These are relatively small numbers as compared to what might be expected if a one-minute chain reaction were possible in accordance with the sequence of 1, 2, 4, 8, etc.

A sequence in which the *ratio* of each term to its predecessor is constant is termed *geometric*. This name was probably selected because the corresponding lengths in a set of similar geometric figures form just such a sequence. Later we shall discuss the general properties of such series that make them suitable for describing different phenomena of growth or decay, whether the increase is one of atoms under fission or money in the bank, the decrease that of radioactive decay or depreciation of a plant.

Geometric sequences need not all be associated with destructive activity. There are happier instances, like that of the frequencies (number of vibrations per second) in a musical scale. For the middle octave of the piano, which is a musical instrument with an

'equally tempered' scale, the frequencies are approximately as follows:

c	c♯	d	d♯	e	etc.
264	280	297	314	333	

The ratio of each frequency to the preceding is approximately 1.06.
The numbers constitute a geometric sequence, which is the meaning
of 'equal temperament' in music.

A ratio like 2:1 for a chain reaction in uranium would not be
likely either in the natural product or in a man-made atomic energy
contrivance. In the first place, most neutrons produced after fission
would be lost either by escaping from the uranium pile, or by capture without fission by Uranium 238, the isotope (see page 106)
forming the greater part of natural uranium, or by atoms of im-
purities mixed with the uranium. In bringing about a chain reaction, scientists found it necessary to produce pure U235 or plutonium to lessen loss of neutrons to U238. By increasing the size of
a pile they lessened loss by escape.

In the bomb, the chain reaction is initiated by stray neutrons from
cosmic rays. The geometric progression is permitted to grow until
there are about 9 billion billion nuclei undergoing fission. After that,
a further increase is undesirable, and it is a matter of keeping the
number splitting constant until all fissionable atoms are destroyed.
There are many problems connected with accomplishing this. The
pile has to be the right size and the neutrons must be 'slow' in motion—
only about a mile per second. If they are fast—1,000 miles or more
per second—they bounce off nuclei instead of entering. As fission
occurs, the new neutrons thrown out of nuclei are of the fast variety
and are not likely to maintain a chain reaction. Hence they must be
slowed down by the use of a *moderator* like *heavy water* or graphite,
the latter being used because it is cheaper and more plentiful. Control
is maintained by the use of cadmium strips, which prevent too large
a geometric ratio and which can be removed at any instant when
violent explosion is desired.

The geometric sequence is not the only type occurring in science.
To introduce some other types let us picture a not improbable scene
in the life of our protagonist, Sonya Kovalevsky.

Sonya is directing her daughter Foufie in the use of an educational toy, a bag of brightly colored marbles and a board with
grooves in which the marbles can be deposited.

Foufie deposits one marble in the first row, two in the second, three in the third, etc. (fig. 99) and then perceives what a pretty array is thus obtained. She notices that the shape of the design is always the same; mama supplies the word 'triangle,' and points to a flock of birds flying overhead in the same formation (airplanes, too, arrange themselves in just this way for a long flight, for science says it is the easiest way).

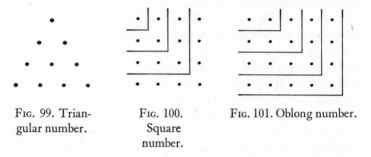

FIG. 99. Trian-   FIG. 100.   FIG. 101. Oblong number.
gular number.   Square
                         number.

Then, instead of counting 1, 2, 3, 4, 5, etc. in succession, Foufie skips numbers and builds the design indicated in fig. 100, based on the odd numbers 1, 3, 5, 7, 9, etc. She is told that this time she has designed a square. She then plays with the even numbers and builds

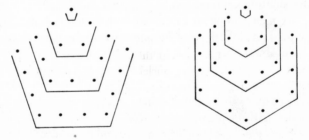

FIG. 102. Pentagonal and hexagonal numbers.

the rectangle of figure 101. By skipping three numbers at a time she obtains the series 1, 4, 7, 10, 13 and the pentagon (fig. 102). Skipping four numbers yields the set 1, 5, 9, 13, 17 and the hexagon.

In playing this game of marbles Foufie is really repeating some of the motions of that famous group of philosopher-mathematicians, the Pythagoreans. When she reaches the number 4 in her count and has built the triangle in figure 99, she has actually constructed that

Holy Tetraktys which the ancient Pythagorean brotherhood worshipped. Throughout, she is studying numbers concretely or geometrically, much as they did.

What do the pictures tell? How can such information be used? The manipulation with marbles can provide a first lesson in arithmetic, algebra, geometry, number theory, history, and philosophy. Foufie's first design shows that if she starts with 1 the *sum of any number of successive integers is a triangular number.* In other designs she shows that the *sum of a series of odd numbers is always a square number,* and the sum of *even* numbers is always an *oblong* (rectangular) number. In these 'Greek games' Foufie is actually developing *formulas* for the sums of various types of number series. For instance, the formula for the series of odd numbers (fig. 100) might be written:

$$1 + 3 + 5 + 7 + \ldots \text{ to } n \text{ terms} = n^2$$

If we look at figure 103 we see that the total number of marbles in successive figures is $2 \cdot 3$, $3 \cdot 4$, and $4 \cdot 5$, etc., since there are 1 row of 2 marbles, 2 rows of 3 marbles, 3 rows of 4, 4 rows of 5, respectively. Hence the figure shows that for the sum of any number of even numbers, we have the formula

$$2 + 4 + 6 + 8 + \ldots \text{ to } n \text{ terms} = n(n + 1)$$

Again, the diagonal lines in figure 103 show that any oblong number is equal to the *sum of two equal triangular numbers.* If the oblong number is $3 \cdot 4$, then the longest row in each of the two equal triangles contains 3 marbles. Hence

$$3 \cdot 4 = \text{double } (1 + 2 + 3)$$

or
$$\frac{3 \cdot 4}{2} = 1 + 2 + 3$$

Again, the oblong $4 \cdot 5$ is composed of two equal triangles with the longest row containing 4. Thus

$$4 \cdot 5 = \text{double } (1 + 2 + 3 + 4)$$

or
$$\frac{4 \cdot 5}{2} = 1 + 2 + 3 + 4$$

We generalize to obtain the formula

$$n(n + 1) = \text{double } (1 + 2 + 3 + \cdots n)$$

or
$$\frac{n(n + 1)}{2} = (1 + 2 + 3 + \cdots n)$$

It is only natural that since the day of the great Hindu arithmeticians more abstract thought should gradually supplant kindergarten tactics in obtaining such results as the sum of a series of natural numbers, odd numbers, or even numbers. Let us then group all the series in Foufie's game and abstract a common attribute:

Natural numbers	1, 2, 3, 4, 5, etc.	Triangular sum
Odd numbers	1, 3, 5, 7, 9, etc.	Square sum
Even numbers	2, 4, 6, 8, 10, etc.	Oblong sum
Counting by 3's	1, 4, 7, 10, 13, etc.	Pentagonal sum
Counting by 4's	1, 5, 9, 13, 17, etc.	Hexagonal sum

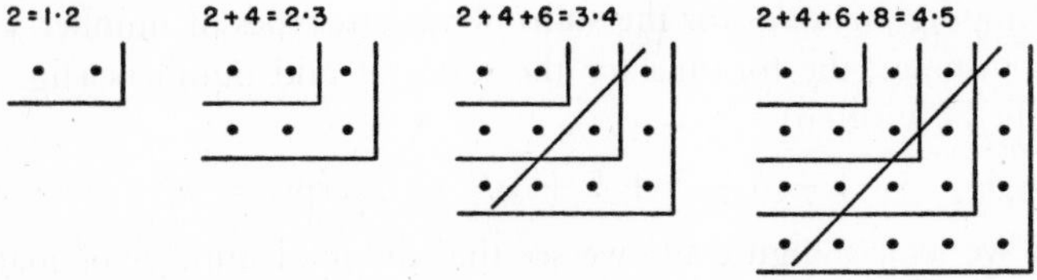

Fig. 103. Illustrations of the formula $2+4+6+8+ \ldots$ to n terms $= n(n+1)$.

We find that in each series there is a common *difference* between successive pairs of numbers. In the first case this difference is 1, in the next 3, and so on. Since such series are so closely connected with the process of counting, the mathematician has labeled them *arithmetic*.

As an instance of arithmetic series [1] consider the distances a falling body covers in successive seconds. They constitute the progression 16 ft., 48 ft., 80 ft., 112 ft., etc. The sums to which money will amount, if placed at simple interest, form an arithmetic series: $100 on which 3% simple annual interest is paid will amount in successive years to $103, $106, $109, etc. Any repetition of figures like a weekly pay check, $75, $75, $75, etc., is an arithmetic sequence with common difference zero, or a geometric progression with ratio 1.

Our next illustration comes from astronomy. Hipparchus and Ptolemy classified stars visible to the unaided eye into six 'magnitudes,' the brightest stars being marked first magnitude, and the faintest visible sixth. This method of rating has persisted in essence

[1] We have been using the terms *sequence* and *series* interchangeably. Usually mathematicians employ the term sequence when numbers are listed in order according to some rule of formation, and series when they are to be added.

until modern times and has been extended in both directions. Sirius, the brightest star in the heavens, has a magnitude of -1.58; the Sun's magnitude is -26.72 and the faintest star that has been photographed is approximately of 22nd magnitude. We might think that there is a constant difference or arithmetic progression between these magnitudes. But, no! There is a *psychophysical law* formulated by the psychologist Fechner which states that if the intensity of a sensation varies in arithmetic progression, then the intensity of the stimulus producing it must be in *geometric progression*. The ratio of the geometric progression of stellar magnitudes is roughly about 2.5, or exactly $\sqrt[5]{100}$. Multiplication five times by $\sqrt[5]{100}$ is equivalent to $100^{\frac{1}{5}} \times 100^{\frac{1}{5}} \times 100^{\frac{1}{5}} \times 100^{\frac{1}{5}} \times 100^{\frac{1}{5}} = 100$, by the law of exponents in multiplication. Hence a first magnitude star is 100 times as bright as one of sixth magnitude.

Let us see why compound interest also illustrates geometric progression. Evidently every dollar invested at 4% annually becomes $1.04 and $100 becomes $100(1.04), $1000 becomes $1000 (1.04), P dollars becomes $P(1.04)$ dollars. Hence we may formulate the rule: Multiply by $1.04 to obtain the amount of 4% for one year. Let us watch the progress of a dollar invested at 4%.

Year	Principal at beginning of year	Common ratio or multiplier	Amount at the end of year
1	1.00	1.04	1.04
2	1.04	1.04	$(1.04)^2$
3	$(1.04)^2$	1.04	$(1.04)^3$
4	$(1.04)^3$	1.04	$(1.04)^4$
5	$(1.04)^4$	1.04	$(1.04)^5$

Evidently we obtain the geometric series:

$$1, \ 1.04, \ (1.04)^2, \ (1.04)^3, \ (1.04)^4, \ \text{etc.}$$

In this connection, let us imagine that the $24 paid the Indians for Manhattan Island could have been invested at 6%. This would have accumulated in the years 1626–1950 to the sum

$$24(1.06)^{324} = \$3,800,000,000 \ (\text{roughly})^2$$

This sum could still buy back a fair part of the island.

One of the most common types of problem is that of setting up an annuity, that is, a uniform annual payment for such varied pur-

---

[2] Result found by logarithms.

poses as providing a pension, making good a loan, or establishing a depreciation fund for factory equipment. Common sense suggests such problems as: How much shall the government invest now at 3% to provide such and such annual pensions for its workers? How much must be put aside each year to furnish $10,000 with which to replace worn-out machinery 10 years hence? I borrow $20,000 now to start my business going and agree to return the sum (with interest) in 10 equal annual payments. How large should they be?

All these questions will result in geometric series. Let us imagine the simplest type of annuity—$1 set aside at the end of each year for 10 years—and let us figure the cumulative amount at the end of 10 years. If the rate is 3% the first dollar will amount to

$$(1.03)^9$$

and the second dollar to

$$(1.03)^8$$

and the third to

$$(1.03)^7$$

etc. and the

total $= (1.03)^9 + (1.03)^8 + (1.03)^7 + \cdots + (1.03) + 1$

or turning things around

total $= 1 + (1.03) + \cdots + (1.03)^8 + (1.03)^9$

This total can be found with the assistance of logarithms or a compound interest table to be $1 + 1.03 + 1.0609 + 1.0927 + \ldots + 1.3047$, which yields $11.46 (approximately). If you set aside $100 annually instead of $1, your total will be $1146 (approximately).

Such sums can be computed readily, but since annuities may be of more than ten years duration, or may involve semi-annual or quarterly payments, any abbreviation of the arithmetic is naturally a boon to the computer. What is evidently needed is a *formula for the sum of a geometric series*. Thus we see that the Greek number games were headed in the right direction. If you play around with a number series, perhaps it will be useful sometime—in which case it is really important to try to discover a formula for its sum. The formula for the sum of a geometric series is derivable by simple algebra. It is

$$S = \frac{ar^n - a}{r - 1}$$

where
a = first term of the series

r = the common ratio

n = the number of terms

Let us work out a more impressive annuity by the use of this formula. Let us consider \$1 invested for 25 years at 4%. Then

$$S = (1.04)^{24} + (1.04)^{23} + \cdots + (1.04) + 1$$
$$= 1 + (1.04 + \cdots + (1.04)^{23} + (1.04)^{24}$$

Then
$a = 1$

$r = 1.04$

$n = 25$

and
$$S = \frac{1(1.04)^{25} - 1}{1.04 - 1} = \frac{(1.04)^{25} - 1}{.04}$$

Since $(1.04)^{25}$ is readily found by logarithms or a compound interest table to be 2.6658

$$S = \frac{2.6658 - 1}{.04} = \$41.65$$

This is surely easier than computing twenty-five terms.

A somewhat different progression is presented by the case of the man who wishes to deposit a sum now and collect his annuity later. He is interested not in the eventual amount of an annuity but in its *present value*. He asks, 'What sum shall I deposit now at 4% to get an annuity of \$1 for 10 years?' He must provide a sum now that will yield \$1 at the end of a year, a sum that will yield \$1 two years hence, a sum that will yield \$1 three years hence, and so on. Thus, to provide \$1 a year hence he must set aside x dollars such that

$$x(1.04) = 1$$
$$x = \frac{1}{1.04}$$

To have \$1 two years hence he must set aside y dollars such that

$$y(1.04)^2 = 1$$
$$y = \frac{1}{(1.04)^2}$$

He must deposit in all

$$\frac{1}{1.04} + \frac{1}{(1.04)^2} + \frac{1}{(1.04)^3} + \cdots + \frac{1}{(1.04)^{10}}$$

which is another geometric series. We leave, as an exercise for those readers who are not afraid of a little elementary algebra, the job of applying the formula for the sum of a geometric series to show that in this case the present value is $8.11 (approximately). In other words $8.11 will supply a $1 annuity for 10 years, and $811 will supply a $100 annuity. Statisticians, financiers, brokers, economists, and actuaries must make so many computations of this sort that the sums of those geometric series occurring in annuity computations are recorded once and for all in tables, and in this way excessive computation is avoided.

As another illustration of a lengthy geometric series, consider the recurring decimal 0.33333. . . In arithmetic this is the result obtained when $\frac{1}{3}$ is converted to a decimal. We now prove the converse fact, that this decimal converges to the value $\frac{1}{3}$.

$$0.333 \cdots = 0.3 + 0.03 + 0.003 + \cdots$$

which is a geometric progression with ratio 0.1.

$$S = \frac{a - ar^n}{1 - r} = \frac{0.3 - 0.3(0.1)^n}{1 - 0.1}$$

The value of n becomes larger and larger as the decimal goes on and on. Even if n were only 10,

$$0.3(0.1)^{10} = 0.00000000003$$

which is very small. The second term in the numerator will surely have a negligible value for $n = 100$, 1000, etc. For all practical purposes,

$$S = \frac{0.3}{0.9} = \frac{1}{3}$$

or the series *converges* to the limit $\frac{1}{3}$, as the number of terms increases beyond all bounds.

What we have just done is to find the *sum of an infinite series*. One cannot literally add an infinite number of terms, for this would be a never-ending job. Therefore we must define what is meant by the 'sum' of an infinite series. The procedure in the case of the recurring decimal will serve as a model. We considered the sums of 10 terms, 100 terms, 1000 terms, etc. and found that as we took more and more terms these sums came closer and closer to $\frac{1}{3}$. The number $\frac{1}{3}$ is the *limit* of these sums. If, in an infinite series, all sums after a certain number of terms are very close to some particular number, this number is called the limit of the sequence of sums. If such a limit exists, the series is said to converge and the limit is considered the *sum* of the series.

Infinite series need not be geometric progressions. Consider the infinite series:

$$1 - \frac{1}{2} + \frac{1}{2} - \frac{1}{3} + \frac{1}{3} - \frac{1}{4} + \frac{1}{4} - \frac{1}{5} + \cdots \text{ forever}$$

The sum of the terms listed is

$$1 - \frac{1}{5} = \frac{4}{5}$$

since all the terms balance except the first and last. If we take an odd number of terms of this series, even as many as 1,000,001, the sum of terms will obviously be 1. If we go out to $-\frac{1}{1,000,000}$, the sum will be

$$1 - \frac{1}{1,000,000} = 0.999999$$

We see that no matter how far out we go, the sums are alternately 1 and numbers closer and closer to 1. Therefore, this infinite series converges and its sum is said to be 1.

Consider the infinite series:

$$1 - 1 + 1 - 1 + 1 - 1 + \cdots$$

Notice that the sums will fluctuate between 1 and 0 forever, no matter how far out in the series we go. Therefore, the sums do not get closer and closer to any single number; that is, they do not approach a limit. The series is said to be *divergent* and there is no meaning to the term sum as applied to it.

The layman sometimes has the idea that the sum of an infinite number of terms ought to be infinite. We have just seen that this is not generally true, but in some cases it is, however. Consider an increasing geometric series like that of the chain reaction originally discussed. There,

$$S = 1 + 2 + 4 + 8 + \cdots \text{forever}$$

$$S = \frac{ar^n - a}{r - 1} = \frac{1(2)^n - 1}{2 - 1} = 2^n - 1$$

As n grows greater and greater, 2^n increases beyond all bounds. In this case the series diverges, since the sequence of the sums $2^n - 1$ approaches no limit.

Infinite series are perhaps the keynote to the work of the nineteenth-century mathematical renaissance. They were a major concern of Weierstrass and Kovalevsky. Why? Because it has turned out that so many entities needed in mathematics and science can be expressed advantageously in this way. The fundamental quantity π is one of these. An infinite series expressing its value is:

$$\pi = 6 \left[\frac{1}{2} + \frac{1}{2} \cdot \frac{1}{3} \left(\frac{1}{2}\right)^3 + \frac{1 \cdot 3}{2 \cdot 4} \cdot \frac{1}{5} \left(\frac{1}{2}\right)^5 + \frac{1 \cdot 3 \cdot 5}{2 \cdot 4 \cdot 6} \cdot \frac{1}{7} \left(\frac{1}{2}\right)^7 + \cdots \right]$$

By means of this series [3] the approximate value of π can be found to as many places as desired. An evaluation of the first three terms gives 3.14. After a while this series 'chokes off,' as we would expect since it converges. The terms become very small, so that not much arithmetic is necessary for a good approximation.

Before presenting the infinite series for another basic constant e, let us discuss its meaning. To do so, we return to compound interest. In our previous examples we assumed that interest was compounded annually. Let us now ask what $1 would amount to if invested at 4% compounded semi-annually. At the end of 6 months it would amount to $1.02. If $1000 were invested, it would amount to $1000(1.02) in 6 months. A general rule for obtaining the amount at the end of half a year, if the rate is 4% semi-annually, would be to multiply the principal by 1.02. Then at the end of a year $1 would amount to $(1.02)(1.02) = (1.02)^2 = 1.0404$. Since we multiply by 1.02 twice, the amount at the end of 1 year at 4% compounded semi-annually is the same as the amount for 2 years at 2% compounded annually. We see that the amount is somewhat greater when interest is compounded semi-annually. If the interest is compounded

---

[3] The reader can compare this series with that given for π in chapter 2. The series used here has the advantage of converging more rapidly.

quarterly, there is an even greater advantage. At the end of 3 months $1 will amount to $1.01 and at the end of a year $(1.01)^4$, which is the same as if $1 had been invested at 1% for 4 years. The oftener the interest is compounded, the greater the advantage to the investor.

For the sake of mathematical theory, let us violate banking tradition and assume a 100% interest rate and in addition, 100 interest payments a year. Then the amount at the end of the year would be $(1.01)^{100} = \$2.70$. (This value can be computed by the use of logarithms or investment tables.) Now keep the 100% interest rate but increase the number of interest periods. Logarithmic computation would show that the amount for 1000 periods would be $2.717, that is, almost but not quite $2.72.

We can keep on increasing the number of interest periods. The results would show that even if banks did pay 100% interest and were ever so generous in the frequency of interest payments, $1 would never amount to a tremendous sum within one year. The sequence of values approaches a limit that mathematicians have proved to be not only irrational but transcendental. Its value is a little less than $2.72. The exact irrational, transcendental limit is symbolized by the letter e and can be represented by a convergent infinite series:

$$e = 1 + 1 + \frac{1}{2!} + \frac{1}{3!} + \frac{1}{4!} + \frac{1}{5!} + \cdots$$

If the reader will compute the first 8 terms of this series, he will find $e = 2.7181$. One reason why e is important in mathematics is that it turns out to be the best base for logarithms in the calculus, and for this reason it will inevitably make its appearance in all laws of nature that are exponential or logarithmic functions. Logarithms with e as base are called natural or Napierian, since Napier's concept of logarithms implied that e is the base.

Logarithmic tables are worked out by approximating the sums of convergent infinite series. Let x symbolize the natural logarithm of 2. Then

$$e^x = 2$$

or, approximating e,

$$2.72^x = 2$$

This equation shows that x is less than 1, for 2.72^1 would be greater than 2. The natural logarithm of 2 is given by the series

$$\log_e 2 = 1 - \frac{1}{2} + \frac{1}{3} - \frac{1}{4} + \frac{1}{5} - \frac{1}{6} + \cdots$$

By adding a sufficient number of these terms the reader can find the approximation

$$\log_e 2 = 0.69$$

This can be converted into the common logarithm of 2 (base 10) by multiplying by the conversion factor 0.43 (approximately) giving

$$\log_{10} 2 = 0.30 \text{ (approximately)}$$

Trigonometric tables are also worked out by the use of convergent infinite series. For example, the series

$$\sin x = x - \frac{x^3}{3!} + \frac{x^5}{5!} - \frac{x^7}{7!} + \cdots$$

will give the value of the sine of an angle if the size of the angle, x, is expressed in *radians*. A radian is an arc of a circle equal in length to the radius, hence the name radian. It is equivalent to about $57°17'45''$. There is no need for us to go into any technical explanation of why radian measure is necessary. Suffice it to say that just as it may sometimes be more convenient to measure lengths in meters rather than feet, so it makes some mathematics easier to measure angles in radians rather than degrees. To obtain an approximation of $\sin 10°$ from the series above, substitute $x = 0.174$ radians and compare with the value of $\sin 10°$ in the table on page 128.

Whereas some series may give the appearance of 'choking off,' they do not actually do so.

$$1 + \tfrac{1}{2} + \tfrac{1}{3} + \tfrac{1}{4} + \tfrac{1}{5} + \tfrac{1}{6} + \tfrac{1}{7} + \tfrac{1}{8} + \cdots$$

is very innocent looking, and yet it diverges. We might add up 50 or 100 terms of this series, and thus become convinced that no limit is being approached, or we may argue as follows: Compare the two series

$$1 + \tfrac{1}{2} + \tfrac{1}{3} + \tfrac{1}{4} + \tfrac{1}{5} + \tfrac{1}{6} + \tfrac{1}{7} + \tfrac{1}{8} + \tfrac{1}{9} + \cdots + \tfrac{1}{16} + \cdots$$
$$1 + \tfrac{1}{2} + \underbrace{\tfrac{1}{4} + \tfrac{1}{4}}_{} + \underbrace{\tfrac{1}{8} + \tfrac{1}{8} + \tfrac{1}{8} + \tfrac{1}{8}}_{} + \underbrace{\tfrac{1}{16} + \cdots + \tfrac{1}{16}}_{} + \cdots$$

Every term in the top series is equal to or larger than the corresponding term of the bottom series, and hence the top sum must be larger than the bottom. But, condensing the $\frac{1}{4}$'s, the $\frac{1}{8}$'s, the $\frac{1}{16}$'s, the $\frac{1}{32}$'s, the $\frac{1}{64}$'s, etc. in the bottom series we have

$$1 + \tfrac{1}{2} + \tfrac{2}{4} + \tfrac{4}{8} + \tfrac{8}{16} + \tfrac{16}{32} + \tfrac{32}{64} + \cdots$$
$$= 1 + \tfrac{1}{2} + \tfrac{1}{2} + \tfrac{1}{2} + \tfrac{1}{2} + \tfrac{1}{2} + \tfrac{1}{2} + \cdots$$

An infinite number of half-dollars would make an infinite fortune. The bottom series thus exceeds all bounds, and hence

$$1 + \tfrac{1}{2} + \tfrac{1}{3} + \tfrac{1}{4} + \tfrac{1}{5} + \tfrac{1}{6} + \tfrac{1}{7} + \cdots$$

will do likewise. It is divergent, first impression to the contrary.

Our discussion should give some indication of the task of the mathematician in connection with series. Of course, his chief aim is to obtain the proper series for the entity he is measuring. Certain tricks of the calculus will do this for him. Secondly, he examines for convergence the series he has obtained. Here he resorts to various techniques. In our work with geometric series, we proceeded as follows. We studied the formula for the sum of a finite number of terms and discovered that it approached a limiting value as the number of terms exceeded all bounds. But, since such formulas are often impossible to obtain in the case of other series, other methods must be employed.

If a series fails to converge, this means further work for the mathematician, for he must then decide whether the particular machinery for obtaining the series is at fault. Again, the series may be convergent, but the machinery may trick him in a different fashion —the series may converge to a value that does not represent the thing he is looking for. Again, it may converge too slowly to please him. If he is a theoretical mathematician, this fact will not disturb him. If, however, he is a computer, he will seek a different series for the same quantity. Any one would prefer adding ten numbers rather than a hundred.

When convergence questions are settled, the mathematician requires an arithmetic of series. Can they be added, subtracted, multiplied, and divided at will? If so, how? Again the reader may wonder why such questions should be of more than theoretical importance. We shall point out that mathematical formulas often consist of sums, products, quotients, and the like, of quantities represented by series. Certain vibrations are represented by sums, each term of which can be approximated by infinite series. Particularly interesting are the Fourier series so necessary to harmonic analysis. An illustration of such a series is

$$y = \sin x + \tfrac{1}{2} \sin 2x + \tfrac{1}{3} \sin 3x + \tfrac{1}{4} \sin 4x + \cdots$$

Each term: $\sin x$, $\tfrac{1}{2} \sin 2x$, $\tfrac{1}{3} \sin 3x$, etc., is itself represented by an infinite series. Thus the question arises: How can we add an infinite set of infinite series?

We may *not* play around with infinite series in the rough and ready fashion in which finite series are handled. The series for the logarithm of 2 (with e as base) is

$$\log 2 = 1 - \tfrac{1}{2} + \tfrac{1}{3} - \tfrac{1}{4} + \tfrac{1}{5} - \tfrac{1}{6} + \cdots$$

Doubling both sides of this equation, we have

$$2 \log 2 = 2 - 1 + \tfrac{2}{3} - \tfrac{1}{2} + \tfrac{2}{5} - \tfrac{1}{3} + \tfrac{2}{7} - \tfrac{1}{4} + \cdots$$

On collecting terms with a common denominator,

$$2 \log 2 = 1 + \tfrac{1}{3} - \tfrac{1}{2} + \tfrac{1}{5} + \tfrac{1}{7} - \tfrac{1}{4} + \tfrac{1}{9} + \cdots$$
$$= 1 - \tfrac{1}{2} + \tfrac{1}{3} - \tfrac{1}{4} + \tfrac{1}{5} - \tfrac{1}{6} + \cdots$$
$$= \log 2$$

Since it comes out that $2 \log 2 = 1 \log 2$ we are led to the fallacy

$$2 = 1$$

Hence the manipulations by which we doubled both sides and then collected and rearranged terms must be at fault. If we rearrange terms in a finite series, the sum total will be unaffected; but this fact does not carry over into the theory of infinite series.

The literature of infinite series is lengthy. The reader has been exposed merely to the elements of the subject that is the gateway to one of the most important practical branches of the mother science, namely modern *analysis*.

10

A World in Flux

> Nature and Nature's Law lay hid in night,
> God said, 'Let Newton be' and all was light.
>
> POPE

Intra

Isaac Newton (1642–1727), often cited as the greatest genius the race has ever produced, established the classic pattern of *dynamics* by setting down his three famous *Laws of Motion*. Because Newton felt that these laws were justified by physical phenomena, he used them as the axioms or foundation stones of a branch of physics that was to produce locomotives, automobiles, airplanes, artillery, and industrial machinery. *Stop*

The wonders of the anticipated age of rocket power or jet propulsion will all stem from Newton's Third Law of Motion: *To every action there is an equal and opposite reaction.* When a shell is fired, the cannon kicks back. The action, the force thrusting the shell forward, is equal to the reaction, the force producing the backward motion of the gun. If a man in a rowboat jumps to shore in landing, the boat moves away from the shore. The man's forward thrust is equal and opposite to the backward push imparted to the boat. The air forced down below the wing of a plane in flight reacts and pushes up, producing in this way almost one-third of the total sustaining force or lift of the plane. The difference between the applications of the Third Law in the illustrations just cited and its use in rockets is that in the former the action is the significant or useful factor, and in the latter the reaction is fundamental. *Reaction motor* is a synonym for *jet-propelled engine.*

The ordinary skyrocket of display fireworks was the forefather of the more recent 'Jato,' 'Chase-me Charlies,' 'Blastards,' and V-2 bombs, which, translated into everyday language signify respectively Jet-Assisted Take-Off (initial letters used, as in radar), the inaccurate predecessors of the German robot bombs, the actual German V-1 rocket bombs, and finally the most deadly of the German *Vergeltungswaffen* (vengeance-weapons).

Figure 104 shows a cross section of a skyrocket. This simple mechanism for fireworks and the principles of its construction and operation are in essence those of the more advanced and dignified reaction motor. The conic cap (A) is a streamlining device to assist the flight. Beneath it is a paper cylinder (B) containing the display material—the stars and streamers that will burst forth at the summit

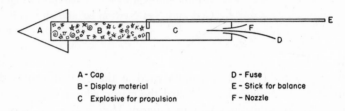

A - Cap   D - Fuse

B - Display material   E - Stick for balance

C   Explosive for propulsion   F – Nozzle

FIG. 104. A simple rocket.

of the rocket path. Beneath (B) is another cylinder (C) containing the fuel or propellant charge, usually a form of gunpowder mixed with charcoal or some other material to slow down the rate of combustion. This fuel is packed solidly, and hence the flame from the fuse (D) cannot penetrate rapidly; only the surface of the explosive is burned. Thus continuous flight is achieved instead of a sudden violent explosion. At the end, the flame spurts through the channel connecting the two cylinders and the display material is ignited. The stick (E) is for balancing and guiding the rocket flight. In the more practical rockets used for throwing a lifeline to a sinking vessel or harpooning a whale, wings may be used instead of the stick; the designs for jet planes of the future show wings of this type, which resemble those of the paper airplanes which boys fold and fly to amuse themselves. The thrust mechanism or motor of the rocket is completed by a nozzle (F).

When the fuse ignites the fuel, considerable pressure is built up in the cylinder (C), since hot gas is formed rapidly and cannot escape through the narrow nozzle. As a result, a stream or jet of gas is expelled through this orifice, tending to draw the rocket downward. The reaction to this force thrusts the rocket upward.

But a reaction motor cannot be as flimsy an affair as a paper rocket nor, to be serviceable, can the flight it produces be as random. Materials and the form of construction, types of fuel, the control of gas pressures, and efficiency become serious questions, and the elementary skyrocket is much modified and refined in the present war missiles and jet planes. In spite of the great progress to date, the rocket application of Newton's law will require much additional research before the anticipated new speeds and new horizons are realized.

To come back to Newton the man and the many other branches of science he launched, it is quite possible that in childhood his un-inhibited imagination envisioned an age of wings and an era of rockets long before he set down formally the theories of his mature years. Like many talented children, he found school a complete bore. In lieu of studying, he devoted himself to the construction of kites, water wheels, tops, mechanical toys, sundials, ingenious clocks, and all sorts of amazing gadgets. His academic record was so poor that his mother decided farming would be the ideal vocational choice for Isaac. His father, who had died shortly before the boy's birth, had been a Lincolnshire farmer, and it seemed natural to have the son continue in the same work. Newton's uncle had a better understanding of the boy's talents. One day he discovered Isaac reading under a hedge instead of performing his agrarian duties. That clinched matters, and he persuaded Newton's mother to send the boy to Trinity College, Cambridge.

In the years 1665–6, when the Great Plague was raging in England, Newton went back to the farm and in spare moments started his work on gravitation, optics, and calculus. In connection with the latter subject, he developed the *binomial theorem,* which was no mean stunt for a young man of twenty-three.

When Newton was twenty-six years of age, his teacher Isaac Barrow, himself a mathematician of note, resigned from the Lucasian professorship at Trinity to devote himself to theology. He named his pupil as his successor. Many tales, some of which may be spurious, are told of Newton, the absent-minded professor. One relates that he cut two holes in his door, a large one for his cat and a little one for her kitten. Another tells of one occasion when he left his guests at dinner to fetch a bottle of wine, but on his way to the cellar forgot why he had started, went to his room, donned his surplice, and appeared in chapel.

Whatever the validity of these tales, there is at least one true story of Newton's forgetfulness. At the age of nineteen, when he was attending grammar school, he fell in love with a certain Miss Storey. She was the stepdaughter of a Mr. Clarke, the village apothecary with whom Newton was lodging. He became engaged to the girl, and although he seems to have remembered his fondness for her the rest of his life, he never recalled his promise to marry her. She consoled herself by marrying a lesser genius.

Newton's first work at Cambridge was in the field of optics. He built his own reflecting telescope, which won him a membership in the Royal Society. He advanced the corpuscular theory of light, which later scientists rejected in favor of the wave theory. Recent developments in atomic physics and quantum mechanics have caused scientists to reconsider Newton's notions about the nature of light, and the present opinion is best described by saying that for some phenomena it is convenient to accept Newton's view. Light in these cases is considered as particles of energy called quanta or *photons*. In other situations, theories are simplified by picturing light as one type of electromagnetic wave.

Newton presented the fruits of his most profound thought in the immortal *Principia* (1686). A brief summary can hardly convey a true impression of the monumental nature of this work. It contained, among other revolutionary scientific material, Newton's dynamics, his law of universal gravitation, and his 'system of the world.' The *Principia* seems to have ended the most important part of Newton's scientific career, and it was certainly a grand finale. After the publication of his work, Newton started life anew in a political capacity. A chance incident was the cause of it. In 1687 James II sought to impose his will on Cambridge University. Newton led the group that resisted and, as a reward for his courage, was elected to represent the University in Parliament the following year. This 'opportunity' was fatal. He was later (1696) appointed Warden of the Mint and finally Master of the Mint (1699). He was one of the best Masters the Mint ever had.

Some mathematicians feel regret that a 'high priest of science' should have wasted his genius in public office. Others cite Newton as a shining example of a scholar who deserted his ivory tower. Still others feel that Newton had spent himself early, that he realized his power for scientific thought was waning and hence sought other occupations. Some biographers assert that Newton's financial need was the cause of his action. We must remark that, whatever the evaluation of Newton's latter-day intellectual power, he was mathematically active to the day of his death at the age of eighty-five, although he did not produce any other work comparable to the *Principia*.

As for critical estimates of Newton's work, we first quote the generous tribute of his rival Leibniz, who said that, taking mathematics from the beginning of the world to the time when Newton lived, what Newton did was much the better half. Many still agree with Leibniz on this point. Lagrange, whom Frederick the Great named the 'greatest mathematician in Europe,' once remarked humorously that Newton was the greatest genius that ever lived and the most fortunate, since only once can the system of the universe be established.

Newton's modesty is revealed in his own appraisal of his work:

> I do not know what I may appear to the world; but to myself I seem to have been only like a boy playing on the seashore, and diverting myself in now and then finding a smoother pebble or a prettier shell than ordinary, whilst the great ocean of truth lay all undiscovered before me.

Newton died in 1727 and was buried in Westminster Abbey. Voltaire attended the funeral, and it is said that, at a later date, his eye would grow bright and his cheek flush when he mentioned that a professor of mathematics, only because he was great in his vocation, had been buried like a king who had done good to his subjects. From a purely mathematical point of view Newton's greatest invention was that of the calculus. The fundamental idea of this branch of mathematics is that of *rate of change*. We shall discuss this concept in detail very shortly, and at this point we merely cite velocity as one example of such a rate. If velocity is variable, as it usually is, say for automobiles, planes, rockets, and electrons, then an *average* rate for a sizeable interval of time may be inadequate. A car that averages only 30 miles per hour between 2 and 4 p.m. may nevertheless have been speeding at 60 miles per hour at 2:15 p.m. Thus it is 'instantaneous' rates that are considered in the calculus. Newton's laws of motion and the dynamics to which they led required consideration of the *abstract* concept 'rate,' and the calculus that resulted has become an indispensable tool of scientific activity.

It would be neither accurate nor just historic fact to allow Newton undivided laurels for the creation of the calculus, since it was invented simultaneously and independently by Gottfried Wilhelm Leibniz (1646–1716). The English school of mathematicians made many a bitter attack on the honesty of the great German contemporary of Newton. There is no doubt in modern minds, however, that Leibniz worked without ever consulting Newton's results. His symbolism, moreover, has the advantage of greater simplicity, and we follow it today in preference to Newton's.

The scientific genius of Leibniz was not of the same high order as that of his rival. On the other hand, he exhibited an all-round development, working in the varied fields of law, religion, history, economics, statesmanship, philology, logic, metaphysics, and speculative philosophy. In addition to inventing the calculus, which was a natural outgrowth of previous mathematical thought, he formulated certain concepts that have come to fruition only recently, in the work of the twentieth-century logicians Whitehead and Russell. In the opinion of some, this work of Leibniz was the more important of his two great contributions to mathematics. Professor Wiener's cybernetics, mentioned previously, may bear this out. Leibniz formulated these particular ideas of logic at the early age of twenty.

Leibniz had taken his bachelor's degree in philosophy at seventeen, his doctorate in law at twenty. He was at once offered a university professorship of law, but refused. The essay he had written for his doctor's degree, however, came to the attention of the Elector of Mainz, who engaged Leibniz as his diplomatic assistant. In the course of duty Leibniz visited London, exhibited his remarkable calculating machine at meetings of the Royal Society, and learned what English mathematicians were doing. After this he developed the calculus and popularized it on the Continent. His work on the calculus was printed before Newton's, although Newton had actually conceived the idea earlier. We omit the sad details of the Newton-Leibniz controversy. Suffice it to say that it was fostered by the British mathematicians rather than by the inventors of the calculus themselves. From the scientist's point of view, Leibniz's active life ceased at thirty, for he spent the last forty years of his life as historian of the Brunswick family.

His last days were unhappy ones. In 1714, his employer, Elector George Louis of Brunswick, left for London to become George I of England. Leibniz would have liked to go with him for one last round with the English mathematicians and Newton, Master of the Mint. George, however, left him at Hanover. Two years later Leibniz died and was buried in an obscure grave. Newton survived him by eleven years and was given an honored niche in West-

end

NO
J

minster Abbey. Newton had won the battle. Let us forget this unhappy ending and turn to our theme—the branch of mathematics
that two great men invented for the proper handling of a world
in flux.

'Wages have gone up 20 per cent this year.' 'And what about
prices?' you ask before rejoicing at the approach of an era of pros-
perity. Johnny has gained fifteen pounds this year, but still wears
that lean and hungry look, for he has also grown three inches. The
ocean has made an inroad of five miles on this coastline. 'What a
disaster!' you feel, until you learn that it has taken a million years
for this change to take place. A *comparison of two related changes*
is called for in each case. We compare increases in wages with rise
in prices before concluding that times are improving, increase in
weight with growth in height before prescribing for Johnny, change
in distance with change in time to realize that the speed of shoreline
advance is slight.

Now let us see how to make such comparisons when formulas for
the quantities are involved. Take, for example, the *amount* in a
simple interest problem in which the principal is $100 and the rate
4%. Initially the amount is $100; at the end of each year the amount
is increased by the annual interest of $4, so that the amounts are

$$100 + 4 \cdot 1 \quad \text{at end of 1st year}$$
$$100 + 4 \cdot 2 \quad \text{at end of 2nd year}$$
$$100 + 4 \cdot 3 \quad \text{at end of 3rd year}$$
$$\text{etc.}$$

The formula connecting amount and time is obviously

$$A = 100 + 4t$$

where A is the amount and t the number of years.

Note that this formula is linear. Its graph is the line of figure
105, the table for which is found below. In this table we have indicated changes in time in one column and changes in amount in
another.

Change in time	Years t	$ A	Change in amount
	0	100	
1	1	104	4
1	2	108	4
1	3	112	4
1	4	116	4

The ratio

$$\frac{\text{change in amount}}{\text{change in time}} = \frac{4}{1} = \frac{8}{2} = \frac{12}{3}$$

$$= \$4 \text{ per year}$$

NO ⨍

We see that this ratio represents the change in amount for one year, or the *rate of change* of amount, as we shall term it. In other words, the annual interest is the rate of change in amount.

In mathematics the symbol used for change is Δ, *delta,* the Greek d. Notice that d is the first letter of the word difference, synonymous with change. Between each pair of successive points in our table and graph, $\Delta A = 4$ and $\Delta t = 1$.

$$\frac{\Delta A}{\Delta t} = \frac{4}{1} = 4 = \text{rate of change}$$

The fact that the ratio $\frac{\Delta A}{\Delta t}$ is the same between any pair of points is a characteristic of a straight line graph. We shall shortly see that this ratio varies from point to point when a graph is not linear. For practice, let us consider another straight line

$$y = \tfrac{2}{3}x + 5$$

This time we shall not attach concrete meanings to x and y. To avoid fractions we select the values 0, 3, 6, 9, 12, etc. for x and find

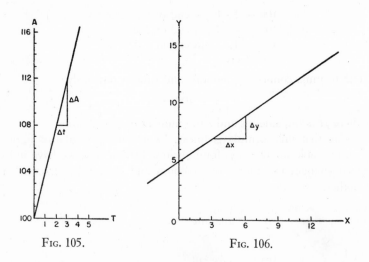

FIG. 105.   FIG. 106.

the corresponding values of y. These are listed in the table and plotted on the graph (fig. 106).

Δx	x	y	Δy
	0	5	
3	3	7	2
3	6	9	2
3	9	11	2
3	12	13	2

We see that

$$\frac{\Delta y}{\Delta x} = \frac{2}{3} \quad \text{for this line}$$

In other words, whatever the meanings of y and x, the rate of change in y is $\frac{2}{3}$ of a unit for each unit change in x.

The rate of change $\dfrac{\Delta y}{\Delta x}$ is also termed the *slope of the line*. It is evident that this ratio is actually connected with the ordinary 'slope' of an incline. Δy represents the *vertical* rise from point to point, Δx the *horizontal* progress. The ratio tells what the rise in height is for one unit of horizontal advance. The greater the ratio, the steeper the slope. In our first illustration, the slope 4 gives a steeper line than the slope $\frac{2}{3}$ of our second illustration.

By an examination of

$$y = 4x + 100 \quad \text{and}$$

$$y = \frac{2x}{3} + 5$$

we see that the slopes 4 and $\frac{2}{3}$ appear as the coefficient of x in the equation. We shall now prove that this is generally true. When a linear equation is put into the general form

$$y = ax + b$$

we can consider any two points satisfying this relationship. Let the x-co-ordinates of these points be c and d respectively. Then, by substitution in this equation, the corresponding y-co-ordinates are $ac + b$ and $ad + b$. Studying changes, we have

$$\Delta x = d - c \left\{ \begin{array}{c|c} x & y \\ \hline c & ac + b \\ d & ad + b \end{array} \right\} \Delta y = ad - ac = a(d - c)$$

and slope $\dfrac{\Delta y}{\Delta x} = a$

since the factor $d - c$ divides out. Then the slope of

$$y = -\frac{3x}{2} + 5$$

is $-\dfrac{3}{2}$. In other words

$$\frac{\Delta y}{\Delta x} = -\frac{3}{2} = \frac{-3}{2} = \frac{3}{-2}$$

This means that when x increases 2, y decreases 3 (see fig. 107), or when x decreases 2, y increases 3.

Let us apply the notion of rate of change to some concrete situations. The following is a timetable showing the time of arrival and

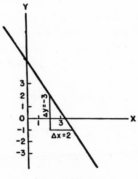

FIG. 107.

departure of a train at various stations. We have filled in the columns t (time), s (distance), Δs, Δt and $\dfrac{\Delta s}{\Delta t}$ and plotted the data in figure 108.

Δs (miles)	s (distance in miles)	Town	t (time in hours)	Δt (hours)	$\dfrac{\Delta s}{\Delta t}$ (miles per hour)
	0	dep. A	9:00		
25				$\frac{1}{2}$	50
	25	ar. B	9:30		
0				$\frac{1}{6}$	0
	25	dep. B	9:40		
20				$\frac{1}{2}$	40
	45	ar. C	10:10		
0				$\frac{1}{6}$	0
	45	dep. C	10:20		
15				$\frac{1}{4}$	60
	60	ar. D	10:35		

In the picture we have five different line segments representing the various portions of the trip. The five values of $\frac{\Delta s}{\Delta t}$ indicate the slopes of these segments, and also the velocity of the train from point to point. From A to B this velocity was 50 miles an hour; during the first stop the velocity was naturally zero; then the train proceeded at 40 miles an hour, etc.

To get the average rate for the entire trip, we seek the constant rate the train would have followed if it had proceeded uniformly

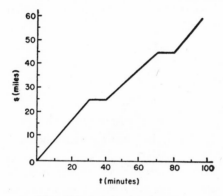

FIG. 108. Graph of train trip.

from A to D without stopping. The picture of its motion would have been a straight line from the first to the last points of the graph. The slope of this line would have been the uniform velocity followed. In other words, this slope represents the average rate from A to D. Reading either from the graph or the table, we see that, from the first to the last points

$$\Delta s = 60$$

$$\Delta t = 1\tfrac{7}{12}$$

$$\frac{\Delta s}{\Delta t} = \frac{60}{\frac{19}{12}} = 37.9 \text{ miles per hour}$$

This exercise illustrates how the quotient $\frac{\Delta y}{\Delta x}$ (above $\frac{\Delta s}{\Delta t}$) is useful even when the picture of a situation is not a single straight line. In our example the picture was a broken line, and in other cases it will be a curved line. We see that in such situations $\dfrac{\Delta y}{\Delta x}$ will give an average rate of change between two points.

As a further illustration let us now consider the famous apple whose fall is supposed to have initiated the theory of universal gravitation. It is shown in this theory that the formula

$$s = 16t^2 \quad (t \text{ seconds, } s \text{ feet})$$

governs the motion of the apple.[1] Let us suppose that it took the apple exactly 1 second to fall. By the formula, we see that it fell 16 feet. Then

Δt	t	s	Δs
	0	0	
1			16
	1	16	

$\dfrac{\Delta s}{\Delta t} = \dfrac{16}{1} = 16$ feet per second (*average velocity during the second*)

Was the apple moving 16 feet per second when it hit the ground? Evidently not for, as we know, the apple started with no velocity at all and increased its speed under gravitational attraction. Hence, since it averaged 16 feet per second, its velocity must have been greater than this at the end of the first second to balance its slow initial speed. Using the formula we can find where the apple was at the end of half a second. Then

Δt	t	s	Δs
	$\frac{1}{2}$	4	
$\frac{1}{2}$			12
	1	16	

Thus $\dfrac{\Delta s}{\Delta t} = \dfrac{12}{\frac{1}{2}} = 24$ feet per second (*average velocity during the half-second preceding impact*)

Similarly,

Δt	t	s	Δs
	$\frac{3}{4}$	9	
$\frac{1}{4}$			7
	1	16	

$\dfrac{\Delta s}{\Delta t} = \dfrac{7}{\frac{1}{4}} = 28$ feet per second (*average velocity during the last quarter-second*)

[1] Strictly correct only if the apple falls in a vacuum. The factor 16 is approximate also.

Again,

Δt	t	s	Δs
$\frac{1}{8}$	$\frac{7}{8}$	$\frac{49}{4}$	$\frac{15}{4}$
	1	16	

$$\frac{\Delta s}{\Delta t} = \frac{\frac{15}{4}}{\frac{1}{8}} = 30 \text{ feet per second}$$
(average velocity during the last eighth second)

Finally,

Δt	t	s	Δs
.01	.99	15.6816	.3184
	1	16	

$$\frac{\Delta s}{\Delta t} = \frac{.3184}{.01} = 31.84 \text{ feet per second}$$
(average velocity during the last hundredth of a second)

It requires no Sherlock Holmes to sense that this last approximation is the best indication of the velocity of the apple when it hit the ground.

Now this simple fact is at the basis of the calculus. To get the *instantaneous rate,* in this case, we let Δt get smaller and smaller. Notice that Δs gets smaller too. The *limiting value* of $\frac{\Delta s}{\Delta t}$ is called the *instantaneous rate of change* or *derivative* of s with respect to t. In our particular problem, we have taken Δt as small as .01. We could take Δt as small as .001, .0001, etc. If we did so, we should find $\frac{\Delta s}{\Delta t}$ to have a value closer and closer to 32. We could get a value as close to 32 as we pleased by taking Δt small enough. This value, 32 feet per second, is called the limiting value of $\frac{\Delta s}{\Delta t}$ as Δt approaches zero. Better and better average rates are obtained by taking smaller and smaller intervals, but there is no 'best' average rate, since if the rate for any interval, however small, is figured, you can always furnish a still better rate by decreasing the interval further. The *limit* does the trick because it is a number to which all 'good' rates are close.

Since we are not always dealing with distance and time, let us define instantaneous rate of change or derivative for any two variable quantities y and x, such that the value of y is determined by the value of x. If there is a limiting value of $\frac{\Delta y}{\Delta x}$, as Δx approaches zero, we shall call it the instantaneous rate of change of y with respect to x, or the derivative of y with respect to x. Newton originally called this the 'fluxion' of y, and calculus was called 'fluxions.' The process of finding the derivative is called *differentiation*, and hence the term *differential calculus*.

Let us illustrate differentiation, that is, the finding of an instantaneous rate. Suppose that a 2-inch metal cube is heated. Just how fast will it expand? The formula for the volume of a cube is

$$V = x^3$$

By substituting values of the edge close to 2 and using this formula to find V, we shall be able to obtain good *average rates of expansion*. Using the accompanying table, we see that, if the edge were to increase

x (ins.)	2	2.01	2.1	2.5	3	4
V (cu. ins.)	8	8.1204	9.3	15.6	27	64

from 2 to 2.5 inches, then

change in $x = \Delta x = 0.5$

change in $V = \Delta V = 7.6$

and $\quad \dfrac{\Delta V}{\Delta x} = \dfrac{7.6}{0.5} = 15.2$ cubic inches per inch

If the edge increases from 2 to 2.1,

$$\frac{\Delta V}{\Delta x} = \frac{1.3}{0.1} = 13 \text{ cu. ins. per inch (see table above)}$$

If the edge increases from 2 to 2.01

$$\frac{\Delta V}{\Delta x} = \frac{0.1204}{0.001} = 12.04 \text{ cu. ins. per inch}$$

The rates 15.2, 13, 12.04 are evidently getting closer and closer to 12 cu. ins. per in. By taking $\Delta x = 0.001$, 0.0001, etc. the average rate would come still closer to 12, which is the *limit* of the series of numbers, and the instantaneous rate of expansion of the cube with respect to its edge is 12 cubic inches per inch when $x = 2$.

Naturally, serious workers in the calculus do not use the excessive computation we have employed for determining a limit. They have

exact meanings and systematic methods. We shall shortly indicate
the nature of such techniques.

Since graphs have proved themselves so revealing on previous
occasions, let us see what they will do for our concept of the derivative. Let us graph the formula $V = x^3$, which we have just used, for
those values of the edge selected in the table above. In figure 109
we have plotted points and joined them by a smooth curve. Notice
the relative positions of the lines PA, PB, PC, and PD with rela-

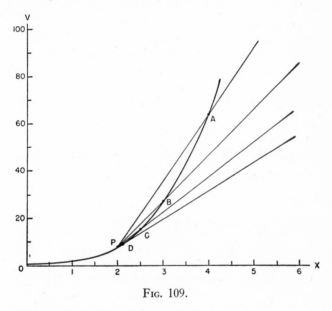

Fig. 109.

tion to the curve of the formula. They cut across it, and hence are
called *secants*. But PC and PD cut off much less of the curve than
PA and PB. PC cuts off a very small segment and PD barely grazes
the curve. PC has the slope $\dfrac{\Delta V}{\Delta x} = \dfrac{7.6}{0.5} = 15.2$ and PD has the slope
13. The *limiting* line, which all these secants approach is called the
tangent to the curve at P. It will touch the curve at P only. Thus,
the geometric meaning of a derivative, or instantaneous rate is the
slope of a tangent to a curve.

It is important in many practical problems to be able to construct
the tangent to a curve at some point. The derivative, by furnishing
us with the value of the slope, enables us to do this. To give just

one illustration of how the tangent may be needed, we may recall that the normal to a curve plays an important part where the reflection of sound, light, etc. are concerned. Now the normal at a point of a curve is the perpendicular to the tangent at that point, and once the derivative furnishes us with the tangent, the normal can be consructed. There are many other types of questions in which the slope of the tangent to a curve is important.

Before attacking such problems, let us get a more efficient way of finding derivatives. Let us take the function $y = x^2$ and obtain

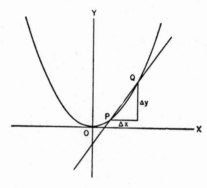

FIG. 110.

a formula for the derivative for any value of x, that is a formula for the slope of any tangent to the parabola $y = x^2$. In figure 110 let P with co-ordinates (x, y) be any point on the curve. Then the co-ordinates of an adjacent point Q will be $(x + \Delta x, y + \Delta y)$.

The slope of the secant PQ is $\dfrac{\Delta y}{\Delta x}$. To find a formula for $\dfrac{\Delta y}{\Delta x}$, let us take cognizance of the fact that Q and P are points on the curve and hence their co-ordinates must satisfy the condition $y = x^2$, that is

for Q, $y + \Delta y = (x + \Delta x)^2$

or $y + \Delta y = x^2 + 2x\Delta x + (\Delta x)^2$

and for P, $y = x^2$

Subtracting the second equation from the first,

$$\Delta y = 2x\Delta x + (\Delta x)^2$$

Dividing both sides by Δx,

$$\frac{\Delta y}{\Delta x} = 2x + \Delta x$$

This is the formula for the *slope of any secant* to the curve. If we desired the slope of the secant between the points whose x-coordinates are 3 and 5 respectively, we should have

$$x = 3 \qquad \Delta x = 2 \quad \text{and}$$

$$\frac{\Delta y}{\Delta x} = 2x + \Delta x = 6 + 2 = 8$$

To find the derivative or slope of the tangent we want the limit of the slope of the secant as two points approach coincidence. If, in the formula just applied, namely

$$\text{slope of secant} = 2x + \Delta x$$

we let Δx approach zero, that is, become smaller and smaller, the limit approached will obviously be $2x$, and this will be the formula for the derivative or slope of the tangent.

A symbol usually used for the derivative is $\frac{dy}{dx}$. Then, in this case,

$$\frac{dy}{dx} = 2x$$

Applying this formula, the slope of the tangent at the point where $x = 3$ is

$$\frac{dy}{dx} = 2x = 2 \cdot 3 = 6$$

and the slope of the tangent at any other point is readily found.

We might use this result a little differently. If we think of $y = x^2$ as the formula for the area of a square, $\frac{dy}{dx} = 2x$ is the formula for instantaneous rate of change of area relative to length of a side. Then if a square is expanding (as a result of temperature change, for example), its rate of expansion at the instant when its side is 3 inches is 6 square inches per inch.

In the study of differential calculus, formulas for the derivatives of many types of function are established. The technique of doing this is similar to our scheme for $y = x^2$. We shall not present the algebraic work for the various cases. Instead we shall give one or two mechanical rules which we shall ask the reader to take on faith.

In a fashion similar to that just used for showing that the derivative of $y = x^2$ is $\dfrac{dy}{dx} = 2x$, it can be shown that the derivative for any power of x

$$y = x^n$$

is

$$\frac{dy}{dx} = nx^{n-1}$$

Putting the symbols into words, the derivative is equal to the *exponent multiplied by the base with exponent reduced by* 1. In formal calculus this rule is proved to hold where n is *any* number. Hence n may be positive or negative or zero, integral or fractional, and so on.

Thus the derivative of

$$y = x^4$$

is

$$\frac{dy}{dx} = 4x^3$$

and the derivative of

$$y = x^7$$

is

$$\frac{dy}{dx} = 7x^6$$

and the derivative of

$$y = x, \text{ that is, } y = x^1$$

is

$$\frac{dy}{dx} = 1x^0 = 1$$

If a coefficient is present, then the derivative of

$$y = ax^n$$

is

$$\frac{dy}{dx} = nax^{n-1}$$

The fact that the coefficient is carried along may be justified by a specific instance. Let us refer to page 224 where we derived the fact that if

$$y = x^2$$

then

$$\frac{dy}{dx} = 2x$$

If we go through a similar derivation for

$$y = 5x^2$$

then $$y + \Delta y = 5(x + \Delta x)^2$$

or $$y + \Delta y = 5x^2 + 10x\Delta x + 5(\Delta x)^2$$

But $$y = 5x^2$$

Hence, by subtraction,

$$\Delta y = 10x\Delta x + 5(\Delta x)^2$$

and $$\frac{\Delta y}{\Delta x} = 10x + 5\Delta x$$

Let Δx approach zero. Then, in the limit,

$$\frac{dy}{dx} = 10x$$

Now compare this procedure with that on page 224 and notice that the effect of the coefficient 5 is merely that all terms in the right member of each equation are multiplied by 5. Hence the net result is to get a derivative 5 times as great.

Thus the derivative of

$$y = 3x^5$$

is $$\frac{dy}{dx} = 15x^4$$

and the derivative of

$$y = 3x$$

is $$\frac{dy}{dx} = 3x^0 = 3$$

and the derivative of

$$y = 4, \text{ that is, } 4x^0$$

is $$\frac{dy}{dx} = 0 \cdot 4x^{-1} = 0$$

(if we assume that the fundamental law holds for $n = 0$).

The derivative of any constant is zero, for if

$$y = a, \text{ that is } ax^0, \text{ then}$$

$$\frac{dy}{dx} = 0 \cdot ax^{-1} = 0$$

The derivative of a sum is equal to the sum of the derivatives of the individual terms. The reason why this law holds is that a derivative is a limit and a fundamental fact is that the limit of a sum is equal to the sum of the limits of terms. As an illustration of this statement let x, y, z, and w represent four variables and S their sum, so that

$$S = x + y + z + w$$

Let us suppose that x, y, z, and w approach the limits 2, 4, 5, 10 respectively. We claim that S will approach the limit $2+4+5+10 = 21$, for this reason: At some stage of their variation, x, y, z, and w will be within 0.001 of their goals. Suppose that at this stage each is 0.001 less than its limit. Then

$$S = 1.999 + 3.999 + 4.999 + 9.999 = 20.996$$

We see that S will be within 0.004 of 21. If the variables x, y, z, and w are within 0.000001 of their limits, then, at worst, S will be within 0.000004 of 21, so that S evidently approaches 21 as a limit. In fact, to repeat, it is generally true that the limit of a sum is equal to the sum of the limits of its terms.

Thus if

$$y = 2x^4 - 3x^3 + 7x^2 - 4x + 5$$

$$\frac{dy}{dx} = 8x^3 - 9x^2 + 14x - 4$$

and the derivative of

$$y = 3x^5 - 4x^3 + 2x - 7$$

is

$$\frac{dy}{dx} = 15x^4 - 12x^2 + 2$$

If the slope of the tangent to the curve

$$y = 3x^5 - 4x^3 + 2x - 7$$

at the point where $x=1$ is desired, we merely substitute $x=1$ in the formula for the derivative, thus obtaining

$$\text{slope} = \frac{dy}{dx} = 15 - 12 + 2 = 5$$

The fact that the derivative of

$$y = 3x$$

is

$$\frac{dy}{dx} = 3$$

that is, the derivative is a *constant,* can be readily interpreted graphically; $y = 3x$ can be pictured as a *line*. The tangent at any point is the line itself, and therefore its slope is always the same.

Since the slope of any line is a constant, the derivative of a linear expression should always be a constant. We see that this is actually the case. The derivative for any line

$$y = ax + b \quad \text{is}$$

$$\frac{dy}{dx} = a \quad (\text{a constant})$$

The fact that the derivative of

$$y = 4 \quad \text{is}$$

$$\frac{dy}{dx} = 0$$

can be interpreted by plotting the line $y = 4$ (see table and fig. 111).

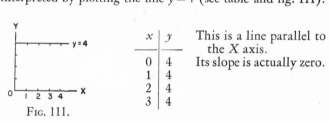

x	y
0	4
1	4
2	4
3	4

This is a line parallel to the X axis.
Its slope is actually zero.

Fig. 111.

Let us apply our rules to a few practical problems. The distance s for stopping an automobile under normal conditions is given by the formula $s = 0.097V^2$, where s is measured in feet and V in miles per hour. Find how fast s increases with V when $V = 20$.

$$\frac{ds}{dV} = 0.194V$$

Substituting $V = 20$

$$\frac{ds}{dV} = 3.88 \text{ ft. p er mile per hour}$$

that is, at the velocity under consideration (20 miles per hour), *the distance for stopping was increasing about 3.9 feet for each mile per hour increase in velocity.*

Along an arch of a bridge the height (y ft.) above the water at any horizontal distance (x ft.) from the center is $y = 80 - 0.005x^2$. Find the slope of the bridge at any point (that is, the slope of the tangent) and, in particular, the slope 40 feet from the center.

$$y = 80 - 0.005x^2$$

$$\frac{dy}{dx} = -0.01x$$

$$= (-0.01)(40) = -0.4 \quad \text{when} \quad x = 40$$

This means that for a horizontal advance of 10 feet, the tangent drops 4 feet (see fig. 112).

To put the derivative to other uses, we remark that graphs of parabolas exhibit *maximum* or *minimum* points. Notice that at

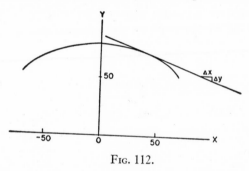

FIG. 112.

these highest and lowest points the tangent is horizontal, that is, its slope $\frac{dy}{dx} = 0$. Even if a graph is not a parabola, the derivative will be zero for *extrema*.

The fact that $\frac{dy}{dx} = 0$ at maximum and minimum points is useful in solving important practical problems. Suppose that a rectangular pasture, one side of which is bounded by a river, is to be fenced on the other three sides. What are the dimensions of the largest pasture that can be enclosed with 4000 feet of fence? In figure 113 we have represented the unknown width of the pasture by x. Two sides of the fence are x feet in length, and the third side must be

$4000 - 2x$. Let us call the area y. Then, since the area of a rectangle is equal to the product of the length by the width,

$$y = x(4000 - 2x)$$
$$y = 4000x - 2x^2$$

Now, it is just this quantity y, or $4000x - 2x^2$, which we desire to be a maximum. We could, of course, graph this equation for dif-

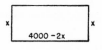

$$x \qquad 4000 - 2x \qquad x$$

Fig. 113.

ferent values of x (different widths), and then, from the graph, estimate which value of x will produce the greatest area. Incidentally, this graph will be a quadratic parabola with a maximum point. If we recall, however, that the slope of the tangent is zero at a maximum point, we can avoid the work of graphing.

$$y = 4000x - 2x^2$$
$$\frac{dy}{dx} = 4000 - 4x$$
$$4000 - 4x = 0 \text{ at a maximum point}$$
$$\therefore 4x = 4000$$
$$x = 1000$$
$$4000 - 2x = 2000$$

The dimensions of the rectangle should be 1000 feet by 2000 feet.

Maximum and minimum problems can be solved approximately by the reading of a graph, but often this graph is difficult to construct with accuracy. Hence the technique of equating the derivative to zero is a most useful one. To give another simple illustration of this fact:

An agency agreed to conduct a tour for a group of 50 people at a rate of $400 each. In order to secure more tourists the agency agreed to deduct $5 from the cost of the trip for each additional person joining the group. What number of tourists would give the agency maximum gross receipts? (It was specified that 75 was the upper practical limit for the size of the group.)

If 6 people were to join the group, the reduction in the cost of the tour would be $30 per person. If 10 joined, it would be $50, etc. If we represent by x the unknown number of additional tourists, the reduction will be $5x$ dollars, and

$$\text{cost of tour} = 400 - 5x$$

$$\text{number of tourists} = 50 + x$$

If we multiply the number of tourists by the cost of the tour, we shall obtain the gross receipts of the company. Let y symbolize these gross receipts. Then

$$y = (400 - 5x)(50 + x)$$

or
$$y = 2000 + 150x - 5x^2$$

To find the maximum gross receipts, we use the technique of finding the derivative and equating the result to zero.

$$\frac{dy}{dx} = 150 - 10x$$

$$150 - 10x = 0$$

$$10x = 150$$

$$x = 15$$

If there are 15 additional tourists for maximum receipts the number in the group will be 65.

We have furnished a bird's-eye view of the sort of problem the differential calculus will handle. The *integral calculus* is obtained by following Jacobi's advice, '*Mann muss immer umkehren.*' This branch of the calculus is even more useful to the scientist than its inverse. In the differential calculus, derivatives, slopes, or instantaneous rates are found from formulas. In the problems of the integral calculus the situation is reversed—the derivative is known and the formula is to be determined.

Suppose it is known that a ball is rolling down an incline, and that its velocity is changing at the constant rate of 10 feet per second for each second. Rate of change of velocity is termed *acceleration*. Here we know that the acceleration

$$\frac{dV}{dt} = 10$$

It is not difficult to see that

$$V = 10t + c$$

for, if a derivative is constant, it must come from a linear function. In the equation c is a numerical quantity or constant, to be determined by known physical conditions. For example, if we know that the ball was started down the incline with a velocity of 30 feet per second, that is, for

$$t = 0, V = 30$$

we can substitute this information in

$$V = 10t + c$$

and get $\qquad 30 = 10 \cdot 0 + c$

$$c = 30$$

thus determining the constant in question. Then the formula for the velocity of the body at any time is

$$V = 10t + 30$$

We can use this formula to obtain another for the position of the ball at any time. *Velocity* is another name for *instantaneous rate of change of distance,* so that

$$V = 10t + 30$$

is equivalent to $\qquad \dfrac{ds}{dt} = 10t + 30$

where s represents distance.

It is a little harder to guess this time, but not too difficult to see that

$$s = 5t^2 + 30t + k$$

where k is once again a constant to be determined by known physical conditions.

If we know that the ball started at a position 20 feet from the top of the incline, that is for

$$t = 0, s = 20$$

we can substitute this information in the formula for s in order to obtain k.

$$20 = 5 \cdot 0 + 30 \cdot 0 + k$$
$$k = 20 \quad \text{and}$$
$$s = 5t^2 + 30t + 20$$

Many geometric and physical problems are of just this type—by theory or experiment a formula for the rate of change of some quantity can be obtained, and then it remains to find a formula for the quantity itself. If

$$\frac{dy}{dx} = 3x^2 + 4x - 5$$

it is easy to guess that

$$y = x^3 + 2x^2 - 5x + c$$

and to sense the rule: *In each term raise the power by one and divide by the new exponent.*

It is not always easy to guess the formula for y. Integral calculus has its set of rules and regulations for doing this. In this respect, however, it forms a marked contrast to differential calculus. Whereas most of the functions that occur in elementary mathematics and science can be differentiated, even the most innocent-looking expressions may fail to be *integrable,* that is, they may not be the derivatives of elementary functions. Then, too, it is evident that there will always be an unknown constant in the answer. Unless some additional information is given, it will not be possible to determine this constant.

In spite of these difficulties, integral calculus will handle many vital problems. Chief among the geometric types are the calculations of the *length* of a curve, or the *area* enclosed by a curve, or the *volume* bounded by a surface. Even where the integration is impossible, good approximate results can be obtained. Since Euclidean methods can handle only a limited number of curves and solids, the calculus is a far superior metric tool. The variety of problems in the sciences to which integration can be applied is very great.

We shall give one illustration of how calculus will determine an area. Let us say that the shaded area, marked A in figure 114, is a growing quantity, for our point of view demands that we consider

all things in a state of flux. The small amount by which it grows
when P (x, y) moves to Q $(x + \Delta x, y + \Delta y)$ is marked ΔA. It is
bounded by the curve, the X-axis, and the ordinates of P and Q.
The area ΔA is made up of a rectangle, surmounted by a small

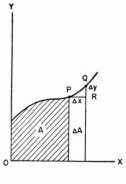

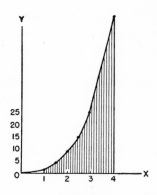

Fig. 114.   Fig. 115.

triangular area, PQR, one side of which is the curve. We shall treat
this little triangle as if it were a right triangle. If Δx, and hence Δy
and ΔA were very small, the error in this assumption would be
negligible. Then

$$\Delta A = \text{rectangle} + \text{triangle}$$

$$\Delta A = y\Delta x + \tfrac{1}{2} \Delta x \Delta y$$

since the area of a triangle is one-half the product of base and
height. Dividing both sides of this equation by Δx, we have

$$\frac{\Delta A}{\Delta x} = y + \tfrac{1}{2}\Delta y$$

Now if Δx approaches zero (see fig. 114) Δy and ΔA will do likewise. The limit of $\dfrac{\Delta A}{\Delta x}$ in this case is $\dfrac{dA}{dx}$ and

$$\frac{dA}{dx} = y$$

that is, *the rate at which the area is changing at any point of a curve
is equal to the height of the curve at that point.*

This proof lacks the mathematical rigor of twentieth-century
standards, but even the great inventors of the calculus depended on

intuition rather than logic at many points. Emulating them, we have given a demonstration sufficient for our present purpose.

To illustrate the use of the formula

$$\frac{dA}{dx} = y$$

let us find the area (fig. 115) under the curve $y = x^3$, and bounded by the curve, the X-axis, and the ordinates at $x = 1$ and $x = 4$.

$$\frac{dA}{dx} = y$$

or

$$\frac{dA}{dx} = x^3$$

in this case. We readily guess

$$A = \tfrac{1}{4}x^4 + c$$

Now if we consider this as the formula for a growing area that starts at $x = 1$ and ends at $x = 4$, we know that $A = 0$ when $x = 1$, that is, that initially there was no area. Substituting this information in the formula

$$A = \tfrac{1}{4}x^4 + c$$

we have

$$0 = \tfrac{1}{4} \cdot 1 + c$$

$$-\tfrac{1}{4} = c$$

and

$$A = \tfrac{1}{4}x^4 - \tfrac{1}{4}$$

is our formula for the growing area.

We want the value of this area when it has grown to the position $x = 4$. Substituting this value, we have

$$A = \tfrac{1}{4} \cdot 4^4 - \tfrac{1}{4} = 63\tfrac{3}{4} \text{ square units}$$

This is an area Euclid could not measure—in fact, would not have considered—since the curve $y = x^3$ was unknown to him. Thus a little simple algebra will measure an infinite variety of areas unknown to Greek geometers.

An extension to three dimensions of the work involved in obtaining $\frac{dA}{dx} = y$ will give $\frac{dV}{dx} = A$. By increasing the dimension of each quantity by one, we can get this formula by analogy. A (area) becomes V (volume); y (length) becomes A (area). In the first of these formulas y is the length of a line-segment that varies its position, that is, moves so as to generate the required area. Then by analogy A is a generating area forming a volume as it moves. Therefore we can find the volume of those solids for which it is possible to express the area of a moving cross section in terms of the distance from some fixed point, providing we can integrate the expression thus obtained.

Suppose we desire the volume of the cone of figure 116, which

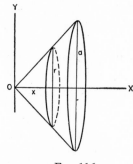

FIG. 116.   FIG. 117.

is such that the radius of the circular cross section is always equal to the distance from the origin, in other words, $r = x$. Then

$$\frac{dV}{dx} = A$$

$$\frac{dV}{dx} = \pi x^2$$

$$V = \tfrac{1}{3}\pi x^3 + c$$

But the growing volume was just starting when $x = 0$; that is, $V = 0$ when $x = 0$. Then

$$0 = \tfrac{1}{3}\pi \cdot 0 + c$$

$$0 = c$$

and $V = \tfrac{1}{3}\pi x^3$

If the total height of the cone is a, and accordingly the radius of the base is also a, then the volume $V = \tfrac{1}{3}\pi x^3$ will grow until $x = a$ and

$$V = \tfrac{1}{3}\pi a^3$$

Again, suppose the volume of the horn in figure 117 is desired, and we are told that the radius of a cross section is given by the formula

$$r = .04x^2$$

and the depth of the horn is 10.

$$\frac{dV}{dx} = A$$

$$\frac{dV}{dx} = .0016\,\pi x^4$$

$$V = .00032\,\pi x^5 + c$$

Since

$$V = 0 \quad \text{when} \quad x = 0$$

$$0 = 0 + c$$

$$c = 0$$

$$V = .0032\,\pi x^5$$

Since the depth is 10

$$V = .0032\,\pi(10)^5$$

$$V = 320\,\pi \text{ cubic units}$$

Again, just as many different areas can be measured by integration, many different volumes can be found in the same way. A problem that sounds simpler, but is somewhat more difficult, is the measurement of the *length* of a curve—the rectification of a curve, as it is called. We shall not go into the technique of this procedure but will shortly explain the principle in back of it.

Numerous physical quantities can be found by integration—for example, *the work done by a variable force*. Thus

$$\frac{dW}{dx} = F$$

or the *instantaneous rate of change of work with respect to distance is equal to the force.*

If the force required to stretch a certain spring x inches is $F = 20x$, how much work will be done in elongating the spring 5 inches?

$$\frac{dW}{dx} = 20x$$

$$W = 10x^2 + c$$

Since

$$W = 0 \text{ when } x = 0, c = 0 \text{ and}$$

$$W = 10x^2 = 250, \text{ for } x = 5$$

We have treated integration as the inverse of differentiation. There is another, perhaps more important, point of view on the nature of this process. To return to the problem of rectification— the approximate length of a curve PQ (fig. 118) can obviously be

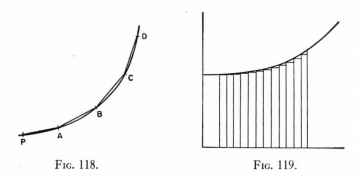

Fig. 118.   Fig. 119.

found by measuring the length of the numerous small straight chords PA, AB, BC, etc. The closer together A, B, C, etc. are, and the shorter the chords, the better they will approximate the arcs PA, AB, BC, etc. The sum

$$PA + AB + BC + \cdots$$

is the approximate length of the curve. The limit of this sum as the chords become smaller and smaller, but more and more numerous, is called the *length* of the curve. This can be found by integration.

Again, the area under the curve in figure 119 can be approximated by finding the sum of the numerous small rectangles. The more numerous and the narrower these rectangles the better the approximation. The limit of the sum as the rectangles grow more and more numerous, and their widths tend toward zero, is defined as the required area. We have already seen that this area can be found by integration.

In the same way, the series of telescoping cylinders in figure 120 will approximate the volume of a solid. The so-called 'circular pyramid' of Cuicuilco in Mexico is a graphic illustration of the approximation of the volume of a solid by cylinders. The actual volume of a solid can be defined as *the limit of a sum of numerous cylinders (or prisms) of small altitude.*

Integration from this point of view is a *summation*. The customary notation used by Leibniz indicates this, for the *integral sign* is a medieval *S*, standing for *summa*. Instead of writing

$$\frac{dA}{dx} = x^3$$

it is customary to write

$$A = \int x^3 dx$$

The concept of integration as a summation of infinitely many infinitesimal quantities, for example, the infinitesimal rectangles whose

Fig. 120. The sum of telescoping cylinders of small height approximates the volume of the solid.

sum yields the required area, makes possible the solution of many important geometric and scientific problems. A study of the theoretical and technical aspects of performing such summations constitutes the subject called integral calculus.

11

From Alice to Einstein

> Your way of saying things is strange
> Your fluent phrases twist and change
>
>   ·   ·   ·
>
> How shall I find out what you mean
> With true and false to choose between?
>
> GRACE HAZARD CONKLING

THE prim young don paces up and down, glancing now and then at the open book in his hand. He takes several deep breaths. Then, in a high-pitched, nervous voice, he recites:

> When he himself might his quietus make
> With a b-b-b-bare b-b-bodkin? who would
>   fardels bear,
> To grunt and s-s-s-s-

With a sigh, the reader closes the book abruptly and replaces it among the numerous volumes which line the shelves.

Is the slim, well-built man, with the perfect, almost feminine features and the long wavy hair, a young actor attempting a burlesque? Is the impediment in speech some clownish pose? No, for the streaks of gray in the thick crop of hair, the austere garb, something severe in the lines about the mouth, the slightly melancholy look in the gentle blue eyes, tell a different story.

The gentleman approaches his desk. From one of the pigeonholes he removes a sheet of paper and commences to write:

Text: Job xxviii.28—And unto man he said 'The fear of the Lord, that is wisdom.' Prayer in the Litany—'Give us an heart to love and dread thee.'

He remains deep in thought for a while, hunched over the desk, from time to time passing his long delicate fingers through his hair. Then he arises, and with quick, uneven steps approaches a cabinet at the other end of the room. Having found the correct heading in his files, he places the paper among the other neatly arranged records. He draws a smaller sheet from the desk, fetches a different pen and inkwell.

He paces up and down, then suddenly leans over the desk, and without seating himself, writes:

> All teetotalers like sugar.
> No nightingale drinks wine.
> Therefore, no nightingale dislikes sugar.

As an afterthought, he changes his pen and ink and goes over the word 'teetotalers' in black, so that it will form a dark and serious contrast to the violet 'nightingale.'

He leans against the side of the desk and, in a few minutes, bends over and adds to his previous statements:

> Babies are illogical.
> Nobody is despised who can manage a crocodile.
> Illogical persons are despised.
> Therefore, babies cannot manage crocodiles.

For the first time he smiles and his eyes twinkle as he inscribes:

> All jokes are meant to amuse.
> No act of Parliament is a joke.
> Therefore, some things meant to amuse are not acts of Parliament.

Suddenly something catches his ear. At the sound of childish voices and laughter in the corridor, he opens the door and hides behind it. Three little girls make their way into the room. All at once our dignified scholar is down on all fours shouting, 'Oh frabjous day! Callooh! Callay! Beware the Jubjub Bird, and shun the frumious Bandersnatch!'

The children are not intimidated by this injunction and begin to chase him. The smallest mounts on his back, while the others pretend to flee in great fear. The girls beg for a story and he recounts at length the tale of the 'Whistling Chinaman on the Chimbley-Piece.'

'And now that will be enough until next time!' he concludes.

'Oh, but it's next time already!' Florence protests.

'No, it's just time for little girls to go home for tea. You may leave me now—to ruminate. I'm as jolly as the day is long except when it's necessary to ruminate on some very difficult subject. Remember, all of me, all of me, that isn't Bonhomie is Rumination!'

'You always send us home the same way,' Florence complains, 'all of me that isn't Bone-disease is Rheumatism.'

'Whether it's Bonhomie or Bone-disease, I have a lesson in Euclid in half an hour.'

'What's Euclid?' The girls are sparring for time.

'Something no Oxford chiel will ever comprehend. And so good-bye.' Uncle Charles is firm.

Within the hour he is transformed once more into the formal figure of the Reverend Charles Lutwidge Dodgson, Mathematical Lecturer of Christ Church. 'So, my friend! That's the way you prove 1.19, is it? Assuming 1.20? Cool, refreshingly cool! Write it on your examination paper, and it will earn you that peculiar mark which cricketers call "a duck's egg," and thermometers "zero"! And now, Fleetwood, define parallel lines!'

'Right lines are said to be parallel,' Fleetwood mutters, 'when they are equally and similarly inclined to the same right line, or make equal angles with it toward the same side.'

'That is very s-s-s-soothing. Just as-s-sume that a pair of lines which makes equal angles with one line, do so with *all* lines. You might just as well say that a young lady, who was inclined to one young man was "equally and s-s-s-similarly inclined" to all young men! Now Fleetwood, I suppose you've been consulting Legendre or Wilson or Cooley! Give them up, if you want to avoid a logical muddle! Euclid is the only text for those who s-s-study with me.'

In the evening the Reverend Dodgson continues the work on his *Symbolic Logic*. We leave him as he writes:

All members of the House of Commons have perfect self-command.
No M.P. who wears a coronet should ride in a donkey race.
All members of the House of Lords wear coronets.
Hence no M.P. should ride in a donkey race unless he has perfect self-command.

*　*　*

Everyone knows Lewis Carroll as the creator of the immortal Alice. His nom de plume was derived by translating his given name Charles Lutwidge into Latin—Carolus Ludovicus—and then reversing and anglicizing the result. As straightforward Charles Lutwidge Dodgson he was a mathematics teacher and a writer on mathematical subjects. His dual personality gave rise to many legends. One story, denied by Carroll, claimed that Queen Victoria, delighted with *Alice in Wonderland,* ordered that Carroll's next book be delivered to her as soon as released. She was somewhat taken aback to receive *The Elements of Determinants (with their application to Simultaneous Linear Equations and Algebraical Geometry).*

Carroll, or Dodgson, was also an ordained minister. He seldom preached, however, because he had an impediment in his speech. His habit of stuttering was probably one reason for his lack of ease with adults and his fondness for children. He attempted all his life to overcome this speech defect; daily he would practice correct enunciation by reading aloud a scene from Shakespeare.

For us Carroll's mathematics must be the question of major interest. The subject which interested him most was that of the logical foundations of mathematics. Although he was not an original worker in this field, he showed an exceptionally keen, almost prophetic understanding of the points at issue. It happens that the problem which interested Carroll is the most basic of all questions in twentieth-century mathematics and science. The creator of delightfully whimsical nonsense literature also possessed rare mathematical insight.

To understand Carroll's mathematics, we now prepare to make good the promise of an earlier chapter in which we omitted the methods of Greek geometry but said we should discuss them later. Now that we have developed some background for more abstract geometry, let us give the details of the geometrical part of the 'glory that was Greece.'

Let us review ancient Babylonian geometric procedures much as the logical Carroll would have done. What about the practical tools that were used? How were their rulers and 'protractors' made? Did they not by chance use these instruments to 'prove' some of the very facts on which their construction was based? May they not have reasoned in a circle? How was the first straightedge constructed? If we wish to be exact, what is a straight line anyhow?

Or even if the use of these instruments should not involve a logical mix-up, a precise thinker could hardly be entirely satisfied with the results. In trying to establish the fact that the sum of the angles of a triangle is 180°, the experimenter might easily obtain 179° or 181° with a crude instrument. Or again, even if the sum of the angles were 180° in the triangles that were measured, would this sum be 180° in all triangles?

Such are the difficulties connected with the experimental method and the procedure of *inductive* reasoning that follows it. When we reason, we draw inferences from certain *propositions* or statements. When these propositions are the result of experiment or observation, the reasoning is termed *inductive,* and we have seen how probability theory aids in pronouncing judgment on hypotheses that grow out of induction.

Experimental methods are not always entirely satisfactory in mathematical situations. To the Greeks must go the initial credit for realizing this. About 600 B.C. Thales, who lived in the city of Miletus in Asia Minor, was the first to experience discontent with the intuitional and pseudo-inductive methods of the Orient. The biography of this Greek mathematician, who has been called 'the first man of science,' furnishes a sharp contrast to that of the Victorian Carroll and all our latter-day notions of the typical scholar. For Thales started life as a merchant and achieved considerable success in the business world. He retired early and devoted his leisure to the hobbies of mathematics, astronomy, philosophy, and travel. His trips abroad (to Egypt and Babylonia) were meant to be recreational, but in the end Thales always took a busman's holiday and conferred with Oriental scientists.

Although we are interested mainly in the mathematical side of Thales' life, one story recounted of his business methods can bear repetition. Olive oil was as important a commodity in his time as wheat or sugar in ours. One year, when the olive crop was particularly good, Thales, fearing that the supply would be greater than the demand, quietly bought all the olive presses and thus 'cornered' the olive-oil market. Thus Thales created one of the earliest instances of a monopoly—in 600 B.C.

Thales was the first to substitute logical reasoning for intuition in a considerable portion of his work in geometry. His pupil Pythagoras absorbed the idea of logical proof, transmitted it to his followers, and so it became a Greek tradition. The pattern of *demonstrative geometry,* started by Thales and finally established by Euclid, is an illustration of *deductive* reasoning. Whereas the propositions or statements at the basis of inductive reasoning are experimental in nature, those in deductive reasoning need not be.

The pattern of deductive thought in traditional Aristotelian logic is based on the *syllogism,* although modern symbolic logic shows that not all deduction is syllogistic. The classic syllogism consists of three propositions: a *major premise,* a *minor premise,* and a *conclusion.* Thus:

Major premise: All voters are citizens.
Minor premise: Smith is a voter.
Conclusion: Smith is a citizen.

Major premise: A regular polygon is a polygon which is both equilateral and equiangular.
Minor premise: P is a regular polygon.
Conclusion: P is both equilateral and equiangular.

An argument usually consists of a series of syllogisms, stated or implied.[1] Thus, 'Since all of you have suffered the hardships of the war, vote for my candidate—he will push an international peace policy,' can be analyzed somewhat as follows:

Premises

(1) People who have suffered from the war are in favor of international peace.
(2) You have suffered from the war.
(3) People who favor international peace should vote for my candidate.

Syllogisms

Major premise: People who have suffered from the war are in favor of international peace (premise 1).
Minor premise: You have suffered from the war (premise 2).

Conclusion: Therefore you are in favor of international peace (a new proposition—4).

Major premise: People who favor international peace should vote for my candidate (premise 3).
Minor premise: *You* are in favor of international peace (proposition 4, previously proved, not an original premise).
Conclusion: You should vote for my candidate (a new proposition—5).

Thus the premises (1) and (2) yield a new proposition (4), which is used along with (3) to yield another new proposition (5).

If you reject any of the premises, you cannot accept conclusions drawn from them. Thus, if you accept (1) and (2) but reject (3), you will agree with (4) but deny (5).

---

[1] To avoid artificial language, we have not used the conventional logical form for a proposition—*subject* and *predicate* connected by copula.

Let us take a sample of Euclid to show that the type of deductive reasoning our political orator employed in the illustration above is also used in demonstrative geometry. We shall furnish the method by which modern texts on plane geometry deduce the *Pons Asinorum* (see page 41). At a certain point in such texts we have the right to employ the following premises, which have either been assumed originally or proved prior to the *Pons*.

Premises
(1) There exists one line and only one that will divide any angle into two equal angles (that is, will bisect any angle).
(2) Anything equals itself.
(3) Two triangles are congruent if they agree in two sides and the included angle.
(4) Corresponding angles of congruent triangles are equal.

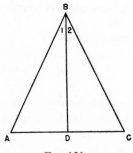

FIG. 121.

Suppose we now take as additional premises that, in figure 121

(5) *ABC* is a triangle (a polygon having three sides and three angles).
(6) *AB=BC*.

Let us see what new propositions we can deduce by a series of syllogisms.

Syllogisms
1. Major premise: There exists one line and only one that will divide any angle into two equal angles.

   Minor premise: There is an angle *B* in figure 121 (part of premise 5).

   Conclusion: Angle *B* can be bisected. Hence draw in bisector *BD*, making angle 1 = angle 2.

II. Major premise: Anything equals itself.

Minor premise: BD is a segment ('thing') created by the conclusion of syllogism I.

Conclusion: $BD = BD$.

III. Major premise: Two triangles are congruent if they agree in two sides and the included angle.

Minor premise: Triangles ABC and BCD are two triangles that agree in two sides and the included angle, for

$AB = BC$	(premise 6)
angle 1 = angle 2	(conclusion of syllogism I)
$BD = BD$	(conclusion of syllogism II)

Conclusion: Triangles ABD and BCD are congruent.

IV. Major premise: Corresponding angles of congruent triangles are equal.

Minor premise: Angles A and C are corresponding angles of congruent triangles (by the conclusion of syllogism III).

Conclusion: angle A = angle C.

In other words, *if two sides of a triangle are equal, then two angles are also equal.*

To be strictly rigorous in our deductions, we should have had a slightly lengthier series of syllogisms, but we have avoided excessive detail for the sake of clarity.

Now let us return to the argument of the orator for a moment. Whether or not you accept his conclusions depends on whether you accept his premises. Let us say that you accept only premises (1) and (2), namely that people who have suffered from the war are in favor of international peace, and that you have suffered from the war.

Let us say that you reject premise (3), namely that people who favor international peace should vote for the speaker's candidate. Then you will accept proposition (4) and reject proposition (5); that is, you will grant that you are in favor of international peace, but reject the conclusion that you should vote for the speaker's candidate.

If you reject any of the premises, the speaker may offer further syllogisms to establish these. Since so many people assert the speaker's premise (2) daily, this premise will probably be accepted without further proof. In proving premises (1) and (3), the speaker will have to assume other propositions. If you refuse to accept these, he will have to prove them in turn but assume still others. If you are obdurate, the argument will continue until long after respectable citizens have retired, the speaker has a bad case of laryngitis, and the argument has become an excellent soporific for all but the hecklers.

You will just have to accept some premises in order to get started, and this holds for the speaker's argument as well as our geometric one. In mathematics these original assumptions are called *axioms* or *postulates*. Whereas in books on logic or argumentation, there is considerable discussion about what sort of propositions should be accepted as premises for launching an argument, the feeling of modern mathematicians is quite different. Theoretically, we have the right to choose our axioms rather arbitrarily.

For those who learned at school or from textbooks that axioms are 'self-evident truths,' this point of view may raise grave doubts. If the axioms are not 'true,' then how can any of the facts derived from them be true? Is geometry true or isn't it? We assert—that is not a proper question. The axioms are like the rules of a game. We agree to abide by them and play accordingly. No one would think of asking whether a game of bridge was 'true.' A proper inquiry would seek to find out whether it had been played according to the rules. No South Sea Islander would deny the 'true' existence of a seminude Balinese woman or charge her with indecency, since local rules of dress make her costume quite conventional.

The point of view we have just elucidated is a rather modern one. Thales and Pythagoras had no such notions. Euclid, who compiled the work of Greek geometers into a great classic, was far from having such ideas. From his time until the nineteenth century, mathematicians were attempting the proof of certain axioms, and calling others 'common notions.' The philosopher Kant, for example, considered axioms *a priori* truths. Less than a century ago, a general attitude, voiced by Edward Everett, was: 'In the pure mathematics we contemplate absolute truths, which existed in the divine mind before the morning stars sang together and which will continue to exist there when the last of their radiant host shall have fallen from heaven.'

Geometry, or algebra, or any mathematical science is merely the set of new propositions, called theorems, that can be deduced from certain original ones. Let us say that in some particular science there are half a dozen of these postulates. Perhaps postulates (1) and (2) will result in a new proposition, which we shall call (7). Perhaps (3) and (7) will yield a proposition (8). Perhaps (4) and (5) will yield (9). Perhaps (8) and (9) will yield (10); (6) and (10) may yield (11), etc. It is possible that a very large number of new propositions can be deduced from the original six. At any rate, *the postulates and all the theorems that can be deduced are said to constitute the mathematical science.*

Benjamin Peirce's definition of mathematics as 'the science which draws necessary conclusions' reflects its deductive nature. A quip of Bertrand Russell's has its serious side. 'Mathematics is the subject in which we never know what we are talking about nor whether what we say is true.' Many will give a literal interpretation to this definition and agree with it heartily. Russell alludes to the fact that we cannot discuss the 'truth' of our propositions, since they are deduced from assumptions. He also refers to the fact that, in addition to the axioms, we must have certain *undefined elements* to which our axioms are applied. Just as we get into an endless chain of argument by trying to prove all premises, we find similar difficulty in trying to define everything. Apropos of this, we quote Born's story [2] of a professor's response to a young lady who asked if he would explain relativity 'in a few words.' The professor's reply was

Of course I will—provided you let me tell you this little story first. I was going for a walk with a French friend and we got thirsty. By and by we came to a farm and I said: 'Let's buy a glass of milk here.' 'What's milk?' 'Oh, you don't know what milk is? It's the white liquid that . . .!' 'What's white?' 'White? You don't know what that is either? Well the swan . . .!' 'What's swan?' 'Swan, the big bird with the bent neck.' 'What's bent?' 'Bent? Good heavens, don't you know that? Here, look at my arm! When I put it so, it's bent!' 'Oh that's bent, is it? Now I know what milk is!'

Some textbooks still define a point as 'that which has no dimensions,' a line as 'something with one dimension,' and so on. Then, what, pray is a dimension? And when you have defined that, we shall have more questions, like the character in Born's story. So make your choice of a starting place. You will just have to leave some things undefined. In relativity and in all sciences, the story 'in a few words' is the listing of axioms and undefined terms. The

[2] Born, Max, *The Restless Universe,* New York, Harper, 1936.

rest is just logic—creating, as Lewis Carroll did, syllogism after syllogism in a logical chain. The Einstein theory 'in brief' is implicitly such a list, the genius of its creator being that it is not a Carrollian collection involving teetotalers and crocodiles, but a group of assumptions from which deductive logic can readily draw a set of theorems that fits nature far better than the propositions of Newton or any scientist preceding the author of the theory of relativity.

We quote another definition of mathematics, from the German mathematician David Hilbert, considered by many to have been the foremost worker of modern times in the field of logical foundations of mathematics. 'Mathematics is a game played according to certain simple rules with meaningless marks on paper.' This definition has the same diplomatic quality as Russell's—it will please those who love mathematics as well as those who don't.

Whether we are disciples of Russell or Hilbert, we must initiate a pure science with *unproved* propositions about *undefined* terms. Let us state that the avoidance of a logical tangle is not the only advantage in leaving some elements and relations undefined. Undefined entities are the equivalent in abstractness to algebraic symbols and possess the same great advantage of generality. In the equation

$$x + a = b$$

x, a, and b are variables. They represent any three quantities such that the sum of the first two is equal to the third. We could have $x=1$, $a=2$, $b=3$, or $x=\frac{1}{2}$, $a=-\frac{1}{4}$, $b=\frac{1}{4}$, etc. Thus $x+a=b$ represents an infinite number of different equations. If we subtract a from both sides of this equation we obtain

$$x = b - a$$

whatever the values of a and b.

If instead of $x+a=b$, we were to consider the equation with concrete numerical values,

$$x + 3 = 1$$

a person unacquainted with negative numbers would be unable to proceed to a solution for x. As soon as we use concrete, specific instances instead of abstract, variable ones, it is only natural that thinking will become confused by such issues as 'truth' or 'reality.'

We find the same factor appearing in logical terms. Who would worry about the proposition *x is a believer in y*? No one! For *x* and *y* are variables. On the other hand, if we make *x* and *y* specific— *Mr. Jones is a believer in Communism*—we have a proposition to which people are sure to react.

In the fact that numerous (indeed sometimes infinitely many) interpretations of the *x*'s and *y*'s are possible lies their great advantage. If we apply the method of deduction to a set of postulates about these variables, we can later furnish the undefined terms with many different physical meanings and thus arrive at many different sciences. The same postulate systems may lead to a *plane geometry,* a *hemispherical geometry,* or something that is not our idea of a geometry at all. These sciences would all have the same logical pattern—the *postulates* with *x*'s and *y*'s plus the *theorems* deduced from the postulates. Such sciences are termed *isomorphic.*

Do we then make no demands whatsoever on postulate systems? May we use as an axiom: *The moon is made of green cheese.* The answer is: For a pure science, yes, providing axioms are *consistent.* We cannot go ahead if one postulate tells us that the moon is made of green cheese and another says that it is purely vegetable.

In addition to consistency, which is an essential property of a set of axioms, we usually ask for another quality merely on aesthetic grounds. While oratory demands that a man be described as honest, upright, reliable, and so on, such redundancy does not appeal to the mathematician. Even concealed repetition seems to the mathematician a blemish which destroys the perfect beauty of a set of axioms. He asks for *independence* in a set of postulates, that is, that no one of the axioms be deducible from the remaining ones. He asks: Have we the most economical set? Or could we get along without a couple of our postulates?

If our assumptions are

(1) In a democracy all the people must receive some schooling.
(2) The U.S. is a democracy.

then we need not assume also

(3) The U.S. should provide universal education.

since proposition (3) is implied by (1) and (2). Let us emphasize again, however, that absolute independence is not an essential attribute of a set of postulates but is only called for by an ideal of logical perfection.

An interesting question comes up when the mathematician is asked to show that a postulate system is consistent. He does this by finding some *concrete* interpretation that will satisfy all the postulates; in other words, he must find at least one applied science of which it is the basis. Thus, *physical* 'points,' 'lines,' etc. help to establish the consistency of a set of postulates about *x*'s and *y*'s. In this way we are virtually forced back to intuition again. In truth, then, there is really *no logical way* of establishing the consistency of a set of axioms.

Bertrand Russell has given the name *propositional function* to propositions containing variables like *x is a believer in y*. The term, propositional function, is used because these statements, like functions, are determined by the values of their variables. Russell reserves the name *proposition* for the statements resulting from the substitution of concrete values for the variables of a propositional function. Thus, *Smith is a believer in God* is a proposition obtained by substituting values in the propositional function above. The analogy with the ordinary function concept (see page 120) is evident. The area of a square is a function of the side given by the formula

$$A = s^2$$

When the value of the variable *s* is given, the value of the function *A* is determined. If $s = 4$, $A = 16$, etc.

A *pure* mathematical science can be thought of as a body of assumed propositional functions and all the propositional functions deduced from these. An *applied* mathematical science is one obtained by substituting concrete values for the variables in the pure mathematical science. If the applied mathematical science is to be of any practical value to us, the values substituted should be in accord with our physical observations. For the pure science, we are interested only in the logical technique of deduction.

In an applied mathematical science such as the physicist or astronomer uses, he may choose several alternative sets of postulates, if each of these agrees equally well with observed data. Moreover these sets are not generally derived from the same set of propositional functions; that is, they differ not only in the interpretation given to undefined terms, but in their actual pattern. The alternative sets of deduced propositions are called *theories*. Having built up his theories, the scientist conducts further experiments to test the propositions in the alternative theories. He then selects that one of his

theories which checks best in the light of these experiments. If the
tests fail to verify any of the theories, he must go back to the beginning and start with a new set of postulates. On the other hand,
instead of this sort of failure, he may be successful in all experiments and find that several theories explain the observed facts
equally well. Then, if he makes a selection of any one, it will be
because it is more convenient—it may involve less computation, simpler formulas, etc. Let us point out that the method of the physicist
and astronomer illustrates the great advantage to science of the
logical processes of the mathematical sciences, which furnish the
pattern for the applied. The process of deduction furnishes the scientist with facts that might be difficult or even impossible to discover by experimental methods. Even where experiment is possible,
the process of deduction tells him what experiments to try in order
to test his theories. For example, application of the Copernican theory led to the discovery of Neptune and Pluto, whose existence had
not been previously suspected.

As for the fact that different theories may explain observations,
we remark that the Ptolemaic and Copernican theories of the solar
system are almost opposite in point of view, but nevertheless describe equally well the motions of the planets, provided a few modifications are made in Ptolemy's theory. Ptolemy conceived the Earth
as being at rest with the stars and the Sun moving in circular orbits
around it as center. In the modifications made by Tycho Brahe the
planets move on circles whose centers are at the Sun and move with
the Sun. The paths of the planets, as observed from the Earth, are
called 'epicycloids.' When some modifications in this theory have
been made, it is suitable for astronomic purposes. In the Copernican
theory, of later adoption, the Sun is the central body and the stars
are fixed. Kepler's laws state that the Earth and the other planets
move about the Sun on ellipses which have the Sun at one focus.
Modern theory is not superior to ancient so far as its convenience
for the numerical work of astronomy is concerned. The Copernican
theory is, however, much the simpler in its geometry and other
mathematical aspects. Thus it was adopted and developed because
it is easier, not because it is more accurate.

Euclid, who in 300 B.C. wrote a geometry that has been the basis
of all elementary textbooks on the subject ever since, did not realize
that his axioms were merely assumptions, that he was using numerous undefined terms, and that his geometry was only a series

of *relative* truths. Moreover, his list of postulates is actually incomplete—Euclid unconsciously assumed many facts. In preparing the rebuttal in a debate, it is easy to reveal assumptions concealed by your opponent. To detect Euclid's omissions, however, is a process of much more subtle analysis. Only recently Hilbert remedied the defects and devised a logically satisfactory set of axioms for Euclidean geometry.

Other sets complying with strict logical standards have also been prepared. There is a set by Veblen, an American mathematician, and one by Pieri, an Italian mathematician. We have already alluded to the fact that several theories may explain an applied science equally well. The 'theories' of Veblen and Pieri for Euclidean geometry do not differ from one another as do the Ptolemaic and Copernican theories for the universe. The theories for Euclidean geometry are all equivalent in that they arrive at the same theorems. The axioms and the undefined terms that initiate the sciences, however, are different. Veblen uses a set of twelve postulates containing only two undefined terms—'point' and 'between.' Pieri's set contains twenty axioms with two undefined terms—'point' and 'motion.' Hilbert's axioms are twenty-one in number with five undefined terms —'point,' 'line,' 'plane,' 'between' and 'congruent.' Veblen's geometry has the advantage of few assumptions, but the fact that Hilbert and Pieri have assumed more makes the derivation of fundamental theorems in their geometries easier and more elementary. In Hilbert's geometry 'congruence' is the basic idea; in Pieri's it is 'motion.'

We shall give a few illustrations of Hilbert's postulates. Before doing so, let us remember that to obtain the proper notion of these postulates as propositional functions we should substitute x, y, z's or other symbols. If this is done in all the postulates and in all the propositional functions deduced from them, then this Hilbertian science is a pure mathematical science furnishing the pattern for the applied mathematical science of Euclidean geometry. The substitution of the physical 'points,' 'lines,' and 'planes' of the draughtsman, surveyor, and architect turns Hilbert's propositional functions into propositions and his pure science into the applied science of Euclidean geometry. The substitution of other values for Hilbert's undefined terms will lead to other applied sciences, so that Hilbert's postulate system need not be thought of as leading merely to the single applied science of Euclidean geometry.

Hilbert's axioms are of six types—'connection,' 'order,' 'congruence,' 'parallelism,' 'continuity,' and 'completeness.' Some are equivalent to facts that Euclid used, some are items that Euclid unconsciously assumed or completely overlooked.

There are seven axioms of connection, one of which is the classic: *Through two points only one straight line can be drawn.*

There are five postulates of order. We quote the one: *If three points lie on the same line, then one and only one of them lies between the other two.* Since this is one we wager you did not have when you studied high-school geometry, let us play with it for a bit. Put 'fi' for point and 'fo' for line. *If three 'fi's' lie on the same 'fo,' then one and only one of them lies between the other two.* Now re-interpret 'fi' as a point and 'fo' as a closed curve, and we have: If three points lie on a closed curve, one and only one of them lies between the other two (see fig. 122). This is false, if our physical intuition is correct, for *A* can lie between *B* and *C*. *C* can lie between *A* and *B*, and *B* can lie between *A* and *C*.

Again, take 'fi' as a line and 'fo' as a point. As for the English, if you do not like to say 'If three lines lie on a point, one and only

Fig. 122.   Fig. 123.

one of them lies between the other two,' then change the postulate to 'If three lines pass through a point, one and only one of them lies between the other two.'

This contradicts common sense (see fig. 123). We see here an axiom that certainly is not a 'self-evident' truth, for the order of points on a circle or lines through a point is not the same as our common notion of the order of points on a line. Thus, in the matter of *order*, which Euclid took very much for granted and which might never disturb the peace of mind of an inexperienced thinker, some agreement on assumptions is actually necessary at the outset of work. The failure of Euclid to list axioms of order makes possible some well-known paradoxes. For example, using Euclid's axioms alone, it is possible to prove that 'every triangle is isosceles.'

To proceed to Hilbert's axioms of congruence, of which there are six, we quote: *If two triangles agree in two sides and the included angle, they agree in their remaining angles.*

As an example of a postulate of continuity, Hilbert gives the one usually named the Archimedean, although it was well known to Euclid: *If* A *and* B *are any points on a line, then starting at* A *and laying off equal segments successively we can always ultimately pass the point* B.

As an axiom of parallelism we have the most famous axiom in mathematical history, which is called Euclid's parallel postulate and can be stated in many equivalent forms. If we define two lines that lie in the same plane, but never meet, as parallel, Euclid's parallel postulate becomes: *Through a point* P *outside a line* l *there is one and only one line parallel to* l. We shall presently explain why this postulate, rather than any of the others, has played such an important role in mathematics.

If we invest the terms 'point,' 'line,' etc. with the usual interpretations and sketch the figure for the last two axioms with pencil on paper, they appear to be in accord with common sense. However, let us imagine not the small sheet of paper in front of us but a very large sheet, extending indefinitely in all directions. Are we then sure that other assumptions would not serve equally well? If the plane of the sketches is thought of as being *infinite,* is it not possible that lines which we picture as parallel may meet if extended indefinitely? Would it not be equally in accord with common sense to picture all lines as meeting and to assume 'Through a point *P,* outside a line *l,* there is no line parallel to *l'?* As for the axiom of Archimedes, we can check its 'truth' if *A* and *B* are 10 inches apart; but what about the case when *A* is here and *B* is very, very far away?

Hilbert's postulate of completeness is one which would never have seemed necessary to early geometers. It reads: '*To a system of points, lines, and planes it is not possible to add other elements such that the system thus generalized shall form a new science in which all the postulates of the foregoing five sets are valid.*' The question of completeness arises more naturally in the modern mathematician's mind from many experiences similar to those we considered in solving equations: Are these all the possible solutions or will someone else be able to find some additional ones? When is our work complete?

Again, Euclidean geometry is only one applied science furnishing an interpretation of Hilbert's pure science; spherical geometry is another. There are an infinite number of others besides—some vital, many trivial, but all possible interpretations.

To return to Euclid—his attitude toward the parallel postulate differed from his belief about the others. While the others seemed 'common notions' to him, this one did not. He realized, only in this one case, that he was making an assumption. If he had used something like our x, y, z scheme, that is, if he had had the concept that initial elements must be undefined, he would have realized that the other axioms were not self-evident either. Since he dared not *assume* the parallel postulate, he tried to *prove* it, that is, to deduce it from the others.

In doing this, he established a precedent for centuries to come (twenty-one of them) for, until the day of the Russian mathematician Lobachewsky (1793–1856), mathematicians were constantly struggling for proofs of the parallel postulate. The problem of finding a proof furnished the same challenge to mathematicians as the famous problems of antiquity. What Lobachewsky did was to challenge this axiom and substitute another. He assumed that *through a point outside a line l there are an infinite number of lines parallel to l*. Then with this axiom and all Euclid's postulates except the one on parallels as basis, he initiated the construction of a logically consistent geometry, that is, one in which there are no contradictions. Somewhat later Beltrami proved that Euclid's parallel postulate is actually independent of the other axioms and not deducible from them. Thus the problem of the parallel postulate is now on a par with the squaring of the circle, the trisection of an angle, and the duplication of the cube. It is solved for all time as far as the mathematical world is concerned. The next natural question would be: How about the other postulates? Mathematicians were led to a reconsideration of the nature of postulates and eventually evolved the point of view that we have set forth in this chapter.

We see that Lobachewsky was the father of the Russian revolution in mathematics. If Lenin was responsible for the most drastic social upheaval in modern times, his fellow countryman was responsible for the most famous mathematical one of all time. But Lobachewsky lived a century earlier than Lenin, and no one thought of erecting special monuments to commemorate the revolution for which he was responsible. Instead, the Government relieved him of his job as head of the University of Kazan, at the age of fifty-four —this with no explanation whatsoever to a mathematician who had served the University well and was renowned throughout Europe. Lobachewsky survived this disgrace for eight years, long enough to see his son die and his own health fail. His last mathematical work had to be dictated, for, as a final blow of fate, he became blind.

At this point we should give credit also to Johann Bolyai, a Hungarian mathematician, who worked out the notion of a non-Euclidean geometry simultaneously with Lobachewsky, but independently. Here we have a recurrence of the Newton-Leibniz phenomenon, the sort of thing that usually occurs when mathematics is ripe for a new discovery. Since Lobachewsky's publications preceded Bolyai's, it is customary to name Lobachewsky as the discoverer of the concept of non-Euclidean geometry. Gauss, the great mathematical giant of the nineteenth century, is said by some to have discovered the same results as Lobachewsky and Bolyai, before either, and to have lacked the courage to publish facts so startling.

As a matter of fact, Saccheri, an Italian priest, had attempted a proof of Euclid's parallel postulate in 1733, in the course of which he actually discovered Lobachewskian geometry without being aware of it. Thus, just as in the case of the calculus the propitious moment for discovery was the age of Newton and Leibniz, so in the matter of non-Euclidean geometry the way was well paved for Lobachewsky or Bolyai or Gauss.

After Lobachewsky had constructed his own particular brand of logical non-Euclidean geometry, the German mathematician Riemann (1826–66) constructed another. Riemann postulated *no* parallels. In other words, he substituted for Euclid's parallel postulate the assumption that: *Through a point* P *outside a line l there is no line parallel to it;* that is, *every pair of lines in a plane must intersect.* When the term non-Euclidean geometry is used in mathematical literature, the geometries of Lobachewsky and Riemann are always meant, although the term might well be applied generically to any geometry that denies one or more axioms of Euclid. After the days of Lobachewsky and Riemann it became the fashion to challenge axioms. Einstein was led to invent his special theory of relativity by challenging classic axioms of physics.

Lest the assumption of Lobachewsky and Bolyai, or that of Riemann, seem too bizarre for the practical man, let us ask him to picture the infinite number of parallels to a line through an outside point as a sheaf so thin that it is not distinguishable from a single line. The Riemannian postulate is easier to imagine—for may not two lines that look 'parallel' meet at an infinite distance? If this interpretation of the two non-Euclidean geometries is too much for our readers to swallow, let us offer another. The modern point of view does not require that we interpret 'point,' 'line,' etc. in the ordinary way. We must first explain a preliminary concept or two. One of Euclid's axioms is 'a straight line is the shortest distance between two points.' That is the assumption for a *plane* surface, but what, then, is the shortest distance between two points on a spherical, cylindrical, or ellipsoidal (egg-shaped) surface? You can find out experimentally by stretching a string taut between two points of the surface. On a spherical surface, the shortest distance is a *great-circle arc,* the path followed by navigators in seeking short-est routes. It is the portion of a circle cut from the sphere by a geo-metric plane passing through the center of the sphere. Any plane section of a sphere will produce a circle, but only a plane through the center will produce a great circle. The shortest paths on other surfaces will be curves of various types. The mathematical name usually assigned to a shortest route is *geodesic.*

Since the geodesic for a plane is a line, this suggests interpreting the undefined term 'line' as geodesic. Let us then consider Riemann's

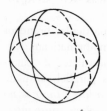

FIG. 124. Every pair of geodesics (great circles) of a sphere must intersect.

axiom first and put it in this way: *Through a given point* P *outside a geodesic l there is no geodesic which does not meet l.* If we pic-ture a *spherical* surface, this axiom will satisfy the demands of com-mon sense (fig. 124). All geodesics (great circles) on a sphere must meet one another, for their planes all go through the center of the sphere and must cut one another (fig. 124)

Let us state Lobachewsky's axiom in the form: *Through a given point* P *outside a geodesic l there are an infinite number of geo-desics 'parallel' to l.* The surface on which this makes sense is prob-ably unfamiliar to the general reader. We shall merely picture it for him. Figure 125a is a curve called a *tractrix.* If this is revolved about the axis, it forms a sort of double-trumpet surface (fig. 125b).

On this surface Lobachewsky's postulate can be pictured in common-sense fashion.

Which then is the correct geometry? This is an improper question —akin to the inquiry: Which is the correct theory of the universe? We have previously seen that a proper question is: Which is the most convenient theory? Which fits observed data best and involves

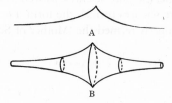

Fig. 125. This surface has a
Lobachewskian geometry.

the least computation and the simplest mathematics? As far as agreement with the result of experiment, the surprising fact is that all three geometries are equally good in the small finite domain of ordinary existence. In the Euclidean geometry there is the oft-quoted theorem, 'The sum of the angles of any triangle is 180°.' The corresponding theorems of Lobachewskian and Riemannian geometries give this sum as less than and greater than 180°, respectively. To test the 'truth' of these theorems, when they were first revealed, a huge triangle with vertices on three peaks in Germany was measured, and after that stellar measurements were brought into play. Even if it made no practical difference which geometry was the true one for small figures, it was felt that it might make some difference if the sides of a triangle were so huge that it would take centuries for light, traveling 186,000 miles a second, to traverse them. All experiments failed to bring about a decisive conclusion. The sum of the angles found was always so close to 180° that the excess or defect in each case could have been readily caused by the unavoidable imperfection in the measuring techniques. Even if the three theories fit experimental facts equally well, they are not equal in convenience of computation. For ordinary everyday purposes, the Euclidean system is the simplest, and hence we use it, not because it is the 'absolute' and only truth, but because it makes our work easier. The Riemannian system happens to be the simplest for use in the Einstein theory.

We hope that the present discussion may have helped to counteract a conventional notion concerning the nature of mathematics, that is, the idea that mathematics is purely a science of measurement. The point of view we have just developed should reveal mathematics as a science of *form*, which need not be restricted to number, space, quantity, or measurement, but is, instead, all-embracing, including logic, the pure sciences, as well as the applied sciences for which the pure sciences furnish the form. For this reason mathematics may be properly termed the 'Mother of Science.'

12

The Realm of Relativity

> If you read about Einstein's theory of relativity you
> will find many references to a peculiar person called
> 'the observer'—the man who has a habit of falling
> down lifts, or getting transported by aeroplanes travel-
> ing at 161,000 miles a second . . . The point is that
> all our knowledge of the external world as it is con-
> ceived to-day in physics can be demonstrated to him.
>
> EDDINGTON

IN ANY current discussion of mathematics or the sciences it mothers,
all roads must of necessity lead to relativity. Einstein's geometry of
the universe has been described as the 'greatest achievement of the
human intellect.' Like Euclid's geometry, it is an abstract science
based on postulates. Just as Euclid's axioms were formulated as the
result of observations of space configurations made by his Babylonian and Greek predecessors, Einstein's were formulated as his
interpretation of experiments carried on by physicists and astronomers prior to his day.

Einstein's forerunners adhered to the axioms laid down by Isaac
Newton and the facts that grew out of these assumptions—the im-
mense structure of classical physics. By 1880 this edifice began to
topple, not as a piece of pure mathematics, since mathematics tolerates any science with a complete set of consistent axioms, but as an
applied science describing natural phenomena. In Euclidean geometry the parallel postulate was the moot point out of which grew
the whole idea of non-Euclidean geometries and the notion of pos-
tulational systems. In Newtonian physics the source of trouble was
Newton's postulation of an *absolute space* and an *absolute time*.

The term 'absolute' describes a fact to which all observers agree;
for example, as a result of counting, people will agree that there are
420 pages in a certain book, or a dozen people seated at a table.
On the other hand, a 'relative' concept is one the estimation of
which may change from observer to observer. Washington is south

of New York City but east of San Francisco. The amount of steak a dollar will buy is relative to the year of purchase.

Is motion an absolute or relative fact? When two trains are side by side in a railroad station and you are a passenger in one of them, you often experience the sensation, when gazing through the window, that your train is moving backward. The fact that you have the station itself as a *frame of reference* enables you to decide that the other train has started while you, like the station, are still at rest. In two balloons flying above the clouds it would not be possible for an observer in one of them to say, when they pass one another, whether one or both are in motion or to decide positively on the direction of possible motion; e.g., both balloons might be moving in the same direction relative to the land below, except that the speed of one exceeds that of the other. As for the motion of heavenly bodies, it is evident that the difficulty of deciding which are at rest and which in motion would be even greater. There are no landmarks or signposts in the far regions of space. An astronomer can consider the speed of the Sun relative to the 'fixed stars,' but are there any stars that are really stationary, or is there anything in the universe we can be certain is fixed?

It would appear that the answer is negative and that all motion is relative. Velocity could only be absolute if there should exist one frame of reference for which the laws of nature would appear simpler to observers stationary in it than for those using any other background. Then this would constitute a *unique* or fixed frame of reference that could be singled out by any observer in the universe, and motion referred to it could be considered absolute. Newton and his successors knew that the laws of mechanics could furnish no such frame, since the laws appear the same, for example, to observers on Earth and those moving at uniform speeds with respect to the Earth. Scientists thought it might be otherwise with electromagnetic phenomena, in particular those involving light.

The 'wave motion' of light was supposed to take place in a medium called the *ether,* which was pictured as filling all of space. The ether theory was gratifying because the ether could be thought of as carrying electromagnetic waves and because it seemed to offer some fixed frame of reference with respect to which there might be absolute motion. In 1887, however, the American physicists Michelson and Morley obtained results that refused to fit into this picture.

To understand the basis of the classic experiment they performed, consider the mundane matter of rowing a boat on a stream that flows at the rate of 4 feet per second between parallel banks 90 feet apart. Two oarsmen, who both row at the rate of 5 feet per second in still water, set out from a point on one of the banks. The first man rows 90 feet downstream and back. Obviously, the current will help him on his way down and hinder him on his return, and his rates of rowing will be 9 feet per second and 1 foot per second respectively in going and returning, and the total time will be

$$\frac{90}{9} + \frac{90}{1} = 100 \text{ seconds.}$$

The second rower sets out simultaneously with the first, proceeding straight across to a point on the opposite bank, and then rows back. To row straight he will have to head diagonally backward (Fig. 126) in order to allow for the effect of the current. While he

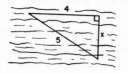

Fig. 126.

pushes the boat 5 feet, the current will carry it 4 feet as in the diagram, and his advance across the stream can be found by using the Pythagorean theorem:

$$x^2 + 4^2 = 5^2$$
$$x = 3$$

His rate of progress across the stream will be 3 feet per second and the time required will be $\frac{90}{3} = 30$ seconds. The story will be the same for the return trip; therefore his total time will be 60 seconds and he will return considerably ahead of the other oarsman.

The same sort of thing can be expected to occur in any race of this type. The man rowing across the stream will have the advantage. If the stream were the ether in which the Earth is moving, the theory was that there would be an 'ether current' somewhat analogous to the breeze felt by a man driving a car. To measure the speed of the ether wind, Michelson and Morley devised an experiment in which the 'oarsmen' were to be two light rays, one of which was to go down the ether stream and back, while the other was to travel the same distance across it and back. The rays were sent on the journey back by reflection from suitably placed mirrors.

Instead of resulting in the earlier return of the transverse light ray, both rays arrived back *at the same time!* The experiment was repeated again and again to take account of any possible errors. Refinements were added so that an ether current as small as $\frac{1}{5}$ kilometer per second would have been detected. The results were still negative! To all appearances, the Earth stood permanently at rest in the ether, which, of course, contradicted the known fact that it speeds around the Sun at nearly 20 miles a second.

The Irish scientist Fitzgerald and the Dutch physicist Lorentz arrived independently at the same explanation of this phenomenon. They suggested that lengths must *contract* in the direction of motion by an amount just sufficient to compensate for the handicap of the longitudinal light ray. If we think of the rival rays as having a normal speed of 5 units per second (each unit equal to about 37,200 miles) in some stream with a speed of 4 units per second, a contraction of longitudinal lengths to $\frac{3}{5}$ of their original size would explain the simultaneity of return. The transverse ray would require 60 seconds for a 90 unit crossing and return. If the 90 units downstream contracted to $\frac{3}{5} \times 90 = 54$, then the total trip down and back would take $\dfrac{54}{9} + \dfrac{54}{1} = 60$ seconds, which checks with the outcome of the Michelson-Morley experiment.

Quite different empirical facts of nineteenth-century science indicated that the difficulties revealed by the Michelson-Morley experiment were not isolated failures of classic physical theories but actually pervaded electricity and optics. We have indicated that Lorentz and Fitzgerald pointed out a partial solution for the apparent contradictions. It was left to Einstein to proclaim in his revolutionary paper of 1905 that the difficulties involved in all the classic experiments with light could best be removed by also scrapping the traditional concepts of space and time. The axioms of the special, or *restricted theory of relativity,* as enunciated by Einstein are:

I. *The principle of relativity:* The laws of physics are the same whether stated in one frame of reference or any other moving with uniform velocity relative to the first.

II. The *velocity of light* is *constant,* that is, the same as measured by all observers in the universe, and is independent of its source.

The first of these postulates is equivalent to the impossibility of defining absolute motion, for to do so we would have to single out a special frame of reference like the ether and give evidence of laws holding only in this frame and no other; this would of course be contrary to principle I, which calls for every natural law to hold in all systems in uniform motion relative to one another.

As for the second axiom, if we consider it a *physical law* that light should have a certain velocity, its constancy would follow from postulate I. That the speed of light is independent of the source is, furthermore, an assumption based on considerable empirical evidence. To understand this experimental basis, we recall that classic theory considered light a wave phenomenon in the ether. *Sound* is actually transmitted by waves propagated in air or some other material medium, and numerous examples can be adduced to show that its speed is neither increased nor decreased by motion of the source.

If supersonic flight becomes general, planes will arrive before they are heard. The velocity of the plane adds not an iota to the speed of the sound it emits. The series of vibrations or 'spheres of disturbance' (see page 61) travel out into the air with a certain characteristic speed whether the source is moving or at rest. On the other hand, speeds of material bodies in the plane acquire the same speed as the plane itself by the 'law of inertia.' If a bomb were dropped from the plane and there were no air resistance, the bomb would be carried along horizontally with the same speed as the plane. At the same time it would descend gradually because of 'gravity' so that it would hit just below the plane, if there were no air friction. If the bomb were propelled forward, its horizontal velocity would be the sum of the speed of propulsion and plane velocity, so that it would fall in front of the plane. The speed of the bomb would be aided by the plane's motion, but the speed of sound is unaffected.

Although this velocity is uninfluenced, the plane's motion has some effect on a sound issuing from it. It seems not to hurry the 'spheres of disturbance' on their way but to push them closer together, that is, shorten the wave-length or *raise the pitch* of the sound advancing in the direction of the plane. For sound in the opposite direction the spheres are pulled away so that pitch is lowered. A trained ear can actually discern whether a train is approaching or receding by the sound of its whistle.

Light waves do not move in a material medium, but Einstein assumed the same independence of the source that existed for sound. That the 'pitch' of light waves is affected by motion is backed up by the experimental *Doppler effect,* the shift in the spectrum of rapidly moving stars or nebulae. There is some empirical evidence, too, of the lack of effect of the source on the speed of light. *Double stars* are stars of about the same mass, close together and revolving about one another. If the speed of the source helped or hindered, then the time taken for light to reach the Earth from the member of the pair moving toward us would be shorter than that for the receding partner. Actually observations show that there is no such effect.

As for the mathematical consequences of the Einstein axioms, let us simplify matters by considering at first only motions on a single straight line or in any direction parallel to it. Then an event taking place somewhere on this

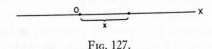

Fig. 127.

line can be described by telling *where* and *when* it occurs. Let O be our point of reference or origin, and let x symbolize the distance from O at which an event occurs and t its time. Next we consider speeds. We can measure them in miles per hour, meters per minute, etc., but since the speed of light is a basic constant of the special relativity theory, we shall take it as one unit and use the letter u to symbolize the relative speed of an observer moving past us on a track parallel to OX in figure 127. The consequences of the Einstein theory are that *distance* and *time* are relative and hence measurements of them by another observer need not agree with ours. We shall not give the mathematical proof, but merely assert that the formulas connecting our distance and time measurements and those of the observer with speed u are

$$x' = \frac{x - ut}{\sqrt{1 - u^2}} \qquad t' = \frac{t - ux}{\sqrt{1 - u^2}}$$

where x' and t' symbolize his measurements, x and t ours. These formulas are called a *Lorentz transformation,* since Lorentz had arrived at them in connection with the contraction theory mentioned above. Einstein employed the same formulas but gave a different interpretation to the results.

If we examine the denominator, $\sqrt{1 - u^2}$, we see that the value of u must be numerically less than 1 if we are to get any *real* meaning from the formulas. If $u = 1$, the denominators are zero and division by zero is meaningless. If u is numerically greater than 1, the denominators are imaginary. The exclusion of values for u numerically equal to or greater than 1 signifies that *no material body can have a velocity equal to or greater than the speed of light*. This is an important theorem of the special theory of relativity.

Consider a case where the speed of another observer, relative to us, has the permissible value, $u = \frac{3}{5}$. Consider the following two events:

$$\text{event i} \qquad x = 0 \qquad t = 0$$
$$\text{event ii} \qquad x = 4 \qquad t = 2$$

This means that the first event occurred at our origin at 'zero hour' and the second occurred 2 seconds later 4 units away ($186{,}000 \times 4 = 744{,}000$ miles away). Then, using the Lorentz transformation, we can find out what the other observer has to say. For event i,

$$x' = \frac{0 - \frac{3}{5} \times 0}{\sqrt{1 - \left(\frac{3}{5}\right)^2}} = 0 \qquad\qquad t' = \frac{0 - \frac{3}{5} \times 0}{\sqrt{1 - \left(\frac{3}{5}\right)^2}} = 0$$

We agree on this event, but for event ii

$$x' = \frac{4 - \frac{3}{5} \times 2}{\sqrt{1 - \left(\frac{3}{5}\right)^2}} = 3\tfrac{1}{2} \qquad\qquad t' = \frac{2 - \frac{3}{5} \times 4}{\sqrt{1 - \left(\frac{3}{5}\right)^2}} = -\tfrac{1}{2}$$

According to the other observer's space standards the second event is not as far away. Even more startling is the estimate $t' = -\frac{1}{2}$, which signifies that in his opinion not only is the time interval between the two events much shorter, but event ii occurred before event i, as indicated by the minus sign, since a positive t signifies time *after* the zero hour, a negative t, time *before*. Thus we see that two observers in the universe may be in complete disagreement on *space* and *time* measurements as well as on the order of events.

When Einstein first pronounced these facts, a Vienna daily carried a headline 'Minute in Danger!' To combat such a fear, we must point out that $u = \frac{3}{5}$ is not an ordinary speed like that encountered in everyday motions like walking, driving, flying, etc.

because it represents $\frac{3}{5} \times 186,000 = 111,600$ miles per second. Even the Earth as it speeds through the heavens covers a mere 20 miles per second relative to the Sun! And so the startling relativity results apply not to observers in trains, planes, even rockets, but to beta particles, for example, which are electrons shot out of the nuclei of radioactive atoms at speeds almost as huge as that of light. The point of view of an individual imagined to inhabit a beta particle would differ so radically from that of the scientist observing him that social life between them could be nothing but a series of violent disagreements!

To see if these observers can agree on anything, or, in other words, to try to find some absolute or *invariant* entities, let us consider a set of observers moving with the respective speeds

$$u = \frac{4}{5}, \qquad -\frac{4}{5}, \qquad \frac{3}{5}, \qquad \frac{12}{13}, \qquad -\frac{7}{25}$$

relative to us, positive and negative velocities signifying motion to our right and left, respectively. Let our observations give

$$\text{event I} \quad x = 0 \quad t = 0$$
$$\text{event II} \quad x = 8 \quad t = 10$$

As before, all observers will agree on event I. Substitution in the Lorentz transformation will yield the following different estimates of the where and when of event II:

speed	u	0	$\dfrac{4}{5}$	$-\dfrac{4}{5}$	$\dfrac{3}{5}$	$\dfrac{12}{13}$	$-\dfrac{7}{25}$
distance	x	8	0	$\dfrac{80}{3}$	$\dfrac{5}{2}$	$-\dfrac{16}{5}$	$\dfrac{135}{12}$
time	t	10	6	$\dfrac{82}{3}$	$\dfrac{13}{2}$	$\dfrac{34}{5}$	$\dfrac{153}{12}$

No invariant is obvious from the table, but if we compute t^2, x^2, and $t^2 - x^2$ in each case, we obtain

t^2	100	36	$\dfrac{6724}{9}$	$\dfrac{169}{4}$	$\dfrac{1156}{25}$	$\dfrac{23409}{144}$
x^2	64	0	$\dfrac{6400}{9}$	$\dfrac{25}{4}$	$\dfrac{256}{25}$	$\dfrac{18225}{144}$
$t^2 - x^2$	36	36	36	36	36	36

Thus, although time and space measurements vary from observer to observer, all will agree that

$$t^2 - x^2 = 36$$

$$\sqrt{t^2 - x^2} = 6$$

It can be shown that this is a general truth, that no matter what the speed u of an observer is, and no matter what event (x, t) we measure, his measurement (x', t') will be such that

$$(t')^2 - (x')^2 = t^2 - x^2$$

This can be proved by performing a little algebraic manipulation on the Lorentz transformation.

This means that although time and space are relative, a certain *mixture* of them is absolute. It is an error to think that because Einstein's theory is called Relativity, all measurements are relative. The

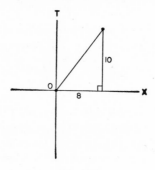

FIG. 128.

mathematician Whitehead chose the name 'separation' for the absolute invariant $\sqrt{t^2 - x^2}$. We can see why and gain more understanding of this new space-time mixture if we chart events on a Cartesian graph. Figure 128 shows that when the events $(0, 0)$ and $(8, 10)$ are points on such a graph, the actual *distance* between them as given by the Pythagorean theorem is

$$\sqrt{10^2 + 8^2} = \sqrt{164}$$

The separation is obtained by changing the sign in the Pythagorean theorem

$$\sqrt{10^2 - 8^2} = 6$$

and can be thought of as a sort of 'pseudo-distance.'

Plotting events on a Cartesian graph and recognizing separation as algebraically similar to distance gives one justification for the name of this invariant. The picture introduces another new element, for we see that to graph events occurring at points of a one-dimensional world gives rise to a two-dimensional picture. If we extend the world of events to all those taking place in a single *plane,* the Cartesian picture will be three-dimensional. If we picture the floor

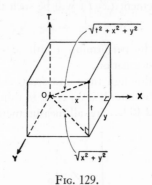

Fig. 129.

of a room as part of the plane of events (Fig. 129), then the values of x and y will be the distances from the side (left) and back walls respectively. The graph of an event (x, y, t) will be a point in the room, the value of the time t being represented by the distance above the floor. The graph of an event will be somewhere in the room on a vertical line through the point in the floor where it occurs.

If the two events are $(0, 0, 0)$—the corner at 'zero hour'—and (x, y, t)—anywhere, anytime—then

$$\text{Pythagorean distance} = \sqrt{t^2 + x^2 + y^2}$$
$$\text{separation} = \sqrt{t^2 - x^2 - y^2}$$

Again, algebra will prove that Pythagorean distance varies with the observer, but that separation is invariant.

To picture events occurring at points of a three-dimensional space, a four-dimensional scheme would be necessary. We are not compelled to resort to visualization in this case, but can nevertheless use the associated invariant,

$$\text{separation} = \sqrt{t^2 - x^2 - y^2 - z^2}$$

numerically and algebraically, thus accepting the idea advanced in 1908 by the mathematician Minkowski. He was the first to state that it is logically simpler to regard the universe as a four-dimensional *space-time continuum* rather than to divide our experiences artificially according to unrelated spatial and temporal aspects, especially since different observers will hold divergent opinions on how the division should be effected.

To return to our one-dimensional world and two-dimensional space-time picture, let us compute the separation of (0, 0) and (4, 2). It is equal to

$$\sqrt{4 - 16} = \sqrt{-12}$$

This is an *imaginary* separation! Whenever x is greater in numerical value than t, the separation will be imaginary. Since the unit is equal to the speed of light, $x = 4$ is the distance light will travel in 4 seconds. Then, with the pair of events (0, 0) and (4, 2), if a light signal were sent from the place where the first event occurs (the origin), describing that event, it could not arrive at the place where the second event occurs *prior to* this second occurrence. Whatever happens at the first locality cannot be a 'warning' to the second, influence it, or exert a 'force' on it in any way. In other words, there can be no *causal* connection between the two events.

A little earlier we saw that a different observer would measure the event (4, 2) as $(3\frac{1}{2}, -\frac{1}{2})$. Still he would obtain the separation as

$$\sqrt{\frac{1}{4} - \frac{49}{4}} = \sqrt{-12}$$

and so would all observers in uniform relative motion. Now we see why the fact that the second observer does not agree on the order of the two events does not matter in this case. The points where the events occurred will, in any frame of reference, be too far apart for causal connection or exertion of any 'force,' since the distance will have to be numerically greater than the time to ensure a negative value of $t^2 - x^2$ and an imaginary separation. This is just another way of saying that *no force can be propagated with a speed greater than that of light.*

In general, then, an imaginary separation signifies no causal connection. By contrast, a real separation would permit signaling. It can be shown algebraically, by using the Lorentz transformation, that in this particular case, although observers may disagree on the length of time intervals, they will never disagree on the *order* of events. When separation is real, then, a causal connection between two events is possible.

We have been considering events occurring at *different* places. If we were following the life history of an individual, however, different events might occur at the *same* place as far as his measurements are concerned. (If the individual were a human being with reference frame on Earth, his personal motion in space would be so tiny in comparison with our unit of 186,000 miles that for practical purposes, he could consider himself permanently at rest). Then for him event $\text{I} = (0,0)$ and event $\text{II} = (0, t)$

$$\text{separation} = \sqrt{t^2 - 0^2} = t$$

The separation of the events would be identical with his measure of the time between them. Hence, for self-observation, *separation is a synonym for time,* and the choice of name for this invariant has additional justification. We remark, in passing, that separation could never be imaginary for events happening to the same individual, since $x = 0$ in such a case, and hence only t^2, which has to be positive, contributes to the value under the square root sign.

For an observer whose world is moving past with speed *u,* if $x = 0$

$$t' = \frac{t - 0 \cdot x}{\sqrt{1 - u^2}} = \frac{t}{\sqrt{1 - u^2}}$$

or, the first observer's time t is given by

$$t = t' \sqrt{1 - u^2}$$

and hence is *less* than the time as recorded by any other observer because the factor $\sqrt{1 - u^2}$ is less than 1 in value.

The measurement by an individual of the time interval between two events occurring at the same place is called the *proper time* for the individual and, as just indicated, is less than the estimate made by any other observer. It is the time as measured by his own clock and, as it gives much smaller estimates of intervals than the clocks of observers moving at tremendous speeds relative to him, the latter observers will say his clock 'runs slow.'

In the early days of relativity, spinners of popular-science yarns had as a favorite plot the tale of two friends parted in youth, one of the pair traveling into space at a velocity close to that of light, while the other remained quietly at home on Earth. When the wanderer eventually returned from his lengthy journey he was still to all appearances a boy in his teens, although by earthly reckoning he had to be counted an octogenarian. His stay-at-home friend looked old enough to be his great-grandfather.

The explanation of this apparent paradox was that the traveler took his clock with him. It was at rest relative to his surroundings and measured his proper time. If we think of his speed as being 0.99 (that is 99% of the velocity of light), then he will think of himself as at rest and consider the Earth to be receding from him with this speed. If the boys part at the age of 8, and 70 years elapse on Earth, then the proper time for the wanderer as measured by his own clock will be given by

$$
\begin{aligned}
t &= t' \sqrt{1 - u^2} \\
&= 70 \sqrt{1 - (0.99)^2} \\
&= 70 \times 0.14 \\
&= 9.8 \text{ years}
\end{aligned}
$$

and he will be only 18 years of age by his own standards, while his friend will be 78.

This is naturally a fantasy, but has some scientific justification in the fact that the human heart vibrates and so, like a pendulum, is a clock. Hence its beating should also be affected by rapid motion if we are to be consistent about the relativity of time. If an individual is in rapid motion relative to the Earth, then by his own standards his heart may beat 72 times per minute. Since the results of *counting* are absolute, we will count 72 heart vibrations, but in a longer interval as measured by our own clocks, for the traveler was considering one minute of his proper time. Put otherwise, we consider all his clocks to run slow, his heart being one of them. Since the same retardation affects all the metabolic processes in the body, it can be said that the wanderer 'ages' less than the person remaining at home.

To consider other consequences of the special relativity theory, let us return for a moment to Minkowski's space-time picture, limiting ourselves once more to events on a one-dimensional straight line as graphed in a two-dimensional chart. Let the creatures existing in the one-dimensional space be insects crawling along OX (they cannot jump or fly). The events occurring in the life of any insect will form a continuous curve, the graph of each event lying on a line perpendicular to OX at the point x where the event occurs. In figure 130, P is the graph of the event at p, Q the representation of

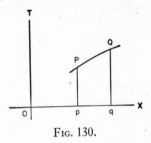

Fɪɢ. 130.

that at q, etc. Different insects will have different curves of events, or *world-lines*, as Minkowski called them. If this picture is generalized, individuals existing in three-dimensional space will have world-lines in a four-dimensional space-time continuum, which is a convenient mathematical abstraction, not something to be visualized.

In the two-dimensional space-time continuum, an insect that remains permanently at rest at the origin will have the t-axis (OT) as its world-line, and if it is at rest at any other point, the world-line will be parallel to the t-axis. There are no world-lines parallel to the x-axis because this would signify that time stands still while the insect moves! Such lines are not world-lines, but can be considered 'cross sections' of the insect's space-time. They give all possible insect locations for a specific time, since t is constant along these lines, while x varies.

If the insect starts at the origin and moves to the right with a constant speed of ½ unit per second, its progress chart will be

$$t \quad 0 \quad 1 \quad 2 \quad 4 \quad \text{etc.}$$
$$x \quad 0 \quad \tfrac{1}{2} \quad 1 \quad 2$$

This is no ordinary insect to be sure, but some atomic particle moving at ½ unit $= 93{,}000$ miles per second. Then the formula connecting distance and time for this 'insect' is

$$x = \tfrac{1}{2}t$$

This is the equation of its world-line, which is straight. If the insect moves with variable speed its world-line is broken or curved. If its speed is any constant k, the equation of its world-line is

$$x = kt$$

Since material things can never achieve the speed of light, k must be numerically less than 1. The equations

$$x = t \quad \text{and} \quad x = -t$$

represent the world-lines of light rays moving right or left from the origin. All other world-lines, straight or curved, are thus restricted to the unshaded sector of the space-time continuum pictured in figure 131. Only a portion of space-time is allotted to material

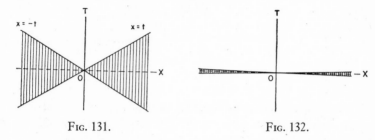

FIG. 131.   FIG. 132.

objects. If we use a more *human* scale in our graph, this restriction will appear slight. If the unit on the X-axis is taken as 1 mile instead of 186,000, the shaded or 'forbidden' area will look like that in figure 132, except that it will be a much thinner sector, and therefore exclude only a small portion of the space-time continuum.

If we study a particular world-line like

$$x = \tfrac{5}{13}t$$

the chart for insect progress is

t	0	13	26	39	52	$\cdots$	104
x	0	5	10	15	20	$\cdots$	40

For the first pair of events, *separation* is

$$\sqrt{13^2 - 5^2} = 12$$

and since the intervals are equal it will be 12 for every consecutive pair. Computing the separation of the first and last events

$$\sqrt{104^2 - 40^2} = 96$$

which is what common sense leads us to expect, since there are 8 intervals of 12 each.

In geometry we learn that a straight line segment is the *shortest* distance between two points. In contrast to this it can be proved that

separation obeys an opposite law. A straight line segment represents
the *longest* separation between two points. If a world-line is curved
or broken (fig. 133) the separation of the last event from the first
is *greater* than the sum of the separations between successive events

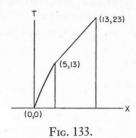

Fig. 133.

measured along the world-line. We shall not give a general proof
but, for the sake of simplicity, limit ourselves to an illustration. Take
the events (0,0), (5, 13) and (13, 23). The separations are

$$\text{I to II} \quad \sqrt{13^2 - 5^2} = 12$$

$$\text{II to III} \quad \sqrt{10^2 - 8^2} = 6$$

$$\text{I to III} \quad \sqrt{23^2 - 13^2} = \sqrt{360} = 18.96$$

The separation of I and III is almost 19, while the sum of the separations is only 18. To realize the significance of this fact, notice that
the world-line from I to II represents a motion covering 5 units of
distance in 13 seconds of time, that is, a motion with speed 5/13.
Similarly, the world-line from to II to III pictures a motion with
speed 4/5. Then the broken world-line from I to II to III shows the
progress of an insect moving *non*-uniformly. It would start with one
velocity and later change abruptly to a more rapid one. By contrast
the straight world-line from I to III represents a *uniform* motion
with speed 13/23.

So it is that insects whose world-lines are straight, signifying that
they are either *at rest* or in *uniform* motion, will have greater separations than if these lines were broken or curved. For an object at
rest, separation has been shown to signify personal or proper time.
If a body is in uniform motion relative to an observer, relativity
permits an individual situated on this body to judge himself at rest
and the observer in motion. Therefore, once again separation becomes that individual's personal time. In the light of this equiv-

alence of separation and personal time, the fact that separation is greatest along a straight line can be stated as: *Proper time between two events will be a maximum for bodies at rest or in uniform motion.* This rule of behavior has sometimes been called the 'Law of Cosmic Laziness,' and in relativity theory takes the place of the 'path of least resistance.'

One consequence of the Einstein theory is that, in addition to the fact that distance and time measurements depend on the observer making them, there is relativity of *mass* as well. Newton described the mass of a body as the quantity of matter it contains and defined it by means of his second law of motion in terms of 'force' and change in *velocity*. Since velocity is no longer absolute in relativity, and 'gravitational force' is ruled out by the general relativity theory, which we shall shortly discuss, we should expect a modification of the concept of mass.

Long before Einstein, physicists J. J. Thomson and W. Kaufmann had found that the movement of electrons with a very high velocity u causes an apparent increase of mass equal to approximately $\frac{1}{2}mu^2$. The mathematics of relativity agrees with this, for it indicates that if m is the mass of a body at rest in a particular frame of reference, which has speed u relative to an observer, this observer will obtain

$$\frac{m}{\sqrt{1 - u^2}}$$

as his estimate of the mass. Since $u = 1$ for the speed of light, u is a fairly small fraction even for high electron speeds. For such small values of u, algebra indicates that

$$\frac{m}{\sqrt{1 - u^2}} = m + \tfrac{1}{2}mu^2 \quad \text{(approximately)}$$

This means that the original mass m is increased by $\frac{1}{2}mu^2$, the same fact obtained in the experiments of Thomson and Kaufmann.

For example, if $m = 1$ and $u = \dfrac{7}{25}$

$$\frac{m}{\sqrt{1 - u^2}} = \tfrac{25}{24} = 1.04$$

$$m + \tfrac{1}{2}mu^2 = 1 + \tfrac{49}{1250} = 1.04, \text{ a } 4\% \text{ increase in mass}$$

The expression $\frac{1}{2}mu^2$ is called the *kinetic energy* of a body, that is, the amount of work it is capable of doing by virtue of its motion.

The term *potential energy* is used for the work it can do by virtue of its position, for example, the work possibility inherent in a compressed spring or a rock at the edge of a cliff. In the expression $m + \frac{1}{2}mu^2$, if the second term is *energy* and the terms are to be combined, the first term must also represent some sort of energy. Since m is the *rest* mass, it is like the rock or spring at rest, and hence m can be thought of as potential energy. Then, in the expression above, the observer's measure of the mass of a body is partly potential and partly kinetic energy, but it is energy of one kind or another. This is the principle of the *equivalence of mass and energy* used in atomic theory.

The term $\frac{1}{2}mu^2$ is a good approximation if u is small, but even if u is as small as $\frac{1}{1,000}$, for example, its value in ordinary units like centimeters per second would be huge—3×10^7—and when squared, tremendously greater—9×10^{14}. If this figure is multiplied by $\frac{1}{2}m$ even for m as tiny as electron mass, the value of $\frac{1}{2}mu^2$, increase in mass, will be enormous in terms of ordinary energy units.

Although the Einstein formula

$$E = mc^2$$

is used in a somewhat different connotation, where matter is 'annihilated' and converted into energy, there is a kinship in form to

$$\tfrac{1}{2}mu^2$$

in that we square a speed to obtain the energy associated with a mass, the speed c signifying that of light, which is 1 unit in relativity reasoning but 3×10^{10} measured in centimeters per second. Hence $c^2 = 9 \times 10^{20}$, so that even if m is the tiny mass of a subatomic particle, the product of its size by 9×10^{20} will be enormous, a fact basic in the atomic bomb and the contemplated peace-time uses of atomic energy.

Such are the facts of the restricted theory of relativity. It is called *restricted* or *special,* because all observers are assumed to have *uniform* velocities with respect to one another. Constancy of speed and direction is an especially simple situation. The general theory of relativity, launched by Einstein in 1917, takes into account frames of reference with *variable* velocity relative to one another. The mathematics involved is not, as originally claimed, so difficult that it is comprehensible to only a dozen mortals. Nevertheless it is technical in nature and does not lend itself to lucid exposition in short accounts. For this reason we shall limit ourselves to a presentation of the basic assumptions and the eventual conclusions to which they lead.

The purpose of the general theory, like that of the special, is to distinguish the subjective impressions of individual observers from the reality of the thing being observed. By the addition of only one new postulate called the 'Principle of Equivalence,' Einstein leads us into the mathematical depths from which emerges a physical concept more adequate than Newton's 'law of gravitation' and one which is able to explain experimental facts that had defied classic theory and puzzled physicists and astronomers for a long time.

To see why 'gravitational force' is not absolute but a matter of relative opinion depending on who is making the observation, we may just as well consider the first observer of the phenomenon, Newton himself, along with the famous falling apple. Suppose that you, instead of Newton, are an observer and that you are located in an elevator with opaque, shut doors. Unknown to you, the supports break and the controls fail. Emulating Newton, you let go of an apple. It remains at rest, poised in mid-air, and hence *you* observe *no force* on it. This will happen because you, the elevator, and the apple are all falling at the same rate without your knowledge of it.

In your frame of reference, then, things do not fall, and no special force or influence makes its presence known. Relative to your frame of reference, there is no gravitation. Just as $+ 32$ will balance $- 32$ in addition, giving zero as sum, gravitational force, as we conceive it, is apparently neutralized by the elevator's motion, and hence must be numerically equivalent to it, but opposite in effect.

This is the basis of Einstein's famous Principle of Equivalence, which states: If attention is confined to a small region of space, *a gravitational field at rest is equivalent to a frame of reference moving with uniform acceleration in a field free of gravitation,* and it is impossible to devise any experiment that will distinguish between the two.

This means that any observer, like the man in the elevator, can select a frame of reference moving in such a way that in his *immediate neighborhood* all gravitational effects are neutralized, and consequently, in this small vicinity, the restricted theory of relativity holds true. By small neighborhood we mean a tiny *space-time* region surrounding a point or event in his world-line, so that to apply the special theory in the presence of matter and its accompanying 'gravitational field,' the observer can pick a neutralizing frame of reference, which will serve for a short time only. He must change this frame as time passes, for he will be in a new space-time region even if he considers himself at rest. For example, in the two-dimensional space-time previously pictured, an observer at rest had a world-line parallel to the *t*-axis. As time passed the events would be pictured on different portions of this line and would occupy different neighborhoods of the two-dimensional space-time world.

In the observer's opinion, if his world-line is straight, signifying rest or uniform motion, the observer's separation will be a maximum, as previously explained. Since separation is invariant, other observers will also agree that it is a maximum, but may not consider the world-line straight because they may not be in the same space-time neighborhood. (An insect may be remote from another in the one-dimensional space previously pictured, or he may live in the same region of this space, but be born long after the first insect has died, etc., so that the time location is different. Even if he lives at the same spot and stays forever at rest, if he lives in a different era, according to the restricted theory, his world-line will be a *different* portion of the parallel to the *t*-axis.) Thus observers who exist far apart in three-dimensional space or are widely separated in time—or in other words those who are remote when the customary mixture of space-time measures their separation—will agree on maximum properties but not on 'straightness' versus *curvature*.

As a result, one fact of the restricted theory must be modified, namely the 'law of cosmic laziness.' The route for maximum separation need not be straight. In the general theory, we say that the presence of matter *distorts* space-time in its neighborhood, and for this reason the world-line of maximum separation (the customary mathematical name for such a line is a *geodesic*) is distorted into a *curve*. Let us picture a crumpling of the paper or two-dimensional space-time on which figures 130-133 are drawn. The straight lines in the diagrams would be wrinkled into curves along with the paper on which they are drawn.

According to Newton, a planet describes an elliptic path around the Sun because there is an attractive 'gravitational force' between Sun and planet, but according to the general theory of relativity, the matter in the Sun causes distortion of the space-time in its neighborhood, and the planet's world-line of maximum separation has to be curved in order to conform to the curved contour on which it is drawn. All we see in three-dimensional space is the elliptic orbit, which is the 'projection' of this world-line, one view of a mechanical drawing of the space-time curve.

Thus, the notion of gravitational force is relinquished. Curved paths or other effects attributed to it by Newton occur only because following particular routes leads to maximum separation in space-time or, stated otherwise, because bodies follow the 'law of cosmic laziness.' Our education has conditioned us to believe to such a degree in a force tugging at things and making them fall that it is hard to get away from the idea. Surely it is easier to believe that we or the other planets are just lazy and fall 'into the groove,' rather than that the Sun exercises some remote control, holding invisible reins 93,000,000 miles or more in length.

Perhaps we can help ourselves out by an analogy. Before 500 B.C. the belief that our Earth was flat was universal. Even later the idea of sphericity was slow in gaining acceptance. Maps were made in accordance with the theory of a flat Earth, and served very well until the new countries discovered and added to the flat map began to introduce inconsistencies. A *Mercator's projection* is a flat map somewhat like this. If you examine one, you will notice the apparent hugeness of Greenland in comparison to its size as mapped on a globe. The ancients did not use a sphere to map the Earth and hence would have supposed that the flat maps just described gave the true size of Greenland. Inevitably, explorers of this region would report that journeys there seemed much shorter than maps indicated. Believing the map to be a correct representation of geographic facts, they might invent a theory that there was a *force* in this part of the world causing distances to shrink whenever explorers appeared on the scene. Our modern knowledge of the spherical shape of the earth would eliminate this theory, show that no force of the sort exists, and indicate that the effect was caused by the curvature of the earth. This is a two-dimensional analogy indicating how a phenomenon produced by curvature might appear, at first conjecture, to be caused by some 'force.'

Space-time is curved here and there, whenever matter is present. The two-dimensional analogy would be the surface of the skin with blisters on certain spots, or a golf course with hummocks drawing a ball off its straight course. The combined distortion of space-time by all the matter in the universe causes it to bend back on itself and close. As a crude two-dimensional analogy, if we take a flat sector of a circle (fig. 134) and curve it sufficiently, we can close it so as to get a conical drinking cup. A cross section of this cup would be circular or oval, a geometric curve that might be described as *finite, but unbounded,* since we can go round and round it in spite of its limited length. This is a one-dimensional cross section of a closed two-dimensional continuum. In the Einstein theory *space* is considered a *finite but unbounded* three-dimensional cross section of a closed four-dimensional space-time continuum. (This is not closed in the *time* direction, much as the conical drinking glass is not,

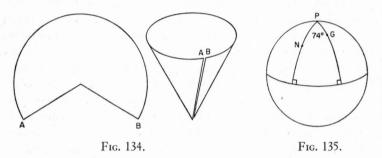

FIG. 134.   FIG. 135.

for some of its cross sections would be two straight lines in V-formation meeting at one end and open at the other.)

Still another item of the general relativity theory becomes clearer through a two-dimensional analogy. If we consider geometry on the surface of a sphere, straight lines would be replaced by great-circle arcs, for these would be shortest distances, or geodesics (term used for minimum *or* maximum, that is for extrema). A triangle would be bounded by three great-circle arcs and the sum of its angles would be greater than 180°. We can visualize, for example (fig. 135), the spherical triangle formed by the half of the prime meridian extending from North Pole to equator, the same part of the meridian through New York City, and the slice of the equator between the feet of these meridians. The angles at the feet, that is between meridian and equator, would each be 90° and the angle at the pole would equal 74°, the longitude of New York, so that the total would be 254°. On the sphere we have a two-dimensional continuum with a non-Euclidean geometry of the Riemannian type. If, however, we think of the space inside and outside the sphere, we have a three-dimensional continuum with straight line geodesics, and we can go back to Euclid after all. By analogy, in the four-dimensional space-time continuum of relativity, distances obey a non-Euclidean geometry. Again, Euclidean geometry can be employed by going outside, but in this case, six extra dimensions have to be added. Since it is all a matter of abstract terminology, we do not have to trouble ourselves as to how this would look.

The ultimate test of a theory is its application, and the Einstein theory has been amply backed up in this way. Where speed is small compared to that of light, or 'weak' gravitational fields exist because of 'small' masses like the Earth, Einstein's predictions agree with Newton's. To find phenomena inconsistent with Newtonian mechanics Einstein had to go beyond mundane space-time neighborhoods. His first case was that of the planet Mercury, close to the Sun, a relatively large mass with a considerable gravitational field to which Mercury is strongly exposed. This planet does not move exactly as predicted by Newton's theory, for then it would describe virtually the same elliptical orbit over and over again relative to the fixed stars. Newton allowed a slight 'perturbation' or shift in the orbit due to the influence of other planets, but the *observed* amount of shift in the orbit was greater than the classic theory permitted, and the discrepancy had never been satisfactorily explained. The calculations of the orbit based on the Einstein theory agree exactly with observation.

The second test of the Einstein theory was more impressive because it was a matter of *complete prediction* from the theory, of facts never before observed. It concerned the effect of the curvature of space on the path of light rays. As light from a distant star passes near the Sun, it is bent toward the Sun. The amount of this deflection as computed by Einstein was double that figured from Newtonian theory. This cannot be checked ordinarily, since the Sun's brilliance makes it impossible to see the star rays passing near, but total eclipses furnish an opportunity. British expeditions to observe such eclipses in Brazil and West Africa in 1919 as well as observations of later eclipses confirmed Einstein's prediction without a doubt.

The third of the tests was connected with a fact mentioned earlier in this discussion, that the vibration of an atom is like the oscillation of a clock pendulum. The mathematics of the general theory indicated that the atom clock is slowed up near the Sun compared to a clock of the same atom on Earth. The effect should be a shift in its spectrum toward the slow or red end. For the Sun this shift is too slight to lend itself readily to experimental verification, but there is a companion star of Sirius, known as a 'white dwarf,' for which it is believed that the density is as much as a ton per cubic inch. Consequently it sets up a gravitational field of so great an intensity in its neighborhood as to make it ideal for testing the hypothesis of spectral shift. Observations made by the astronomer Adams at Mt. Wilson agreed with Einstein's prediction. Very fine measurements made by Evershed in 1927 gave evidence of a shift toward the red even in the vicinity of the Sun, where the amount is slight.

We might have expected that with the acclaim of the general theory, Einstein could have rested from his labors, but instead he has continued along the lines of still further generalization in order to include electromagnetic phenomena, since he holds that the electric and magnetic field strengths are also *relative* and not absolute. Students of elementary classical physics learn that there is an analogy between certain mechanical and electromagnetic laws. To take a specific instance, we refer to Newton's formula for gravitational attraction (page 152)

$$F = G \frac{Mm}{d^2}$$

This becomes Coulomb's law of *magnetic* attraction between the poles of two magnets if we replace M and m by the magnitudes of the poles and G by a magnetic constant. It becomes *electric* attraction if we replace M and m by electric charges and G by another suitable constant. Moreover, if we take Newton's law and think of it as applied to constant masses like those of the Earth and Sun, it reduces to the inverse square law, the attraction between the Earth and Sun varying inversely as the square of the distance between them. But we have seen (chapter 6) that the inverse square law is fundamental in the theory of light. Here phenomena in gravitation, magnetism, electricity, and light seem to be manifestations of one general principle. Matter and electromagnetic entities exert influences or create a *field* in the space around them.

We have seen how Einstein handled the gravitational field, that is, the influence of matter on the space-time continuum. For thirty years or so, Einstein, Hermann Weyl, and others tried to obtain a single theory that would include gravitational and electromagnetic fields as two special cases. Finally, in February 1950, Einstein released to the world a 'unified field theory,' which still awaits the sort of experimental verification that Einstein's earlier work has had. There is no doubt, however, that the new theory, expressed in the language of *tensors* (which can be thought of as generalized vectors), is the greatest contribution to mathematical physics to date.

Instead of attempting a discussion of any phase of this unified field theory, let us return to some other aspects of relativity. The Lorentz transformation was the nucleus of the restricted theory. The notion of *transformation* is a general one and has not only cosmic applications but uses in other parts of mathematics. To illustrate, making maps of the Earth transforms a spherical surface into a flat one. Separation was an *invariant* of relativity. The invariants in map-making depend on the type of map.

Let us suppose that a model of the Earth (fig. 136) is enveloped by a cylinder in such a way that the cylinder touches the equator,

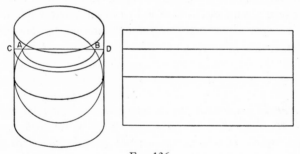

Fig. 136.

and the plane of each parallel, such as *AB*, is prolonged to intersect the cylinder in circle *CD*. If the cylinder is unrolled, the projection will appear as in figure 136. The whole Earth is represented as a rectangle and each parallel is a straight line whose length is the same as that of the equator. The meridians are parallel straight lines spaced at equal distances. It can be proved by the elementary geometry of the sphere and cylinder that *area* is invariant under this transformation. Each strip of the projection is equal in area to the zone on the model it represents, and each small quadrilateral bounded by meridians and parallels is transformed into a plane rectangle of the same area. It is evident that while this transformation preserves area, it distorts shape. This distortion is very slight near the equator but is more serious near the poles. A map projection like this would be valuable, for example, if it was desired to compare the area and distribution of states in the British Empire.

More useful to the navigator is Mercator's projection, which has as invariants the *angles* between curves as well as the *ratio of lengths* in small neighborhoods, and hence preserves the shape of small parts of the Earth's surface while changing areas. Because the similarity of small figures is preserved, a curve drawn on the sphere cutting all the meridians at the same angle—the *loxodrome* by name—is transformed into a straight line, and it is this property that renders Mercator's chart so valuable to seamen. If we join New York City and Southampton by a straight line on the map and measure the angle of intersection of this line with the meridian, we have the bearing that the ship should retain during its entire trip between these points in order to follow a 'rhumb line.'

This is not, however, great-circle sailing, and hence the ship so navigated does not take the shortest path. Great-circle sailing is generally impractical, since it involves continually altering the ship's course. Modern navigators steer a sort of compromise course, which has some of the brevity of the great-circle route, and some of the simplicity of the rhumb line. There are many other types of map projection with different invariants for different purposes.

A set of things like all possible Lorentz transformations (these are infinite in number since the value of u can vary between 0 and 1) has certain properties in common with many other sets in science, leading mathematicians to abstract this essence and give a name to sets possessing it. The name is *group*. One of the characteristics of a group can be illustrated by giving instances of its existence or absence. In the classic picture of the atom, now modified, in which the atom is described as a heavy central nucleus together with a number of light electrons revolving around it somewhat in the fashion of planets moving around the Sun, the electrons are pictured as jumping nimbly from orbit to orbit. If now we choose as transformations for our consideration these 'jumps' of an electron, we may follow a jump from orbit 1 to 3 by a jump from orbit 3 to 6, and the net result will be a jump from 1 to 6. If we compare these leaps of the electron with the moves of a knight on a chessboard, we perceive a remarkable contrast. The difference is this. If the electron makes 2 orbit jumps in succession, it arrives at a state which it could have reached by a single jump; but if a knight makes 2 moves, it arrives at a square which it could not have reached by a single move. The electron jumps are said to possess the *group property;* the chess moves are said to lack it.

Discussing other group characteristics would lead us too far afield. We remark merely that the group concept is a powerful one. By using it Évariste Galois (1811–32), the Keats of mathematics, settled once and for all the matter of solving algebraic equations. He proved that *it is impossible to solve algebraically the general equation of degree greater than four.* For centuries before his time, the greatest algebraists had struggled to solve equations of the fifth degree and higher. His youthful contemporary, Abel, established the same important fact but not by so neat a method. Galois developed the theory of groups and applied it to the question in hand. We shall state Galois' great theorem, which established once and for all a criterion for solvability: *An algebraic equation is algebraically solvable if and only if its group is solvable.* We shall not attempt an explanation of what the 'group of an equation' is, or what a 'solvable group' is, but merely point out the nature of Galois' signal contribution. We know that one of the most important functions of algebra is to solve equations. We have previously seen how to solve equations of the first and second degrees. We may recall the story of the sixteenth-century Tartaglia and his solution of the cubic. The general fourth-degree equation was solved about the same time. From the sixteenth to the nineteenth centuries mathematicians believed that general equations of degree higher than four could be solved and sought for a method of doing so. Of course, there were some *special* equations of higher degree which they found easy to solve. It was the youthful Galois who finally closed the subject. Let us explain what he meant when he said that the solution of higher degree equations is 'impossible.' He showed that the solution cannot be effected if we insist on expressing the unknown by any combination of the coefficients in the equation, using only a *finite* number of additions, subtractions, multiplications, divisions, and root extractions. If we permit an *infinite* number of steps, however, Galois' theorem no longer holds.

In the restricted theory of relativity certain observational phenomena were at hand and a search was made for formulas to fit them. The Lorentz group served this purpose. In Galois' work the fundamental question was the matter of finding the 'group of an equation.' For the philosophic-minded there must be interest in the *general* query: Given some property, what is the largest group of transformations that leaves this thing unaltered? The answer forms the basis for *defining a branch of science.* The material for such a science may already be in existence and merely need the *unification* of a broad underlying principle. On the other hand, the specification of some property that is to be an all-important invariant may lead to a new discovery.

Thus the basic group question may prove a strong stimulus for science. It made it possible for Einstein to

> ... mount where science guides ...
> Instruct the planets in what orbs to run
> Correct old Time and regulate the Sun.

13

The Paradise of Mathematicians

> Cantor's theory of the infinite—one of the most disturbing original contributions to mathematics made in the past 2500 years.
>
> BELL

IF RELATIVITY indicates the lofty height to which applied mathematics has attained, then the concept of infinity represents simultaneously the crowning glory of the nineteenth-century pure mathematical renaissance and the thorn in the flesh of the twentieth-century mathematical philosopher! The domain of the infinite is a disorderly place, says the logician. We must straighten it out lest it have a confusing influence on our finite household.

Before discussing those notions which, as Einstein has said, precipitated the fiercest 'frog-mouse' battle in mathematical history, let us see what manner of man created them. Georg Cantor (1845–1918) came by his imaginative traits naturally, for his heritage was an artistic one. On his mother's side there had been a long line of painters, pianists, violinists, and conductors. He was of Jewish descent on both sides, although sometime and somewhere (Denmark, Austria, or Russia) one side of the family had found it convenient to become Protestant, and the other side had turned Catholic.

Cantor's father tried to force him to be practical and insisted at first that he train for the profession of engineering, but consented finally to his pursuing his bent for pure mathematics. The young scholar studied with Weierstrass, Kovalevsky's teacher, and with the mathematician Kronecker, who was to become his most bitter enemy. Just before he was thirty, Cantor published his first revolutionary paper on the theory of the infinite. The facts as well as the method were fundamentally new in mathematics and marked the man of genius.

Cantor's personal life, like that of so many gifted men, was unhappy. He earned his living by teaching at second-rate colleges.

The most tragic fact of all was the mathematical and personal animosity of his teacher, Leopold Kronecker. The latter disagreed violently with Cantor's point of view, and to this day pitched battles are being fought regularly between Kronecker and Cantor adherents. No decisive victory has been achieved by either side as yet. Poor Cantor lacked the stamina to be a revolutionary; he took things so much to heart that he went out of his mind and spent his last days in a mental clinic.

We shall not decide here whether Cantor's notions will stand the test of time. We present them for their beauty and because they have probably been the greatest stimulus in recent years toward placing mathematics on a firm logical foundation. We feel that no discussion of modern mathematics would be complete without what Hilbert called 'the most admirable fruit of the mathematical mind, and one of the highest achievements of man's intellectual processes.' Thus we devote this chapter to 'The Infinite,' favored topic of mystics, theologians, dialecticians, and scientists.

Whatever the role of the infinite in matters of faith, it is certain that the notion of infinity permeates all mathematics and hence is indirectly a potent factor in modern science. Strangely enough, it turns out that even the logical validity of such down-to-earth elementary processes as addition, subtraction, multiplication, and division depend on the infinite—to say nothing of more complicated mathematical machinery like that of the calculus.

The trouble in the household of the infinite started long before Cantor's day. About 2300 years ago there lived in the Greek city of Elea, in western Italy, a young man by the name of Zeno. Aristotle felt that Zeno and his friends (the Sophists) were a bunch of 'smart alecks' and 'wisecrackers,' and proceeded to banish them intellectually when he was unable to answer their arguments.

Now just what was it in Zeno's teachings that so irritated Aristotle? Before answering, we must explain that Zeno was a follower of the Greek philosopher and mystic, Parmenides. Teacher and pupil alike stressed the doctrine that the world of sense is nothing but an illusion. So it was that Zeno concentrated on a single but ubiquitous aspect of the external world, namely *motion*. 'If motion, which pervades everything,' thought Zeno, 'can be shown to be self-contradictory, and hence unreal, then everything else must assume the same unreal quality. By convincing people of the unreality of motion, I can best teach the doctrine of Parmenides and success-fully discredit the world of the senses.'

Thus it was that Zeno propounded four famous paradoxes on motion, which philosophers and mathematicians are still discussing. Those readers who would convince themselves that modern orthodox metaphysics has progressed little beyond Zeno and Parmenides need only read F. H. Bradley's *Appearance and Reality* and compare this work with Parmenides' poems, 'Reality' and 'Appearance.' Zeno, in pushing Parmenides' notions, may or may not have been guilty of 'sophistry.' Nevertheless it takes a pretty clever man to get himself talked about for over two thousand years. Among those who have given serious thought to these puzzling questions are Thomas Aquinas, Descartes, Leibniz, Spinoza, and Bergson. Zeno's paradoxes in some form have been used as arguments for all the theories of space, time, and infinity that have been propounded from his day to ours.

Zeno's arguments were:

i. The Dichotomy. There is no motion because that which is moved must arrive at the middle (of its course) before it arrives at the end. (And of course it must traverse the half of the half before it reaches the middle, and so on *ad infinitum*.)

In other words, to cover a distance of 1 yard, one must first reach the $\frac{1}{2}$ yard point, before that the $\frac{1}{4}$ yard, before that the $\frac{1}{8}$, and so on, *ad infinitum*. How is it possible to reach an infinite number of positions in a finite time?

ii. The Achilles. The slower when running will never be overtaken by the quicker; for that which is pursuing must first reach the point from which that which is fleeing started, so that the slower must necessarily always be some distance ahead.

A modern version of this states that Achilles can run 1000 yards a minute while a turtle can run 100 yards a minute. The turtle is placed 1000 yards ahead of Achilles. Zeno's argument states that Achilles can never overtake the turtle, for when Achilles has advanced 1000 yards, the turtle is still 100 yards ahead of him. By the time Achilles has covered these 100 yards, the turtle is still ahead of him, and so on, *ad infinitum,* as the accompanying table shows.

Position	Achilles	Tortoise
1	0	1 0 0 0
2	1 0 0 0	1 1 0 0
3	1 1 0 0	1 1 1 0
4	1 1 1 0	1 1 1 1
5	1 1 1 1	1 1 1 1. 1
6	1 1 1 1. 1	1 1 1 1. 1 1
7	1 1 1 1. 1 1	1 1 1 1. 1 1 1
	etc.	etc.

The trouble here is essentially the same as in the first paradox. If Achilles must occupy an *infinite* number of positions in order to overtake the tortoise, will he ever be able to do this in a *finite* time? Thus the solution of both these puzzles will be a matter of clarifying notions about 'infinity.' It would seem that the way to help ourselves would be to permit the number of points in a finite space and the number of instants in a finite time to be infinite.

III. The Arrow. If everything is either at rest or in motion in a space equal to itself, and if what moves is always in the instant, the moving arrow is unmoved.

The tip of the arrow is in one and only one position at each and every instant of time; in other words, at every instant of time, it is at rest. Hence it never moves. Zeno seems to assume that a finite part of time consists of a finite series of successive instants. Throughout an instant, he says, the tip of the arrow is at one point. Imagine a period consisting of 1,000,000 small instants, and picture the arrow in flight during the period. At each of the one million instants, the arrow is where it is, and at the next instant, it is somewhere else. It never moves, but somehow accomplishes the change of position. Thus, motion is an illusory, irregular sort of thing—a succession of stills, like a motion picture—not the smooth sort of transition our senses picture.

IV. The Stadium. Two rows, composed of an equal number of bodies of equal size, pass one another on a racecourse as they proceed with equal velocity in opposite directions, one row starting from the end of the course and the other from the middle. Thus a given time equals its double.

Let us picture Zeno's argument. The first diagram below shows the original position of the rows of bodies. The *A*'s represent a row that is stationary, the B's and C's are the rows that move with equal velocities in opposite directions, B's to the right, C's to the left.

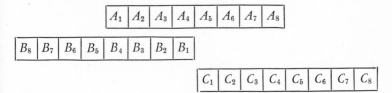

| A_1 | A_2 | A_3 | A_4 | A_5 | A_6 | A_7 | A_8 |

| B_8 | B_7 | B_6 | B_5 | B_4 | B_3 | B_2 | B_1 |

| C_1 | C_2 | C_3 | C_4 | C_5 | C_6 | C_7 | C_8 |

Then there will be a moment when the B's will be exactly under the A's as in the figure below. Thus B_1 has passed alongside

| A_1 | A_2 | A_3 | A_4 | A_5 | A_6 | A_7 | A_8 |

| B_8 | B_7 | B_6 | B_5 | B_4 | B_3 | B_2 | B_1 |

| C_1 | C_2 | C_3 | C_4 | C_5 | C_6 | C_7 | C_8 |

all eight C's while it has passed alongside only four A's. Thus eight moments equal four moments, and a given interval of time is equal to its double.

In the first two paradoxes Zeno voices objection to the *infinite divisibility* of finite portions of time and space. In the last two, he shows that serious difficulties arise as a result of the *opposite* hypothesis, namely that space and time are not infinitely divisible, but are composed of points and instants that can be counted off in a finite number of steps—1, 2, 3, 4, 5 . . . n. Thus all four paradoxes taken together would seem to present a serious contradiction.

Several methods of escape are possible. In the first place, we could do what Zeno wanted his listeners to do—we could *deny the reality* of space and time. Or, instead, we could use the approach of the philosopher Bergson and deny that space and time consist of points and instants, for these entities seem to cause all the trouble. Or we can maintain that, although space and time do consist of points and instants, the number of these in any finite interval is infinite. Most mathematicians choose this last alternative, which naturally demands a clear-cut concept of the nature of the infinite.

Zeno's contribution to the elucidation of the infinite was mainly *negative*. It required more than two thousand years before a *positive* theory was evolved. A definite solution of difficulties was first propounded by Cantor in 1882. Cantor attacked the core of all the trouble by furnishing a new number concept to replace the usual idea of *counting*. Unconsciously man assumes that, in order to have complete numerical knowledge concerning a collection, we should be able to pass its terms in review, one by one. In the case of the Dichotomy, if we wish to count the positions that must be reached— the halfway mark, the quarter, the eighth, the sixteenth, etc., we shall never finish. Or, in the case of Achilles and the tortoise, if we imagine an umpire to say 'Stop—Go!' when Achilles reaches the 1000 yard mark (and the turtle the 1100 yard mark), to repeat this when he reaches the 1100 yard mark (and the turtle the 1110 yard mark), to repeat it again at the third stage, the fourth stage, and so on, then Zeno's contention would be true in practice and Achilles would never overtake the tortoise.

But it is actually possible to reason successfully about a collection without going through such an enumeration as that described. This may be illustrated even in the case of finite collections. We can speak of 'Americans' without having a personal acquaintance with each citizen of the United States. We can do this because we know the essential characteristic that each individual has if he belongs to the group, and that he lacks, if he does not. So it is with infinite aggregates. They may be known by their characteristics even though we cannot complete the task of counting them, one by one.

To appreciate the substitute Cantor offered for ordinary counting, let us journey back in time once again to that era when man first asked, albeit in primitive fashion, 'How many?' We know that the savage found his answer by pairing his clubs with a bundle of sticks and his wives with a handful of pebbles. This process of matching, or *one-to-one correspondence,* was put forward by Cantor as the best mathematical procedure for the handling of all collections, finite or infinite. By means of this criterion he was actually able to furnish an answer to the fundamental question, 'What is number?' Cantor seems to have gone primitive in his selection of a meaning. His primitive moments, however, were truly inspired ones!

When a one-to-one correspondence exists between the elements of one collection and the elements of another, the number in one set is said to be the same as in the other. Let us emphasize the nature of one-to-one matching by calling to mind some familiar illustrations. A telephone directory matches subscribers with telephone numbers in one-to-one fashion (if we exclude those with more than one telephone). On a map where all cities of population over 100,000 are indicated by red dots, there will be a one-to-one correspondence between red dots on the map and large cities in the region mapped. In the Achilles paradox, there is a one-to-one correspondence between the positions of Achilles and those of the turtle.

In this process of matching lies the explanation why the number of stars in the heavens or grains of sand in the desert may inspire the poet but fail to thrill the mathematician. Although no one would particularly enjoy the physical labor of enumerating such aggregates, it would be possible to do so. We know that sooner or later the matching of the stars and the numbers 1, 2, 3, 4, 5, etc. will end and we shall have the number, however large. Let us then carry on a piece of one-to-one matching that will have more startling results! Let us write the positive integers in a row, thus—1, 2, 3, 4, 5, 6, 7, 8, 9, 10, 11 . . . —and agree that each integer has a successor, however far out in the series we may go. Now let us pair each integer with its double, thus:

1	2	3	4	5	6	7	8	$\cdots$	n	$\cdots$
2	4	6	8	10	12	14	16	$\cdots$	$2n$	$\cdots$

Then, since we have agreed that two sets of things are equal in number when they can be paired in one-to-one fashion, there are as many numbers in our first set as in the second; that is, *the number of even integers is the same as the number of all integers.* 'But, surely,' you exclaim, 'this second set is merely a part of the first! The even integers are only part of the whole set of integers!' Evidently we have, in the set of integers, a collection that is *numerically equal to a part of itself!*

Again, let us take a part $A'B'$ of line-segment AB, and compare the number of points in the two. We move $A'B'$ to the position indicated, draw AA' and BB' meeting in P (fig. 137). Then we pair the points of $A'B'$ with those of AB as follows.

To find the partner of any point on $A'B'$, such as C', draw PC' and extend it to meet AB in C. Then C and C' are partners. On the other hand, to find the partner of any point on AB, as D, draw PD and let it meet $A'B'$ in D'. Then D and D' are partners. For every point on $A'B'$ we have a point on AB, and for every point on AB, we have one on $A'B'$. In other words there is a *one-to-one corre-*

spondence between the points of AB *and those of* A′B′; that is, there
are as many points in part of *AB* as in all of *AB*. Once again, *the
whole of something is numerically equal to one of its parts.*

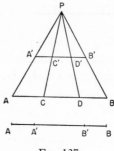

Fɪɢ. 137.

If we maintain one-to-one correspondence as a number criterion,
then we can adduce many other illustrations where the whole of
something is equal to one of its parts. As we have seen, it was Georg
Cantor who decided to make one-to-one correspondence a universal
criterion for determining the number of things in any set—thereby
answering many more serious questions than Zeno's paradoxes.

The Cantorian point of view was anticipated by Galileo, who
showed that there is a one-to-one correspondence between the integers and their squares, although the latter set of numbers is only
part of the first. The correspondence is:

$$1 \quad 2 \quad 3 \quad 4 \quad 5 \cdots n \cdots$$
$$1 \quad 4 \quad 9 \quad 16 \quad 25 \cdots n^2 \cdots$$

Galileo merely saw in this discovery a puzzling fact and did not
develop the matter further. Infinity did not appear in mathematics
as a mature concept until it was discovered by Bernhard Bolzano
(1781–1848), who paved the way for Dedekind and Cantor.

A set of things, whether these are numbers or curves, points or
instants of time, speeds or temperatures, is said to be *infinite* if it
can be put into *one-to-one correspondence with one of its parts.* In
Zeno's paradox, the Dichotomy, we see that the argument hinges
on the fact that a moving point will occupy an infinite number of
positions. The positions to which allusion is made in the paradox
are

$$1/2, \ 1/4, \ 1/8, \ 1/16 \cdots$$

In the fact that these can be put into one-to-one correspondence with the infinite set of positive integers lies the proof that the number of positions to be occupied is infinite. Thus we have the correspondence

1/2	1/4	1/8	1/16	$\cdots$	$1/2^n$	$\cdots$
1	2	3	4	$\cdots$	n	$\cdots$

Then if one-to-one correspondence is a criterion of equality, there is nothing remarkable about having a finite length contain an infinite number of positions. Again, in the Achilles paradox, we have an infinite set of positions. The tortoise's positions can be put into one-to-one correspondence with Achilles', as we see in the table on page 294, and each can be put into one-to-one correspondence with the positive integers. We have

Achilles	0	1000	1100	1110	1111	1111.1	1111.11	etc.
Tortoise	1000	1100	1110	1111	1111.1	1111.11	1111.111	etc.
Integers	1	2	3	4	5	6	7	etc.

Therefore both the turtle and Achilles occupy an infinite number of positions. The fact that puzzled Cantor's predecessors is this: If Achilles were to catch up with the tortoise, the places where the tortoise had been would, on the one hand, be only part of the places where Achilles had been, and on the other, would be equal in number to Achilles' positions (on account of one-to-one correspondence). Thus, by stating as an axiom that the whole of something *can* equal a part, Cantor was able to deny the argument of this paradox.

It is not unlikely that a first reaction to Cantor's concept of the infinite will place his point of view beyond the ken of common sense. It is true, to an extent, that the notion of infinite sets demands a cleavage between the everyday world of practical life and the ideal realm of pure thought. 'Practical pursuits bring to light only finite things,' we may claim. There are no aggregates, however huge, that cannot be counted—the treasures of the mighty, the drops in the ocean, the bacteria in a culture. No totality here is matched by one of its parts. On the other hand, there is that strange new world of infinite things, where each totality contains parts matching it perfectly in number. Surely this is not the domain of banking, taxation, and industry!

Of course we can refute the 'non-practical' charge against infinite sets by asking whether such things as a one-inch line-segment, the ordinary numbers of counting—1, 2, 3, etc.—or the type of motion described by Zeno are such extraordinary affairs. They are not, we must admit. In fact, a proper handling of the idea of infinity turns out to be essential in the practical mathematics Newton and Leibniz invented as a scientific tool. The job of perfecting the logical aspects of this tool was left to Weierstrass, Cantor, Dedekind, and other modern mathematicians, and in the course of this work the new concept of infinity was evolved.

Now that we have adjusted ourselves somewhat to the dizzy heights of the infinite realm, let us renew ambition and ascend still further. Mountain climbing in the domain of the infinite requires fortitude, for we have just begun! There are infinities and infinities! The first peak is a friendly one, for it harbors the infinity that results from the familiar process of counting:

$$1, \ 2, \ 3, \ 4, \ 5, \ \text{etc.}$$

We have proved the number of positive integers infinite. They are said to constitute a *countable infinity,* and any set that can be put into one-to-one correspondence with them is also countable. Since the even integers (or the odd integers) can be put into one-to-one correspondence with all the integers, there is a countable infinity of even integers, and a countable infinity of odd integers. Likewise, since the positions

$$1/2, \ 1/4, \ 1/8, \ 1/16, \ \text{etc.}$$

of Zeno's Dichotomy can be put into one-to-one correspondence with the integers, they constitute another illustration of a countable set.

Just as the mathematician has symbols, 1, 2, 3, etc., for the finite numbers, he has symbols for the *transfinite* ones as well. He represents a countable infinity of objects by the first letter of the Hebrew alphabet $\aleph_0$ (read *aleph null*). The null or zero subscript was used because Cantor hoped to be able to find other examples of infinite sets and then be able to arrange them in order of magnitude: $\aleph_0, \ \aleph_1, \ \aleph_2,$ etc. In spite of poets' descriptions of 'stars unnumbered' and 'countless gems which stud night's imperial chariot,' there are certainly not $\aleph_0$ celestial bodies. The total count of stars of the first six magnitudes yields the trivial finite figure of 7190.

Is the set of all rational numbers (fractions whose numerators and denominators are whole numbers) countable? Let us speculate on this query for a moment. If we consider the set of integers

$$1, \ 2, \ 3, \ 4, \ 5, \ 6, \ 7, \ \ldots$$

and reflect upon the vast number of fractions *between* 1 and 2, those between 2 and 3, between 3 and 4, etc., we begin to suspect that we are on the verge of something new. Consider the fractions between 4 and 5 and select any two, such as $4\frac{1}{4}$ and $4\frac{3}{4}$. Note that between these two there are others, such as $4\frac{3}{8}$ and $4\frac{5}{8}$. Between the last two are $4\frac{7}{16}$ and $4\frac{9}{16}$ and so on, *forever*. Between each pair of whole numbers we have an amazing assemblage of fractions! Surely, since there is an infinite number of integers and between each pair there appears to be an infinity of rational fractions—in other words, an *infinity of infinities*—surely this aggregate should tower over the *countable infinity!* But such is not the case; our Alpine trip has brought us to another summit—with a different view—but Baedeker tells us that it is no higher than the last peak! The rational fractions are merely a one-to-one match for the integers, and therefore merely constitute a countable infinity! There are only $\aleph_0$ rational numbers.

The argument follows. Take a fraction at random, say 3/5. Notice that the sum of numerator and denominator is 8. Notice, too, that there are many fractions having the same sum for numerator and denominator. Arranged in the order of increasing numerators, they are

$$1/7, \ 2/6, \ 3/5, \ 4/4, \ 5/3, \ 6/2, \ 7/1$$

Any other sum will similarly give rise to a set of fractions.

Sum	Fractions
2	1/1
3	1/2, 2/1
4	1/3, 2/2, 3/1
5	1/4, 2/3, 3/2, 4/1
6	1/5, 2/4, 3/3, 4/2, 5/1
7	1/6, 2/5, 3/4, 4/3, 5/2, 6/1
etc.	

By this procedure we are bound to arrive sooner or later at any fraction the reader may designate. If he mentions 99/100, we shall reach that with the sum 199. If he mentions 157/211, we shall arrive at that with the sum 368. Whole numbers will appear among the fractions, such as 4/2 or 4/1, for example. Also the same integer may be repeated, as in 2/1 and 4/2. The same fraction may appear repeatedly as 1/2, 2/4, 3/6, etc. We shall agree, however, to take each but once in the matching process now to follow, in which each fraction is matched with an integer and each integer with a fraction.

1/1	1/2	2/1	1/3	3/1	1/4	2/3	3/2	4/1	1/5	. . .
1	2	3	4	5	6	7	8	9	10	. . .

In this way a one-to-one correspondence is set up, and we see that the number of rational fractions is the same as the number of integers. The set of rational fractions, even though an infinity of infinities, is after all merely *countable*.

Two thousand years ago the Epicurean philosopher and poet Lucretius[1] had some notion of the properties of a countable infinite set. Witness this passage from his writings:

> Nor by prolonging life do we take one tittle from the time passed in death nor can we fret anything away, whereby we may be a less long time in the condition of the dead. Therefore, you may complete as many generations as you please; none the less, however, will that everlasting death await you; and for no less long a time will he be no more in being, who beginning with to-day has ended his life, than the man who has died many months or years ago.

Shall we climb higher in the infinite scale? Over yonder is the Jungfrau, and here is the Matterhorn. The guidebook says that man can no more exhaust the wealth of one of these sky giants by removing from it a countable infinity of elements than he can exhaust a countable infinity by removing from it a finite collection however large. Our heart grows a bit faint, our knees tremble ever so slightly! Perhaps we shall remain content to contemplate the majesty of the snow-caps from a vantage point below and resort to a guidebook for details it might be dangerous to ascertain at firsthand!

[1] Keyser, C. J. 'The Role of Infinity in the Cosmology of Epicurus,' *Scripta Mathematica*, Volume IV, no. 3.

Our Cantorian Baedeker says that the peak glistening in the sunlight as the clouds lift momentarily is the *totality of irrational numbers,* those numbers like $\sqrt{2}$, $\sqrt[5]{7}$, π, e, and that this aggregate is not countable. In other words, the world of mathematics is far richer in irrational numbers than it is in rational ones. The irrational should thus be thought of as the usual number and the rational as exceptional. To compare our plateau of the rationals with the dizzy peak of irrationals—can the human mind fathom the magnitude of the ratio? Contrasting the financial status of miner and Morgan, size of electron and galaxy, we find them mere finite trivialities relative to our infinite jumps! If from the totality of our irrationals we take away a countable infinitude, there will always remain infinitely more than we have taken away. Indeed this will remain true if we take away not merely one countable infinity, but another and another and another—forever,—thus removing a countable infinity of countable infinitudes! In spite of this huge subtraction, the original ensemble remains absolutely undiminished in its wealth. The cold mathematical name for this majestic mountain is the *type of the continuum.*

The name 'continuum' is used because the totality of points in a continuous line-segment of any length, however short, is one example of an infinite manifold of this type. More power to the mathematicians's imagination if he can conceive of a line-segment only 1/100th inch in length, but so wealthy in points that its riches can never be depleted by the removal of one countable infinity of points after another, forever! The number of instants in a second, the number of points on a sphere, the number of lines through a point are all of the type of the continuum. Pity poor Zeno who first hit the seemingly stupendous snag of an infinite number of points in a finite length and the infinite number of instants in a finite unit of time!

Are there peaks above the clouds? Even so. We could mount step by step in an ever-ascending scale of more and more embracing infinitudes, but we shall leave that to the sturdiest of our climbers. In this volume we shall merely point the way by indicating the existence of an imposing hierarchy of infinitudes superior to that of the continuum. Each rank includes all the ranks below it, and taken together these constitute an ever-rising mountain range proceeding upward forever!

The mathematician's symbol for the number of the continuum is C. We have just seen that there are infinitely many transfinite numbers greater than C, and it might be natural to ask whether there are any transfinite numbers between $\aleph_0$ and C. Mathematicians have not yet been able to answer this question one way or another, and Cantor's plan for finding meanings for $\aleph_1$, $\aleph_2$, etc. has not been realized. In fact, Kurt Gödel, a mathematician of our day, has been working on the *Hypothesis of the Continuum,* which states that there is no cardinal number between $\aleph_0$ and C.

The Cantorian theory of the infinite leads us to consider that particular property of certain infinite aggregates which will resolve the paradoxes of the Arrow and the Stadium. The name of this attribute is *continuity*. It is a property that can only be applied when a collection is arranged in some *order,* so that we can always tell which of two objects of the aggregate comes before the other. The points of a line from left to right and the moments of time from earlier to later are illustrations of such ordered collections. We have not hitherto been interested in the question of order, since the number of objects in a collection did not depend on it. There would be as many telephone subscribers as telephones, even if the subscribers were not listed in alphabetical order.

The property of *continuity,* however, does depend in an essential way on the arrangement of a set of things. A set may be continuous when arranged in one order but lack continuity in another arrangement. It is easy to see that a collection can be arranged in many different ways. The integers can be arranged in order of magnitude, thus:

$$1, 2, 3, 4, 5 \ldots$$

Or all the odd integers could be given priority in order of magnitude and then all the even ones could be considered as following, thus:

$$1, 3, 5, 7, 9 \ldots; 2, 4, 6, 8, 10 \ldots$$

We shall call an ordered set a *series*.

When we say that we 'arrange' a set of numbers, the term is not generally used in a literal sense. If magnitude is our criterion, then we can always say of any two fractions between 0 and 1 which is smaller and which is larger; in other words, we can conceive that these fractions have an order determined by their size. We cannot, as we shall now emphasize, list or arrange them in this order.

One particular property of a continuous series or continuum is the characteristic of being *everywhere dense*. A series is called everywhere dense when no two terms are consecutive, but between any two terms there are always other members of the series. The series of rational numbers (fractions) arranged in order of magnitude is everywhere dense, for between any two fractions, however close, there are always others.

> Between
>
> for example, there is
>
> 0.5 and 0.501
>
> 0.5005
>
> Between
>
> there is
>
> 0.5 and 0.500001
>
> 0.5000005

Evidently, between any two fractions, however close, there is an infinite number of other fractions. There is no *next* fraction after 0.5, or after any other fraction.

The characteristic of being everywhere dense is the property of the continuum that is important in the resolution of the Arrow and the Stadium paradoxes. However, it is not the only characteristic of a mathematical continuum. Another requirement for mathematical continuity is that there be no gaps in a series. To see what this means, we return to the set of rational numbers ordered according to size. This series is everywhere dense and yet is not honored by the name continuum, since it does contain gaps.

We may decide to divide this series into two classes in which all rationals whose squares are less than two in value are assigned to one class and all the remaining rationals, to the other. Since there is no rational number whose square is exactly two (see page 78), there will be no highest number in the first class and no lowest in the other. There is no number that will fence off one set from the other. The number we call $\sqrt{2}$, which could do the trick, is not rational and hence does not belong to the series in question. Here then is a gap. Similarly all other irrationals are gaps in the rational series. Recalling the magnitude of the set of irrationals (page 303), it is rather staggering to realize that there are tremendously more gaps in the rational series than there are actual numbers, in spite of their density.

To go into further properties of what a modern mathematician calls a *linear continuum* would carry us beyond the scope of this work. Let us then merely furnish some illustrations. We have already implied (page 298) that a geometric line-segment is a continuum. The Cantor-Dedekind axiom states that there is a one-to-one correspondence between the points of a line and all real numbers—that is, the totality of decimals with an infinite number of places. (If the number of decimal places is finite, the last place can be followed by an infinite number of zeros. Thus 0.25 becomes 0.250000 . . .) When there are an infinite number of non-repeating digits we have the irrational numbers that fill in the gaps in the system of rationals. A line or its equivalent, the real number system, is a one-dimensional continuum. There are mathematical continua of 2, 3 . . . any number of dimensions. For convenience in mathematics it is customary to consider *time* a continuum. In the previous chapter we discussed the four-dimensional space-time continuum of general relativity.

We must now consider what is meant by *continuity of motion*. In our discussion of relativity we pictured the motion of an 'insect' in a one-dimensional continuum and plotted its progress as a world-line in a two-dimensional space-time continuum. Putting matters on a purely intuitive basis, we might say that motion of a point (insect) is continuous if the world-line representing this motion has no gaps or sudden jumps. Analysis of this intuitive concept will lead us closer to an exact mathematical definition of continuity of motion. Examining a graph with a *discontinuity* will be helpful. The graph of $xy = 2$ (fig. 68) has a discontinuity at $x = 0$. If we think of x as representing time and y as representing position in a one-dimensional continuum, the graph will tell us that:

(1) at a certain instant (time $= x = 0$) we cannot say where the point is;

(2) a millionth of a second before this instant ($x = -0.000001$) the point was two million units away from the origin of the one-dimensional continuum ($y = -2,000,000$). A millionth of a second after the instant being considered it was 2,000,000 units in the other direction; that is, there was a change of 4,000,000 units in position in two millionths of a second! If the 'unit' should be the one we used in relativity, just picture this situation!

Certainly items (1) and (2) do not correspond to our experience of physical motion. Observation of the physical world indicates that such things are impossible. Hence it seems sensible to exclude world-lines with gaps or jumps. We must insist that at every instant of time the 'insect' or moving point be somewhere; that is, its position must be defined, and this in a unique manner, since it cannot be in two places at the same time. In mathematical language, the distance s must be a one-valued function of the time t. Secondly, to exclude jumps, if motion is to be continuous at time t, the difference in the positions of the moving point just before and just after this time must be slight. If motion is continuous at time t with corresponding position s, it must be possible to find an interval of time, $t-a$ to $t+a$, such that throughout this entire period the moving point will lie between two positions, $s-b$ and $s+b$, and this must hold however small b is taken to be.

This brings us back to Zeno. If motion is continuous, his arrow cannot jump from one position to another in successive instants, but must always pass by a gradual transition through an infinite number of intermediate positions at intermediate instants. Zeno's thought would yield the world-line of figure 138 with a discontinuity at the

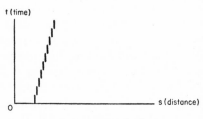

FIG. 138. Placing the space-time axes as in the previous chapter, Zeno's picture of motion would resemble this graph. The length of the time intervals is exaggerated to make the drawing possible. For the same reason the gaps have been enlarged.

end of each short instant. It is true that in continuous motion, the tip of the arrow does occupy one fixed position at each instant, and that nothing happens when a body moves except that it is in different places at different times. This does not imply, however, that it is at rest. Describing it as being at rest would mean that it was in the same position at all instants. Nevertheless, this modern resolution of the Arrow is a partial triumph for Zeno. Although we have destroyed his picture of time and space, we have conceded to him the fact that the 'nextness' or 'from-to-ness' usually ascribed to motion by the senses is an illusion.

We remind the reader that continuity of space and time is postulated concerning *mathematical* space and time. Whether *physical* space and time are continuous is a philosophic question to which there is no clear-cut answer at present. Since, as far as our senses go, a motion picture that is a finite succession of stills can create the same impression as a truly continuous motion might, it is doubtful whether there will ever be direct empirical evidence to decide whether time and space are continuous in constitution or whether motion is merely an ever-so-perfect movie. Nor does conclusive empirical evidence exist in favor of Cantor's theory of the infinite. In a previous chapter we have explained that mathematics does not aim at *absolute truths* but at *logical theories* that seem to offer the technically simplest explanations of observed facts. It is in this sense that the theory of infinity and the continuity of space, time, and motion are tenable.

Again, the paradox of the Stadium can be resolved by considering motion as a continuous phenomenon. The fault in Zeno's argument, as considered by us, was that he believed he could actually list four (or eight) consecutive instants or positions. Since time is a continuum, it is everywhere dense and no two instants can be consecutive. Let us outline our previous presentation of Zeno's argument somewhat differently. In the final diagram of that discussion, imagine the B's to continue their motion to the right and the C's to the left. We show the positions of the moving bodies in two instants that Zeno considered consecutive. At the first moment, B_8, B_7, B_6 and C_1, C_2, C_3 are respectively opposite A_1, A_2, A_3. At Zeno's next moment, B_8 and C_3 are opposite A_2. Thus B_8 and C_3

A_1	A_2	A_3	A_4	A_5	A_6	A_7	A_8

B_8	B_7	B_6	B_5	B_4	B_3	B_2	B_1

C_1	C_2	C_3	C_4	C_5	C_6	C_7	C_8

A_1	A_2	A_3	A_4	A_5	A_6	A_7	A_8

B_8	B_7	B_6	B_5	B_4	B_3	B_2	B_1

C_1	C_2	C_3	C_4	C_5	C_6	C_7	C_8

are opposite one another. Did B_8 actually pass C_2, and if so, when? If we assume continuity of motion, we agree that B_8 did pass C_2, and that such an intermediate position was occupied at an intermediate moment. Hence the instants Zeno considered consecutive could not have been so. Similarly between any two given moments he might have pictured as consecutive, there would be others; we are once again led to the density of time and the entire basis of Zeno's argument is destroyed.

Having reached infinity, it is doubtless time to end our story. We have traveled a long way from the 'one, two, heap' of the savage, to the 'hundred million spheres' of the poet, to the $\aleph_0$ of Georg Cantor. Such a journey is a necessary cultural cruise for mathematician, philosopher, and scientist, as well as for all who would appreciate the current scene in modern science.

General References

Ball, W. W. R., *A Short Account of the History of Mathematics,* London, Macmillan, 1908.

Ball, W. W. R., and Coxeter, H. S. M., *Mathematical Recreations and Essays,* New York, Macmillan, 1947.

Bell, E. T., *Men of Mathematics,* New York, Simon and Schuster, 1937.

Bell, E. T., *The Development of Mathematics,* New York, McGraw-Hill, 1945.

Birkhoff, George D., *Aesthetic Measure,* Cambridge, Harvard University Press, 1933.

Born, Max, *The Restless Universe,* New York, Harper, 1936.

Boyer, Carl B., *The Concepts of the Calculus,* New York, Columbia University Press, 1939.

Cajanello, A. C. Leffler (Edgren), duchessa di, *Sonia Kovalevsky; Biography and Autobiography,* New York, Macmillan, 1895.

Cardano, Girolamo, *The Book of My Life,* New York, Dutton, 1930.

Church, Alonzo, *The Algebra of Classes,* Brooklyn, N. Y., Long Island University, 1938.

Conant, Levi L., *The Number Concept,* London, Macmillan, 1896.

Courant R., and Robbins, H. E., *What is Mathematics?* New York, Oxford University Press, 1941.

Dantzig, Tobias, *Number: The Language of Science,* New York, Macmillan, 1933.

Durrell, Clement V., *Readable Relativity,* London, Bell and Sons, 1931.

Eddington, Sir Arthur S., *Space, Time and Gravitation,* Cambridge, Cambridge University Press, 1920.

Einstein, Albert, *The Meaning of Relativity,* Princeton, Princeton University Press, 1945.

Fisher, R. A., *Design of Experiments,* Edinburgh, Oliver and Boyd, 1949.

Ginsburg, Jekuthiel, 'Rabbi Ben Ezra on Permutations and Combinations,' in *Mathematics Teacher,* vol. 15, 1922, pages 347-56.

Hambidge, Jay, *Dynamic Symmetry in Composition,* New Haven, Yale University Press, 1923.

Hambidge, Jay, *Practical Applications of Dynamic Symmetry,* New Haven, Yale University Press, 1932.

Jacobs, Michel, *The Art of Composition,* Garden City, N. Y., Doubleday, 1930.

Kasner, E., and Newman, J. R., *Mathematics and the Imagination*, New York, Simon and Schuster, 1940.

McDonald, John, 'A Theory of Strategy' in *Fortune*, volume 39, June 1949, pages 100 ff.

Neugebauer, Otto, *Vorlesungen uber Geschichte der antiken mathematischen Wissenschaften*, Berlin, Springer, 1934.

Neumann, John von, and Morgenstern, Oskar, *Theory of Games and Economic Behavior*, Princeton, Princeton University Press, 1944.

Russell, Bertrand, *Introduction to Mathematical Philosophy*, London, Allen and Unwin, 1919.

Russell, Bertrand, *Our Knowledge of the External World*, London, Allen and Unwin, 1926.

Sanford, Vera, *A Short History of Mathematics*, New York, Houghton Mifflin, 1930.

Smith, David E., *History of Mathematics*, Boston, Ginn, 1923.

Smith, David E., and Ginsburg, Jekuthiel, *Numbers and Numerals*, New York, Teachers College Bur. of Publications, Columbia University, 1937.

Walker, Helen M., *Studies in the History of the Statistical Method*, Baltimore, William and Wilkins, 1929.

Wilks, S. S., *Statistical Aspects of Experiments in Telepathy*, Brooklyn, N. Y., Long Island University, 1938.

Young, John W., *Fundamental Concepts of Algebra and Geometry*, New York, Macmillan, 1911.

Index